LƎFT FIELD

DAVID WILSON

unbound

ABOUT THE AUTHOR

Born in Shaftesbury, Dorset in 1945, David Wilson has been a gaucho, sailor, teacher, art agent, film-maker, war crimes witness, aid worker and whistleblower.

He has written four plays and, as an activist, has written for US and UK political websites.

'Do not follow where the path may lead. Go, instead, where there is no path and leave a trail.'
   Ralph Waldo Emerson

This edition first published in 2016

Unbound
6th Floor, Mutual House, 70 Conduit Street, London W1S 2GF
www.unbound.co.uk

'Behind God's Back' © Anne Aylor 2016, reprinted courtesy of the author.
Photographs pp 75, 115, 157 © Thom Hoffman
Photograph p 193 © Decca Records

Typesetting by PDQ

Art direction by Mecob

A CIP record for this book is available from the British Library

ISBN 978-1-78352-226-2 (trade edition hardback)
ISBN 978-1-78352-227-9 (ebook)
ISBN 978-1-78352-282-8 (limited edition hardback)

Printed in England by Clays Ltd, St Ive Plc

1 2 3 4 5 6 7 8 9

David Wilson has lived a life and a half. I was proud to play a minor role in War Child, an organisation in which David was inspirational. The broken world needed people like David then; it still does and it always will.
– *Sir Tom Stoppard*

This is an excellent and inspiring book. David Wilson is an adventurer and a freethinker, who, despite the best efforts of an education designed to equip him for obedient anonymity, somehow did something truly useful with his life. His stubborn and yet self-effacing commitment to his ideals carried him through many daunting situations, and his sense of humour kept him able to see the funny side.
– *Brian Eno*

This is the work of a determined guy who is prepared to expose fraud and injustice wherever he finds it.
– *David Hencke*, former Westminster correspondent for the *Guardian*

David Wilson is a national treasure.
– *Mandla Langa*, author of *The Lost Colours of the Chameleon*, winner of the 2009 Commonwealth Prize

What a life this man has led!
– *Dorothy Byrne,* Head of Channel 4 TV News and Current Affairs

For my grandson Rhys Matteo

Dear Reader,

The book you are holding came about in a rather different way to most others. It was funded directly by readers through a new website: Unbound.

Unbound is the creation of three writers. We started the company because we believed there had to be a better deal for both writers and readers. On the Unbound website, authors share the ideas for the books they want to write directly with readers. If enough of you support the book by pledging for it in advance, we produce a beautifully bound special subscribers' edition and distribute a regular edition and e-book wherever books are sold, in shops and online.

This new way of publishing is actually a very old idea (Samuel Johnson funded his dictionary this way). We're just using the internet to build each writer a network of patrons. Here, at the back of this book, you'll find the names of all the people who made it happen.

Publishing in this way means readers are no longer just passive consumers of the books they buy, and authors are free to write the books they really want. They get a much fairer return too – half the profits their books generate, rather than a tiny percentage of the cover price.

If you're not yet a subscriber, we hope that you'll want to join our publishing revolution and have your name listed in one of our books in the future. To get you started, here is a £5 discount on your first pledge. Just visit unbound.com, make your pledge and type **leftfield** in the promo code box when you check out.

Thank you for your support,

Dan, Justin and John
Founders, Unbound

CONTENTS

GLOSSARY

APC	Armoured Personnel Carrier
BiH	Bosnia-Herzegovina
BM	British Movement
BMJ	*British Medical Journal*
CCF	Combined Cadet Force
CND	Campaign for Nuclear Disarmament
GOSH	Great Ormond Street Hospital
HVO	*Hrvatsko vijeće obrane*, army of the Croatian Republic of Herzeg-Bosnia
INC	Iraqi National Congress
JNA	Yugoslav People's Army
NEPBAT	Nepalese Battalion (of the United Nations)
NMCF	Nelson Mandela Children's Fund
ODA	Overseas Development Administration
OHR	Office of the High Representative in Bosnia-Herzegovina
OSCE	Organisation for Security and Co-operation in Europe
PMC	Pavarotti Music Centre
RAMC	Royal Army Medical Corps
SPANBAT	Spanish Battalion (of the United Nations)
SRT	Serious Road Trip
STWC	Stop The War Coalition
UCH	University College Hospital
UNHCR	United Nations High Commission for Refugees
UNPROFOR	United Nations Protection Force

Chronology

1945	26 March: born in Shaftesbury, Dorset
1946–1956	Bromley, South London
1958–1961	Canford School, Dorset
1962	Argentina
1963–1966	Lawyer's clerk and package holiday to Yugoslavia
1966–1967	Oxfam clerical assistant, Oxford
1967–1970	University of Essex, BA in Sociology
Aug 1968	Married Renata Kasun, Zagreb
1970–1971	University of Warwick, MA in Labour History
Apr 1972	Birth of son, Benjamin
1972–1987	College lecturer, Kilburn Polytechnic, London
Apr 1978	Death of son, Daniel
Jul 1980	Birth of son, Jonathan
1987–1991	Agent for Ivan Rabuzin, Croatian naïve painter
May 1989	*Simple Writings,* performed at the Duke of Cambridge, London
Apr 1990	*The Old Master,* rehearsed reading, Lyric Hammersmith, London
Sep 1991	Attended playwriting course with Anne Aylor, Porthcothen
1991–1992	Producer, BBC Arena: *Croatia: The Artists' War*
Feb 1993	Co-founded War Child with Bill Leeson
Jan 1994	Divorced from Renata
Jun 1996	Visited Soweto and KwaMashu, Republic of South Africa
1997–1999	Director Pavarotti Music Centre, Mostar, Bosnia-Herzegovina
Mar 1999	Visited Luciano Pavarotti, New York City

Feb 2000	Sacked from War Child
Mar 2000	Co-founded Future Trust with Hiroshi Kato
2001–2004	Employed by Fujitsu Ten
Jan 2001	*Guardian*/Channel 4 TV exposé of War Child
May 2003	Man of the Year Award, presented by Mikhail Gorbachev
Nov 2004	*Spitting into the Sky* performed at the Dylan Thomas Festival, Swansea
2005–2009	Press Officer, Stop the War Coalition
Apr 2008	Married Anne Aylor, London
May 2009	*The Trainer* (co-writer Anne Aylor), performed at the Hackney Empire

LEFT FIELD

CHILDHOOD, BOYHOOD, YOUTH

'So many memories of the past arise when one tries to recall the features of somebody we love that one sees these features through memory, as though through tears.'

Leo Tolstoy

The Gondola

The black-and-white photograph sits on the windowsill in my father's care home. He and my mother are in a gondola. In any other city you'd be able to tell the era from the background or the cars, but Venice is a watery city built on larch and alder pilings. It's only by taking a closer look at my parents that I can tell it's the 1950s.

Gondolas are the romantic way to explore Venice, but in this portrait my parents might as well be alone in their black boat. My father's bulldog chin juts out as he stares straight ahead. My mother looks away from him, straight at the camera. In her tweed two-piece suit she could be Donna Reid. My father, in jacket and tie and with hair neatly combed to the side, is leaning forward, smoking a pipe. Not smiling, he looks thoughtful, as if they are setting out to visit the cemetery island of San Michele.

I am 20 years older than my father in this photograph but, to me, the man in this boat is old. I look down at the 99-year-old in the bed. Now that *is* old. He looks like an unbandaged mummy.

I glance back at the picture. I can't tell the season. My parents are dressed for cold weather. The British don't expect sunshine, even in Italy.

My father seems to sense I am here and opens his eyes. 'It's you,' he says, sounding angry. 'I want to go. I have had enough. I've overstayed my welcome.'

I nod, say I understand.

'How am I going to do it?' he says.

I look at his tray of congealed food, his meal all mashed up. He can't wear his false teeth any more. 'You could stop eating.'

'I tried that, but I got hungry and it was boring.' His eyes start to close, then suddenly flicker open. 'How am I going to do it?' he asks again.

I tell him what his grandson in New York told me. 'Dad, if you ever get to 99 and are looking at the ceiling all day, I'll fly to London and bring every Class A drug I can get my hands on. I'll see you out in a haze of chemicals.'

My father raises his head from the pillow. 'Can you call him now?'

We both laugh. He is quiet for a long time, then says, 'I need you to give me some money.'

'What for, Dad?'

'To pay for the theatre we went to last night.'

'What theatre?'

'The Gilbert and Sullivan.'

'How much do you need?'

'Two thousand pounds.'

'That's a lot for the theatre.'

'Yes,' he says, 'but then there was the meal afterwards at Mon Plaisir.' He looks at me sternly. 'You know perfectly well what I'm talking about.'

I won't disillusion him. He hasn't moved from this bed for over a year. Besides, he is falling asleep, the tip of his tongue protruding from the corner of his mouth.

Seeing his tongue like that reminds me that it's a trait I've inherited. When I'm concentrating on a physical task, like carrying dinner plates down a flight of stairs, I too stick my tongue between my teeth: a foolish thing to do. The slightest stagger and it's bitten.

This is something he did when confronted with getting his lawn mower to start, trying to jam a bamboo stick in hard ground to hold up his tomatoes and, more in character with the man and who he was, replacing a ribbon in his typewriter. The lawn mower and tomatoes could always wait, but never the Imperial.

In the Second World War, my father was a neurologist

in the Royal Army Medical Corps and treated servicemen who suffered from what we now call post-traumatic stress disorder. He wrote up his conclusions and, in 1943, submitted a paper to the *RAMC Journal* titled 'Minor Psychological Disturbances in the Services'. A year later, he published 'Somatic Manifestations of Psychoneurosis' in the *British Medical Journal*.

At the end of the war, the editor of the *BMJ*, Hugh Clegg, offered my father a job but, after meeting him, changed his mind. He told him that he was too radical for an establishment journal and advised him to apply for work with *The Lancet*. He did and was there for 30 years, the last 12 as editor.

Throughout my childhood, my memories are of my father spending evenings and weekends proofreading articles or writing the following week's editorial. I can still see the long scrolls of text stretching across the floor of his study.

I loved going with him to his office in Adam Street, off the Strand. *The Lancet* entrance smelled of wine as the building was immediately above Sichel's cellars, the Bordeaux wine dealers. That and a musty dampness. The marshy banks of the Thames once stretched up to the Strand before the construction by Joseph Bazalgette of the Embankment with its road, underground line and gardens.

The next time I visit him he is eating his lunch. I clean the sides of his mouth with his bib and he looks at me sternly.

'Who are you?'

'I'm your son, David.'

'Oh,' is all he says.

It's hard to come to terms with the fact that this man, who once edited a magazine held in high regard throughout the world, is now so confused.

His editorship of *The Lancet* was part of a long series of radical editors which went back to Thomas Wakley, who worked with the social reformer William Cobbett in the 1820s. My father's predecessor, Sir Theodore (Robbie) Fox, was a Quaker and a pacifist ambulance driver on the Western

Front in the First World War. The present editor, Richard Horton, is responsible for reminding the world that the Iraqi war and occupation very likely took in excess of a million lives.

I stare at the wilting rose on his bedside table. 'Who gave you that?' I ask.

He smiles. 'An admirer. I have them here, you know.'

'How's lunch?'

'Good. They have a new chef. She's excellent.'

'You met her?'

'I went to the kitchen yesterday.'

'How did you manage that?'

He smiles. 'You know. First left, second right.'

My father had a few catchphrases and this was one he always used when asked for directions.

I lift a spoon of something to his lips and he chews at it for ages, as though it's rare steak. As I lift the spoon again he says, 'The potatoes are particularly good.'

I look at the mush on his plate and wonder which pile is the potatoes.

The catchphrase my father used to trot out after Sunday lunch was 'The best roast potatoes since last Sunday'. My mother's potatoes were to die for. She would parboil them, drain the water, shake them until the outsides were flaky, then place them in the meat juices which had been kept boiling on the cooker. Well basted, they joined the roast meat in the oven. The result – crispy, hard skins and cotton wool inside. I've never been able to achieve her results. Is it my electric oven? (My mother's was gas.) Was it the potatoes? The quality of the meat and its juices? Is it my memory, like my father's, playing tricks on me?

I arrive to find him holding his arms out. I lean down to kiss the top of his head. He brings his left hand down to touch mine. He doesn't have the strength to hold.

'Look at this arm,' he says. 'It's thinner than the right.'

I can't tell the difference. They are both thin; the veins look like they want to break free of his skin. With each visit he's becoming more skeletal, receding from life.

My father had been one of the first medics to enter the Bergen-Belsen concentration camp when it was liberated. I remember him telling me how British troops handed out high-calorie rations to the prisoners and that thousands died because they were unused to food.[1]

When I was a small boy, he showed me photos he'd taken in the camp. Barrows full of corpses with limbs trailing on the ground. Faces with protruding eyes. The pyjamaed living carrying the naked dead. Bodies lying on top of each other in mass graves. He kept these photos in the bottom drawer of his roll-top desk. When he was at work, I used to take them out and stare at them with horror and fascination.

When I was sorting out his desk after he moved to this home, they weren't there. I would like to have asked him what had happened to them, but I am left to guess his motives. Perhaps he felt guilty about what had taken place in Belsen, that he could have intervened to stop the disastrous food handout. Perhaps he just felt guilty to be in such a place at such a time. That was something I had learned some years before for myself, when I, too, was a helpless witness to death.

Today I tell him this will be a quick visit as I am meeting a friend. He asks what the time is. I push the large clock on his side table towards him. 'Three o'clock.'

'That clock has a story to tell,' he says, then adds angrily, 'It's not mine.'

'Whose is it?'

He is struggling to remember. 'I can't put it together. My mind …' His sentence falls away, replaced with, 'Thank you for coming. You've done your duty. Go.'

I kiss his head. 'I love you, Dad.'

'À tout a l'heure.'

When he wants to say something emotional, he always slips into French.

When I was a child, I didn't call him Dad. He was Pa or

Papa. I remember that I was often frightened of him, especially on days when I'd upset my mother who would say, 'Wait until your father gets home.'

Even when I thought I'd done nothing wrong, I knew he would take her side and that I would be banished to my room with his harsh words following me up the stairs. He only hit me on one occasion. With a belt. When I saw what was about to happen, I locked myself in the lavatory which only delayed the punishment. I can't remember what I'd done to deserve the beating. Normally, his looks and words were punishment enough.

His mother had had a devastating effect on him. She never held him, kissed him or showed the slightest bit of affection for him or his sister, Dilly. Whenever I asked him about his relationship with his mother, he always returned to the same story about her terrible snobbery. How in Harrogate, where his father was a spa doctor, he'd once brought a friend home for tea and his mother wouldn't allow this boy into the house again because he spoke with a Yorkshire accent.

He never talked about his father, Hector. I know nothing about him except that he died, aged 59, of a heart attack. Perhaps he kept himself busy with his spa patients so as to spend as little time as possible with his wife. 'Don't leave me with that woman,' he pleaded with Dilly when his daughter left home for the last time.

My father did have a nanny, Alice Pinder, who retired to Streatham. I remember we used to visit her there on our way to the skating rink. In my father's words, 'she was unburdened by education'.

My grandmother's coldness and cruelty had its effect on my father; he found it almost impossible to express emotion. When my mother tried to touch him tenderly he would recoil. With us children he could be warm and funny, but he rarely kissed us or gave us hugs. He spent his life letting his love out bit by bit, escaping in slow motion from the destructive effect his mother had had on him.

In 1972, following a car crash, my mother had an operation for a cerebral haemorrhage which had the same neurological effect as a frontal lobotomy. For the rest of her life, she needed to be looked after. My father took early retirement to become her full-time carer. He would help her dress, cook her food and hold her hand when she slept in her chair. It was only late in life, and as a result of a personal tragedy, that he was finding a way to express his affections.

This time when I arrive, my father asks me to draw the curtains. He says the sun is in his eyes. I tell him it's raining.

'Close them anyway.'

I push the Venice picture against the window. I look at his defiant chin and think, He's always been obstinate. Perhaps that's another trait I've inherited.

I tell him the news. How there is an Occupy movement spreading across the US and Europe. That it had started in Tunisia and Egypt. That I'm on my way to St Paul's to visit the occupiers camped out there.

His face lights up. 'Good for you,' he says. 'Will there be a revolution?'

I smile. It's not just my tongue-between-my-teeth and his obstinacy I have inherited, but also his politics.

Travelling across Salisbury Plain in October 1956, the A30 is blocked with military convoys on their way to Southampton to be shipped to Suez. Israel, France and Britain have just launched an attack on Egypt after President Gamal Abdel Nasser's decision to nationalise the Suez Canal.

My father is crouched over the steering wheel. 'That bloody man.'

'What bloody man?' I ask.

'Anthony Eden. The bloody Prime Minister.'

My mother taps his arm, turning round to look at my sisters and me in the back seat. 'Don't listen to your father,' she says and turns back. 'Really, Ian. Remember the children.'

I am transfixed by the column of desert-camouflaged tanks,

Bedford lorries and Land Rovers and want to know why my father is so angry. As an eleven-year-old, it looks pretty exciting. 'Where are all those tanks going?'

He spends the rest of the journey telling us, my mother interrupting with. 'Ian, stop talking so much and keep your eyes on the road.'

I remember that during the seven-year Mau Mau insurgency in Kenya, I would watch the BBC News, appalled at images of black men waving spears. The commentary was full of praise for 'our boys' holding back these 'terrorists'. If my father was in the room, he would angrily remove his pipe from his mouth and say, 'We shouldn't be there'.

Sixty years later, the BBC returned to the Kenya insurgency, this time to report the victory of survivors of British terror in the High Court in London. We now know that 70,000 men, women and children were held in concentration camps and that many were subject to torture by British forces.

I tell my father I am writing a book about my life.

'Good. You have a lot to say. You always did. I hope I live long enough to ...' His voice drops away.

'I'll read it to you.'

'Is there anything ready?'

He asks me this every time I visit, but I'm nervous about reading my book to him. He will either not like what I have written about him, or will ask me not to mention him at all. He has always been modest. When he was interviewed on BBC radio, he insisted they introduce him as editor of *The Lancet*, without his name.

He was passionate about speaking and writing coherently. He'd be sure to find my grammatical and syntax errors. Even a missing comma, he said, could have a dramatic effect. He told me that just before the Battle of El Alamein, in November 1942, the *Daily Express* had printed a headline, *EIGHTH ARMY PUSH BOTTLES UP GERMANS*. And just as funny, perhaps with his mother in mind, he'd add another, 'Let's eat Granny'.

I want to ask him questions about his family. There are big gaps in what I know, but it's unlikely he'll remember now.

I keep it simple. 'Has Thomas been to visit you?' I ask.

Thomas Dormandy is my father's oldest friend. He used to write for *The Lancet*. He was the author of books on the history of tuberculosis, pain and opium. He would take along pages from his latest work and read them to my father. I think Thomas did this because my father was always brutally honest with his comments.

'Oh no,' he says. 'He's too ill to come here.'

I don't know how my father knows if Thomas is ill or not, but Thomas is Hungarian and I had hoped this might be a way to ask him about the refugees who stayed with us in 1956.

In October of that year, demonstrations broke out across Hungary, demanding the withdrawal of Soviet troops. The government fell and Imre Nagy became Prime Minister in the middle of a revolution. Workers and students set up militias; troops tore off their insignia and joined them on the barricades. Police were killed at street corners, as well as some Russian soldiers. It seemed that the few remaining Soviet troops would withdraw. But on 4th November they returned in large numbers. The workers and students only had small arms and Molotov cocktails. Thousands were slaughtered. Lucky ones fled.

My father and mother found homes for two of them, a young couple, Lorencz and Ester. They arrived just before Christmas. Lorencz stayed with us and Ester went to the Schields's, my parents' bridge partners. My father told Mr Schield that, as refugees from Hitler, they had a duty to return the favour.

I was fascinated by Lorencz's stories of how he and his fellow fighters had climbed onto the Soviet T-34 tanks and hurled petrol bombs inside. How they had lost many comrades and how grateful they were to have a new home, thanks to my parents.

When Ester came to visit her boyfriend, they would

cook goulash, which made a change from my mother's steak and kidney pie. They were always cheerful, but it was only a front. I remember waking at night to hear Lorencz sobbing in his room.

After leaving us, they went on to qualify as dentists, marry and settle down in Kent. Every Christmas they would send us a card. Ten years after they'd arrived in this country, they rang my parents and said they wanted to visit. They turned up in a Rolls-Royce. My father watched as they turned in to our drive. 'Betty, you answer the door.' He pointed at the car. 'Look at that.'

'It's a Rolls-Royce, Ian,' my mother said. 'They have done well.'

He slammed his study door shut. My mother welcomed them. 'Ian's been very busy this week. He'll join us soon.'

She left Ester and Lorencz with my sisters and me. I could hear her whispering loudly outside his door, 'Ian, come out now. We have guests. Ian, do you hear me?'

While I gobbled up the delicious *puncstorta* jelly roll they'd brought, the conversation was as frosty as the cake's pink icing. My father was disappointed at their success. I suppose he expected them to be revolutionary dentists in Sevenoaks.

It's early May 2012 and my father is going to be a hundred. I tell him about the arrangements for his birthday. 'It's your centenary next weekend, Dad. Family and friends want to visit.'

He frowns.

'What do you want for your birthday?'

'For you to give them the wrong address.'

'You'll be getting a card from the Queen.'

'I'll send it back.'

'Shall I bring some vodka?'

'Don't get me started. I'm proud I've been sober for …' He pauses and looks around the room, '… years.'

Ever since my mother died, I've brought him a bottle of vodka on his birthday. For most of his life he'd been a beer drinker. I remember the large bottles of Whitbread in wooden crates. He'd have them delivered and the empties taken away.

He loved going to the pub and used to tell me he was surprised he graduated, as most evenings he was boozing with other medical students. As he got older, he drank at home with my mother who enjoyed her evening fling at the sherry.

My parents loved giving sherry parties. They were usually on Saturday evenings and guests were invited from six to eight. There was dry and sweet sherry for the women and whisky and soda for the men. There were also cocktail sticks stabbed into squares of cheddar cheese and pineapple. My father would get angry if any of the guests trespassed beyond 8pm. Later at dinner he'd say, 'Norman was asking for a whisky when it was time to go. Some people take advantage of one's hospitality. Not to mention my liquor.'

A regular guest at our house was Karl Henrik Køster, a Danish neurosurgeon who wrote for *The Lancet* and who'd met my father in Bergen-Belsen when they were both serving in the RAMC. They became close friends and my sisters and I called him Uncle Karl. Because he always came to stay in December, this large man with his deep voice and Nordic accent was Father Christmas, though now I realise he looked more like Karl Marx.

Uncle Karl always arrived with a large bottle of Cherry Heering, a Danish liqueur, and gifts for us children. I remember the nine-inch-high brightly-painted wooden soldier with its red tunic and blue trousers. It had moveable arms and a detachable lance which was quickly lost.

Karl Henrik was a surgeon at Copenhagen's Bispebjerg hospital. After operating on a wounded member of the Resistance, medical students asked him to help hide 40 Jews while their escape by boat to Sweden was organised. But how to get them into the hospital? Karl Henrik organised a 'funeral' with dark cars, black clothes and flowers. 140 turned up and all of them had to be hidden.

He then arranged for ambulances to take them to the coast. In all, he and his hospital saved 2,000 Jews.

Then their luck ran out. One day, when leaving his apartment, he passed the Gestapo on the stairs. They asked him where Dr Køster could be found. As he left the building, he passed the body of a medical student shot in the back. He then followed the same route as those he had helped save and escaped by boat to Sweden. He made his way to the UK and joined the British army.

His wife Doris was at home. The Gestapo imprisoned her.

My father lost contact with him when he retired from *The Lancet*. The last he knew of Karl was when he heard from a mutual friend that he had, as my father put it, 'taken up with his secretary'. He had no idea what happened to poor Doris.

Karl committed suicide in the 1980s and didn't live to see the 1998 Disney film made about his life, *Miracle at Midnight*. Directed by Ken Cameron, it starred Sam Waterson as Karl and Mia Farrow as Doris.

I recently came across words of his explaining why he acted as he did. 'It was the natural thing to do. I would have helped any group of Danes being persecuted. The Germans picking on the Jews made as much sense to me as picking on redheads.'

What with Uncle Karl and the Hungarians, I had contact at a young age with people who'd led dangerous political lives. Karl Henrik's booming voice and wry humour has stayed with me. It has always been important to be able to see the funny side of the grimmest experiences. There is always a *Springtime for Hitler*.

It's July and my wife, Anne, and I are planning a month away on the Croatian island of Mljet. I'm nervous about leaving my father and tell him I won't be seeing him for a long time.

'Lucky you,' he says. 'Not having to see me.'

'Promise to hang on until I get back.'

'I promise,' he says, then smiles. 'But if I break my promise, it will be because I forgot I made it.'

My father was a man who kept his promises, faithful to his friends and to his wife.

'I never had any affairs,' he told me after my mother died.

'Are you saying that with regret?'

'When you marry, you have a duty to your partner for life.'

He had few friends, but those he had were lifelong.

A nurse brings my father a cup of tea and a Rich Tea biscuit. 'Thank you,' he says, as though he's been given a gold watch. 'Very kind.' She leaves the room and he adds, 'They're all crazy here, but the biscuits are good.'

His eyes close and I stand up, ready to go. He opens his lids. 'Are you leaving?'

'I thought you were asleep.'

'I will be soon. I'm on the short list. The short list for death.'

It's getting dark so I push the old photo back against the window before closing the curtains. I notice that damp has got inside the frame. The bottom of the gondola is now buckled and white. I look at my mother's carefully permed hair and want to ask him about her. I touch his arm. 'Dad, how did you first meet Mum?'

My sister, Liz, told me they'd met at Smokey Joe's, a night club in Soho. That my father had turned to the friend he was with and said, 'I'm going to marry that girl.' He asked her to dance and she said she was with a member of the band. He said, 'You can still take a chance.' At the end of the evening he asked her to meet him the next day at Speakers' Corner adding, 'If you come there, we will spend the rest of our lives together.' He arrived with a red rose and there she was, waiting for him. But I want to hear this story again, from my father. It may be my last chance.

He looks at me and smiles. 'Go,' he says.

I get up to leave and kiss the top of his head.

'*Je m'ennuie*,' he says.

'You're bored,' I answer sadly. 'I understand.'

'*Tous les jours*. Enough.'

Alice in the Oven

'Can I stay at home, please?'

'Don't be silly,' my mother said. 'Rattling around in this house all on your own. Go and put your coat on.'

I have always hated shopping and I blame my mother for that.

During the long wait while she sat at her dressing table, which was itself dressed in starched crochet frills, I would watch as she powdered her nose, rouged her cheeks, and then the five-minute search for her hat, sometimes a scarf.

First stop: Mr Thomas, the cobbler above the station. I say above as there was a row of small shops built on the bridge. The trains shook the stacked shoes and jangled the blank keys waiting to be cut.

My mother handed him my Clarks school shoes. 'I don't know what he gets up to,' she told him as if I wasn't there. 'He's always running everywhere. Why he can't keep still I don't know.' She looked at me, her face a brief smile. 'You little rascal.'

'Keeps me busy,' said Mr Thomas. 'Wednesday morning all right for you to collect?'

A nod, then on to Cullens, the grocers.

'Good morning, Mrs Douglas-Wilson. May I have your list?'

My mother would sit on a wicker chair at the far end of the counter while Mr Roberts, in his long brown jacket, climbed a ladder which ran on rails along the line of shelves. He called down, 'Two tins of sardines today? These ones in brine are very good. Only half a pound of sugar this week? How's the

15

doctor? Saw him on Masons Hill on Saturday. Appeared to be having trouble with the motor. It was coughing a bit on the way up. I'm afraid this corned beef has gone up a ha'penny.'

'Can we have some ginger snaps?' I always had to remind her to buy biscuits.

Mr Roberts would open a large bin and scoop a dozen pieces into a paper bag. He would then hold the two corners of the bag and twizzle them several times to seal it.

Then to Importers, the coffee shop at the top of the High Street with a café at the back. I liked the aroma of roasting coffee revolving in the drum in the window.

'Half a pound of Continental, please, Mr Barraclough. Ground two and a half. I'll go and have my coffee and pick it up on my way out.'

I had to sit listening as my mother chatted to Naomi Peters, Dorothy Somers and Patty Masterson, her three friends, who were always there and always talking. Occasionally, they smiled in my direction through their unbroken words.

'The tennis match has been cancelled with this rain. My daughter is so upset.'

'My husband gets home so late. It's hard keeping dinner warm for him.'

'You must go to David Greigs. They have some excellent fresh salmon in today and their eels are always good.'

The local library was just across the road. Literature was my escape from my mother and her nattering friends. 'Can I go and get a book?'

'Yes, but be careful how you cross the road. Be back in 15 minutes.'

My favourites were Kenneth Graham's *The Wind in the Willows* and Defoe's *The Adventures of Robinson Crusoe*, an illustrated and probably abridged version. The first was a rural escape from the suburbs, but safely English, while the second took me as far away as you could get.

And as much as I could find of Lewis Carroll so as to escape logic altogether: 'and the moral of that is – be what you would seem to be – or, if you'd like it put more simply – never imagine yourself not to be otherwise than what it might appear to others that what you were or might have been was not otherwise than what you had been would have appeared to them to be otherwise.'

In the winter flu season my mother would place Alice and her Wonderland friends in the oven for an hour 'to get rid of the bugs, dear'. I always had a warm feeling when I read these books and I'm grateful to those talking women at Importers for encouraging my love of literature.

In Market Square there was Medhursts, the local department store, which had an extraordinary contraption for making purchases. The cashier would place the customer's money in an envelope and pin this with a clothes peg to an overhead wire 'track' that whizzed the envelope way across the ceiling. Change and receipt came back the same route.

I remember my mother taking me there to meet Father Christmas for the first time. I sat on his lap and he gave me a Meccano set. How did he know?

That was the year my faith in Santa Claus was destroyed with a little help from my sister Liz. On Christmas Eve my mother told me to call his name up the sitting room chimney and ask him to visit.

I bent down close to the fire and called out, 'Father Christmas, please come tonight.'

A voice came back. 'Yes, child, I will.'

My sister started to laugh and I turned round to see my mother talking in a deep voice through her cupped hands. A dead giveaway, but I didn't want to believe my own eyes or ears.

That night I asked my mother if my sister Joanna and I could leave a glass of sherry for Father Christmas as it was a cold night and he'd appreciate it. We had lost Liz to the faith.

'Yes, of course, dear.'

We put the glass outside my bedroom. The next morning it was empty, with a note beside it. 'Thank you for the most welcome glass of sherry.'

Hang on, that was my father's writing.

I don't remember my mother ever being upset with us children, but she often argued with her husband. That's something I blocked from my mind, but my sisters remind me that plates used to fly. My father worked a seven-day week and had little time for us and her. When she was very old, she told me that he was less than attentive in bed.

Like my father, I think her own childhood had left its scars. My mother and her younger sister, Enid, were the daughters of Rees Bevan, the General Manager of Briton Ferry steelworks in south Wales. His wife had been killed in 1920 when my mother was twelve years old. My grandparents had been travelling in an open-topped car from their home in Pontardawe to Swansea. A lorry pulled out in front of them and because she was standing up to enjoy the sun and wind, her neck was cut by the windscreen.

Two years later, my grandfather married Betts, the under-matron at Malvern Girls' School where he'd sent his daughters. Betts was only six years older than my mother and she saw to it that both girls were cut off from their father's money. Thanks to Betts, there was never going to be help for either sister from their wealthy father.

They had a younger brother, Ken, who died of diphtheria, aged eight. Betts told the two sisters that he was ill because he'd eaten too many sweets. The girls nursed him and my mother told me that his last words were 'I want to see my mother'. She said her brother had been popular in Pontardawe and all the shops closed on the day of his funeral. Throughout her life, she talked about Ken and how much she'd loved him.

At bedtime, if I was fooling around and disappeared under the sheets, my mother would get angry with me. I think it reminded her of Ken's death. When she was dying, she kept mentioning his name.

After my mother left school, Betts made her feel unwelcome at home in Pontardawe so she went to Italy and took a job as a nanny for a *contessa* in Florence. She became fluent in Italian and used to entertain her charges on the piano and violin; she played both well. Her father came to visit her and got a small comeuppance on the journey there. He got off the train in Milan in his pyjamas to buy a newspaper and the train left without him. My mother always laughed when she told us that.

She spent her life trying to fit in with English middle-class conventions. At meals she would say, 'Take your elbows off the table', 'Don't scoop your peas', 'Turn your fork over'. Salt had to be poured in a small pyramid at the side of the plate. When eating soup, the bowl had to be lifted away from you, never towards. Spread over your knees was a table napkin, but never a serviette When the meal was finished, knife and fork had to be placed together and set at six thirty on the dinner plate.

We were told never to say 'toilet', but 'lavatory'. Never 'pardon', but 'I beg your pardon'. We had to greet guests politely and say goodbye when they left. When my mother held her regular coffee mornings, she would call us down from our bedrooms: 'Children, come and say goodbye to Mrs Paterson.' If we were visitors at a friend's house, we should never ask to look around.

Language and behaviour were codified to distance the upper and middle classes from the standards of common people: they were non-U to our U.

My mother had a slight Welsh accent. When she was with her sister, Enid, the accent became broad Swansea. I remember them gossiping about their cousin. 'Do you remember Mathonwy, Betty?'

'Oh yes, I do that,' my mother answered.

'She was a one, she was.'

My mother would then deliver the punchline. 'Only had to hang her knickers on the end of the bed and she was pregnant.'

Dialogue worthy of *Under Milk Wood*.

One of the things I'm most grateful to my mother for are the holidays we took on a farm at Llangennith on the Gower Peninsula where Dylan Thomas had his first kiss. My father rarely came with us and would wave us off at Paddington station. We would visit her father in Swansea – God knows why – and then take the bus to Llangennith where we stayed on a dairy farm.

I loved climbing on the back of the tractor trailer each morning as the farmer loaded his milk churns. He let me sit beside them as he took them to the depot in the village.

Back at the farm, my sisters and I used to spend hours jumping from the barn loft into the deep straw below. When we got bored with that, we would stand on the rails of the gate leading into the field, staring at the cows. They, of course, stared back.

The beaches on the Gower were an adventure playground. My sisters and I played hide-and-seek in the dunes and, when the tide was out, we'd hunt for razor clams. They burrowed below the sand, but left small round depressions. We'd run to the sea line and fill milk bottles with water which we poured into the holes. We'd been told the clams would think the tide had come in and emerge from their burrows to feed through their siphons. Nobody really knows the truth of any of this. We never caught any.

I would have liked to stay on that farm forever because I hated the journey home. I hated Bromley and the London suburbs. North of London's inner periphery road, the North Circular, and south of the South Circular has always been enemy territory to me, their streets living graveyards, their houses full of repressed emotions. Give me the inner city with its noise, sirens, dirt and anger.

We had moved to Bromley in 1946 when I was one. My first memories are from three years later. I remember a lot of snow, followed by a very hot summer. 1950 is recorded as being unusually warm with temperatures in the high 80s.

Perhaps childhood memories play tricks on us, but each trick contains a truth. Snow above the knees and watching my father dig a path to the pavement. The coal man tipping sacks of anthracite down the coal-hole. The bread van, the milkman, the rag-and-bone man with his horse, cart and bell. Running into the back garden to watch the sweep's brush emerge from the chimney stack. The buses coming up Westmoreland Road: the 126 to Beckenham, the 138 to Hayes Common.

Of all the telephone numbers in my life, I can only remember Ravensbourne 4510. Of all the cars, I can only remember the registration of our Morris Oxford, RKE 595. I remember my first bicycle, a black Raleigh which, on summer mornings, I'd ride through affluent streets to the swimming pool at Bickley School on the other side of town. There is a strong smell of roses in those memories and the smell of the swimming pool itself, a chlorine memory. The more adventurous bicycle rides were out past Hayes Common to Westerham. I would cycle past RAF Biggin Hill and watch the Meteor jets take off and land.

There are memories of trains: steam giving way to electric as childhood gave way to adolescence. Standing on the pedestrian bridge at the far end of Bromley South station, waiting for the *Golden Arrow* to Dover to pass underneath my feet, steam enveloping me in a thick cloud. A temporary excitement, unlike the longer-lasting smog that gripped London in the early 1950s. Going to school with a handkerchief over my mouth which turned yellow on the journey, unable to see my hand in front of my face.

One memory still makes me feel guilty. May 1st, 1953, my mother's 45th birthday. It must have been that year because the shop windows were full of Union Jacks and pictures of the new Queen. My sisters gave me one shilling and sixpence and told me to buy our mother a box of chocolates. I walked into Woolworths and spent the money on marbles.

When I got back Liz said, 'We told you to buy chocolates for Mum and you bought marbles!'

I started to cry and ran upstairs to my parents' bedroom. I placed the marbles on my mother's dressing table. My sisters stood at the door.

'What are you doing, David?' Joanna asked.

Through guilty tears, I lied. 'Look, they're a lovely present.'

Elizabeth was born on August 18th 1941, and Joanna two years later on the same date. Curiously, the daughter my mother's stepmother, Betts, had with Rees Bevan – also called Elizabeth – was born on August 18th and Betts died on August 18th. I don't know what a numerologist would make of all this, but a bookie would say the odds are wildly against it.

My mother told me pointedly that my two sisters were 'planned'.

'And me, Mum?'

'You?' She would laugh and give me a hug.

In 1944 my father had been based at a military hospital in Shaftesbury. In July he was in the second wave of the D-Day landings. Although not with the front-line troops, he was entering a war zone to treat the wounded and traumatised. Perhaps on that last night in the house at No 39 Bell Street at the top of Gold Hill (some readers will remember it from the Hovis ads), he and my mother would have said their goodbyes. I can imagine her asking him if he had any condoms. He didn't and probably didn't fancy walking down that steep hill to get them from the hospital. 'Betty,' he might have said, 'we can't worry about that. I'm leaving at dawn.'

'Ah well,' she would have replied, 'I'm probably safe.'

I am proof of how safe she was. Whenever I visit my eldest son in Cornwall, I stop off in Shaftesbury and walk up Gold Hill. I love it. I like to imagine that that hill gave me life.

A year before she died, I visited my mother with my partner, Anne. 'Happy birthday, Mum.'

She turned to my father. 'Is it my birthday?'

'Yes, Betty, it is.'

Her face lit up. 'Oh good.'

'You are ninety today,' I said.

'Am I?' She turned to my father. 'Am I ninety, Ian?'

'Yes, Betty, you are.'

'Oh good,' she said.

I gave her our present. Four packets of Marlboro Lights.

She looked puzzled and handed them to Anne. 'I don't smoke. You have them.'

'Your ashtray is full, Mum,' I said. 'Dad doesn't smoke.'

'Is it?'

'Anne doesn't smoke either, Mum.'

She looked at Anne. 'Oh, I'm so sorry. Are you two married?'

'No, we're not,' Anne said. Then looking at me, 'Not yet.'

My mother looked concerned. 'Ian, are we married?'

He nodded.

She smiled at him. 'Oh good.'

She then turned to me. 'Why aren't you married?'

Before I had a chance to answer, her attention had drifted back to the cigarettes. She fumbled one out of its packet. 'Will you light this for me, Ian?'

She took two puffs and left the cigarette to burn. 'I'm tired. I'm tired, aren't I, Ian? I think I'll go and lie down.'

I took her to her room and pulled back the covers. I kissed her and she smiled up at me. 'I love you. No, I adore you.'

In the last months of her life, and after 20 years of looking after her, it all became too much for my father. He told me that every evening he found her banging on the bedroom window and screaming, 'I want to die. Let me die!' She had to be moved to a care home. At the end of our visits there, we'd say goodbye and get up from our chairs. She did, too. 'Oh good. We're all going home now.'

When my mother died on the eve of the Millennium, aged 91, I didn't cry. I'd been mourning her for years. The operation 28 years earlier had been a success, but as soon as the surgeon's knife left her brain, the mother I had known was no longer there. She was confused and unable to do anything for herself. The only positive result was that she was cheerful for the rest of her life.

As I write this now, my father is clinging on and my mother's ashes are in the attic where they've been for 13 years. She is waiting for him.

When my father dies, my sisters and I will take them both to the Gower where we spent those childhood holidays. We will scatter their ashes at Worm's Head. He'll be able to spend more time with her there than he ever did when we were children.

Commie Wilson

Summer 1958, aged 13, my mother took me to Gorringe's in Buckingham Palace Road to get my school uniform: two pairs of black trousers, a herringbone suit, a school blazer and tie and six white shirts with detachable starched collars.

I looked at myself in the mirror in my first long trousers. 'Can I keep these on?'

'Of course you can and we'll have tea at Lyons Corner House.'

I felt sure everyone was looking at me as we ate our Maryland cookies.

'Are you excited about going away to school?' my mother asked.

'Yes, but I'll miss you.'

'How do you think I feel about you going?' she said as she removed her lace hanky from her purse.

There wasn't much to say to that. If she felt it was out of her hands, what could I do?

The school train left Waterloo station on a wet September morning. We drove there from Bromley in the Morris. My father lifted my leather trunk out of the boot and my mother helped me with the birch-plywood tuck box. She had filled it with her homemade strawberry and raspberry jams, Marmite, Ryvita, biscuits and cake and three bottles of her milk-cloudy ginger beer carefully wrapped in the *Daily Telegraph*.

We followed the porter as trunk and box were taken to a platform with a chalk board marked *CANFORD SCHOOL TRAIN*. The porter put them into the luggage wagon. My father tipped him while my mother hugged me. 'Remember to ring every week. Reverse the charges.'

I nodded, unable to speak.

'And don't forget to write.'

My father shook my hand, then patted me on the back. 'You'll be fine. Come on, Betty. We must go.'

He always brought goodbyes to an end with these words, 'We must go', and I never knew whether this was because he had an appointment to go to, or because he had to go before he dropped his guard and joined my mother and me in our damp farewells.

My mother gave me a last hug and pushed me towards the train.

My starched collar was already itching and I was sweating by the time I reached my carriage, the windows pasted with *NEW BOYS*.

I stood in the corridor, looking back up the platform as the train chugged out of the station. I couldn't see my father, but my mother was still there, dabbing her eyes with her handkerchief, getting smaller and smaller.

And then we were on the London to Weymouth line heading for Wimborne, west of Bournemouth, a route that, five years later, would be gone with the decimation of Britain's railway routes – the Beeching cuts – along with the steam engine that had pulled our train.

Boys in the two carriages ahead were unravelling toilet rolls into the wind. Long lines of paper flew past like white dragons and disappeared into sheets of rain. To keep myself from choking up, I got out my *Eagle Annual* to catch up on Dan Dare and the adventures of extra special agent Harris Tweed, while the boy opposite me picked his nose with one hand and flicked the pages of *The Wide World Magazine* with the other. It was an illustrated monthly which *The Times* described as 'brave chaps with large moustaches on stiff upper lips, who did stupid and dangerous things'.

Four hours later, green Dennis coaches ferried us from Wimborne station for the two-mile journey to the school.

Canford Magna had been built as an extension to John of Gaunt's fourteenth-century kitchen, but John was never there. His son, Cardinal Beaufort, did visit, although I doubt he spent much time in the kitchen.

Five hundred years later, Canford had become the home of Sir John and Lady Charlotte Guest, nineteenth-century iron magnates and owners of the South Wales steel firm, Guest, Keen and Nettlefolds. The Cardiff works were rivals to the Briton Ferry steelworks where my grandfather had been general manager, so I had a tenuous connection with the place.

When I was preparing to go to Canford, my parents had shown me photos of the buildings and its grounds. It looked beautiful, sitting on the banks of the river Stour, with its grey stone walls and manicured lawns bordered with oak, beech, horse chestnut and elm, the old parkland now extensive playing fields. But like the rotting flesh beneath the bindings of a Chinese concubine's slippered feet, appearances are deceptive.

As I entered the building for the first time, we were asked to report to the prefects who stood holding clipboards. I approached one of them.

'Name?' he asked, without looking up from his list.

'David Douglas-Wilson.'

'Surname only.'

'Doug—'

'Over there.' He pointed to a line of boys.

In the 1950s, public schools were run like armies and divided into regiments, known as Houses. There was School House, Franklin, Salisbury, Beaufort, Court, Monteacute and Wimborne. I was to be in School House. My housemaster was a fierce Yorkshireman, Frank Hopkinson, whom we called Hoppy. He was the geography teacher and had a huge world map behind his desk, the fading British Empire in red.

On the first night we were gathered in one of the large classrooms and Hoppy organised a compulsory boxing match. The introduction to my new school friends was not with a handshake, but a punch.

'Welcome,' he said. 'You are privileged to be in School House. We have the best teams, the most cups. I expect all of you to continue this tradition. Life is a test. There will be many tests while you are here. This is the first. Each of you will box one round. Make space. Push the desks back and we'll start.'

With his clipped language, this man had no time to waste.

After the boxing, the prefects were introduced. 'This is Thompson,' Hoppy said, 'Captain of School House rugby. This is Mitchell, Captain of the House hockey team.'

Mitchell looked friendly and after the introductions were over, I went up to him. 'Is there a public phone?'

'What for?'

'I want to ring my parents.'

'Forget it,' he smirked. 'Forget them.'

He put his hand on my shoulder. I thought he was doing this to soften his words, but he was pushing me away.

From the moment I arrived, I hated Canford: the cold corridors, the ox tongue we'd been served for the first meal, a housemaster who looked like Hitler. Then there were the bells. There were bells for everything. For getting up and going to bed, for PT, for starting and ending classes, for meals, for assemblies and, of course, the chapel bell.

In the passageway to the kitchens, where we queued for our dinner trays, there were rows of redundant bells, reminders of the Guest family years. Their numbers and names were on brass plates: *BILLIARD ROOM, SMOKING ROOM, LIBRARY, HER LADYSHIP'S CHANGING ROOM, DINING HALL*.

That first night, in a dormitory with 20 boys I'd never met before, was terrifying. I lay awake, thinking of my bedroom at home: my mother kissing me goodnight, the sound of the TV downstairs, my father locking the back door, the click as the hall light was turned off and Penny, our dachshund, running up the stairs to her basket on the landing.

Here the strip lighting in the corridor was left on. I remember going to the toilet that first night, frightened I would meet someone. What do you say in the middle of the night to a complete stranger?

The next morning I was given a 'tutor', a second-year boy who had three weeks to teach me answers to the School Quiz. Useless information. How many rugby pitches Canford had, the number of oak trees in the grounds, the names of the Masters and their subjects, the distance in yards from the school gates along the towpath to the bridge at Wimborne, the date the school was founded, the number of boys in the school in 1948.

The film maker, Derek Jarman, was at Canford in the 1950s. In his journal, *Modern Nature*, he wrote, 'Smarting under this tortured system, the boys tortured each other, imposed valueless rules and codes of conduct, obeyed imaginary hierarchies where accidents of origin and defects of nature were magnified.'

You were never alone at Canford. Never allowed to be alone. But it was a place of loneliness. The only opportunity to be with yourself was in bed at night, feet away from the next boy, both practising the art of silent masturbation. I don't remember any gay activity in the dormitories. I naïvely never thought about that kind of sex. The only attention I received from a homosexual was during my first summer term, when a prefect stood before me at the running track. I was hugging my knees to my chest before the hundred yards race.

'I can see your genitals,' he said and smiled at me.

I got up and walked away.

Physical abuse at Canford was never far from the surface. Prefects had the role of sergeant majors. There was fagging. For one week every month, each junior had to clean the prefects' studies. This meant getting up before 6am, shining their shoes, scraping dried baked beans from pans and plates, sweeping carpets with a pan and brush and dusting desks. They would inspect our work and, if dissatisfied, would award the fagger a 'blue paper'. These were entered into a ledger which was kept in Hoppy's office.

Each evening a prefect would come into the Junior Common Room and run his hands along the window ledges, tops of cupboards and desks. If there was any dust, one blue paper to the boy who was on cleaning duty.

If a boy was summoned to the Senior Common Room or a prefect's study and failed to fold his arms on entry, or did not go up to the most senior boy in the room, another blue paper.

Three of these papers and you went to bed, shaking with fear, because after lights out, a prefect would come into the dormitory and call out the victim's name. 'Douglas-Wilson, upstairs.' There, in the Senior Common Room, you received six strokes of the cane, delivered by a prefect, while a second attended as a witness. They had cups of coffee they sipped between strokes. We were allowed to put trousers on over our pyjamas, but the wounds left weals.

One evening, sweet papers were found on the gym floor where School House juniors had been watching a film. When Hoppy asked who had dropped them, and in a rare show of student solidarity, we all put our hands up. He then ordered the prefects to beat everyone. All 30 of us were gathered on the stage in the gym and publicly caned, one by one.

For the worst crimes, beatings were given by Hoppy. Dating girls was in this category. We were allowed exeats to go to Wimborne, but these were only long enough to buy a Crunchie bar or a bag of aniseed balls in the sweet shop across the bridge. Not enough time to wander around or date a local girl.

I had fallen in love with the girl in the record shop. She had brush curls and a pink hairband and wore fluffed-out dresses. She was puzzled by my interest in Ray Charles, Howlin' Wolf and Muddy Waters. My only diversion into mainstream pop was when she persuaded me to buy Johnny Tillotson's 'Poetry in Motion'.

One Sunday afternoon on exeat, she had agreed to meet me on Wimborne Bridge to go for a walk. I don't know what would have happened, but nothing did because a master passed us. I was so scared I said a quick goodbye and rushed back to school along the 1,245-yard riverside path, the only fact from the School Quiz that was ever of any use to me.

I should have stayed with her because it would have been compensation for what was to follow. That evening I was in Hoppy's study. 'You were seen with a girl in Wimborne.' He pointed to the far corner of the room as he lifted the cane from the top of his desk. After a caning, we were supposed to say, 'Thank you, sir.' I never did, and he didn't insist on the protocol with me.

Canford was High Church and today I can still recite, not only the Lord's Prayer, but the Apostles' Creed: 'I believe in God the Father, maker of heaven and earth and in Jesus Christ his only Son ...'

Towards the end of the first autumn term, we were 'invited' to put our names down for Confirmation. I didn't and was summoned to Hoppy's study.

'Douglas-Wilson, Reverend Geake tells me that you have not registered for Confirmation.'

'I don't believe in God, sir.'

'That has nothing to do with it. You are letting the House down.'

They couldn't force Confirmation on me, but they could harass me. Summoned a second time, I was told, 'Douglas-Wilson, you're not kneeling in chapel.'

'I told you, sir. I don't believe in God.'

Again I was told this had nothing to do with it.

'Do you believe in God, sir?' I asked.

'My beliefs have nothing to do with you. We are not talking about God here, Douglas-Wilson. We are talking about loyalty.'

The last straw was when I confronted the religious education teacher, the assistant school chaplain, the Reverend Norman Crowder, when he read Matthew 19:24: 'And I tell you, it is easier for a camel to walk through the eye of a needle than for a rich man to enter the gates of heaven.'

My hand shot up. 'Isn't that about socialism, sir?'

31

'This parable is not to be taken literally, Douglas-Wilson. Sit at the back of the class and get on with your Latin.'

There I remained, isolated, but happily free of the Reverend's attentions who liked to rub his crotch against the back of our chairs. After that, I was banned from RE. No Divinity GCE for me, but I got a good grade in Latin.

I also got a good grade in history. I couldn't stand the present so I concentrated on the past. The history master, Basil Rathbone – not the actor – was a large, shambling man who chain-smoked through class. He was the only teacher who left me with love for a subject.

He was also the only master who was anywhere close to being a liberal. At the beginning of term I used to bring CND pamphlets and leaflets into school. They went unread by my fellow pupils, although during the Cuban Missile Crisis my opinions were taken more seriously. Rathbone read them all.

He also had a risqué sense of humour. 'Would you prefer to be in the light with the ten wise virgins or in the dark with the ten foolish virgins?' he would ask us apropos of nothing.

Our headmaster, Mr Hardie, had two beautiful daughters. Once, when we were discussing the four-minute nuclear warning when sirens would announce Armageddon, Mr Rathbone said, 'You will have just enough time to boil an egg, but not to eat it.' Then added, 'but if I were you, boys, I'd forget the egg, make a dash for Hardie's house and hope that he was out.'

I was a member of the school Debating Society which was as intellectual as things got at Canford. I had trouble finding a supporter for the debate on 'Public Schools should be abolished'. And lost that vote. Heavily.

My nickname was Commie Wilson, but there were others far more radical than me. There were boys who refused to be beaten and were expelled. One of my friends ran away and walked the 25 miles to Southampton before he was found, returned to school and then thrown out.

I reluctantly took part in most school activities. I was even a member of the Combined Cadet Force which was compulsory, but I suppose I could have tested the school and said I was a conscientious objector.

There was Army, Navy or Air Force to choose from. I chose the Army because, as a commando, I could swing on ropes across the River Stour. The Navy cadets paddled beneath us in an ancient lifeboat with the school caretaker, Lieutenant Pantlin, nicknamed Plug, standing to attention in the stern as coxswain.

The Air Force had a glider and 12 boys would divide into two teams and pull on two elasticated ropes while the 'aircraft', balanced on its ski, would be anchored to a stake in the playing field. The 'pilot' was strapped to a wooden block on the nose. On an order from the commanding officer, the pilot released the anchor. A good flight would be 30 yards at three feet off the ground, then a nose dive into the rose bushes. It was rumoured that, in the 1930s, a boy had taken off with a strong tail wind and made it over the school before ditching in the river.

When not swinging on ropes, I was a bugler in the CCF band. Every month there was a parade when a visiting officer from the real Army would inspect us. On these occasions boots had to be spit-polished with blacking, belts, buckles and bugle shined with Brasso. The French teacher, Colonel Kirkpatrick, (aka Wump), a *doppelgänger* for Captain Mainwaring in the TV series *Dad's Army*, would stop in front of me. 'Ah, Commie Wilson.' He'd then turn to the visiting officer and say, 'It's good to see we have the communists on parade.'

Once a year we had Field Day, which meant going on recce patrols on Canford Heath, a good opportunity to take cover and smoke cigarettes. Back on duty, we'd fire blanks at each other from First World War bolt-action Lee Enfield rifles. I remember stuffing mine with dirt and firing off at the other boys. When new, these could fire 15 rounds a minute. I used to think about the soldiers who used these guns in the trenches. Many of them didn't survive that minute when they were sent over the top.

33

Canford was a sports school, not so much for the exercise, but for the development of team spirit, essential in every regiment. So rugby and hockey in winter, but not football – working class – and cricket and rowing in summer. Few boys in School House played tennis, a sport discouraged by Hoppy. He considered the game to be individualistic and effeminate.

If your name didn't appear on the list of players for that day, you had to stand on the sidelines, cheering on your team in the never-ending inter-house matches. If you were caught studying in the library, you were a third of your way to a beating.

Because I was small, I played right wing at rugby, but refused to run fast or tackle an opponent. My reluctance to engage in sports was most marked with the annual School Run. At the end of the autumn term, 400 boys would run six miles across Canford Heath, a maze of brambles and thorn bushes. Prefects in blue shirts were stationed at every junction to direct the runners and watch for slackers. When they were out of sight, I would walk to make sure I was always among the last 50.

I left Canford in December 1962. I had a plan. In an inter-house rugby match in the last week, I tackled and scored the winning try. That same week I came in at number 20 in the school run.

On my last day Hoppy invited me to his study. Too late now to be summoned.

'You have been here four years and could have helped your House win more cups. I do not wish you ill, Douglas-Wilson, but I'm glad to see the back of you.'

I stood scowling in front of him, removed my tie, placed it on his desk and left his office. Years later, I found out that Hoppy was sacked for having an affair with a colleague's wife. His obsession with 'loyalty', verged on the tribal. It must have slipped from his mind, along with his trousers. Talk about letting the House down.

I have no idea if that boy reading *The Wide World Magazine* ever came across the adventures of Sir Henry Layard, son-in-law of Lady Guest. A regular visitor to Canford, he would have rambled though that park with Lady Charlotte and told her of his adventures in Nineveh and how he'd stolen an Assyrian frieze from what is today Iraq, a country of a more contemporary and bloodier theft.

In 1994 this frieze was discovered behind layers of paint in the school's tuck shop and sold at Christie's for nearly £8 million. The proceeds went to the school, of course, not to the Iraqi people, from whom it was stolen.

The very name 'public' school carries with it the stench of British hypocrisy. Another robbery, this one linguistic. Canford was as far away from the public and their norms and needs as you can get. Yet secession from the life of the rest of the nation was no barrier to the desire to dominate it. This is something I understood and despised from an early age. And wanted no part in it.

The location for Lindsay Anderson's 1968 film *If* was Cheltenham College, but it would have been more authentic had it been made at Canford, although I never went as far as Malcolm McDowell and organised an armed rebellion. There were too few of us brave enough to hate the place and see it for what it was. And even if we had, we would have been overwhelmed in less time than it took to empty the cartridges from those ancient Enfields.

I had only two friends at Canford: Roger Lavers who was in School House and Norman Boyer in Franklin. It's extraordinary that, during those four years, these two were the only boys I called by their first names. The only two who were real people and in whose company I escaped my loneliness.

When Roger arrived at Canford, his two older brothers were already there, so their names were Lavers Major, Lavers Minor and poor Roger was Lavers Minimus.

Roger was from Westerham in Kent and lived next door to Lord Cromer, the then-Governor of the Bank of England. On summer holidays I used to cycle out there from Bromley to help harvest his Lordship's wheat. It was great fun to ride on the combine harvester. I can't remember what my job was. Perhaps I am one of the few people in his Lordship's life who got a free ride off him.

At Canford you rarely got to know boys from other houses so my friendship with Norman was unusual. Perhaps it was because we shared a hatred of the place and wanted to get out as much as possible, so long as this did not involve the sports field. One of the only ways to do this, when exeat quotas to Wimborne were used up, was to walk across the school fields onto Canford Heath. This was allowed at weekends if there wasn't a rugby, hockey or cricket match to cheer for from the sidelines.

On these walks we discussed our plans for the future. Norman said he was going back to Argentina where his father managed an *estancia*. I said my only plan was to move as far away from Canford as possible. Norman interpreted this literally and told me that if I could get to South America, he would ask his father to give me a job.

'But I can't ride a horse,' I told him.

Norman laughed. 'Commie Wilson, you'll learn in a day.'

Gaucho and Sailor

December 1962 was the coldest on record and the only warm room in our Bromley house was the kitchen. I spent hours helping my mother with the Christmas pudding. She gave me three sixpenny pieces which I had to wrap in greaseproof paper and place into the mixture. Discovering the tiny silver bundle in your helping was exciting because the lucky finder could make a wish.

Even though I was 17, I still made sure I was her sous chef for another lucky dip – being allowed to lick the bowl with the last of the sugar, treacle and raisins. It seemed a good moment to tell her about my decision. 'I'm going to Argentina, Mum.'

She slammed the oven door on the pudding. 'I beg your pardon.'

'A school friend says I can work on his father's farm.'

'How are you going to get to Argentina? On a magic carpet?'

'On a ship.'

'If you think your father and I will help, think again.'

'It won't cost you or Dad a penny. I've saved money.'

That summer I'd worked as an orderly in the geriatric unit at Orpington Hospital. It involved a lot of bottom cleaning, but the bottoms belonged to some extraordinary old men. I remember one of them had been an infantryman in the First World War. He seemed very old, but couldn't have been more than 70 in 1962. He'd had a stoke and required the complete works when taken to the toilet.

'David, you are such a disappointment to your father and me. I don't know what he's going to say.'

My father closed the door of his study and pointed to

the chair beside his desk. I was nervous because I knew this preceded a lecture. I was ready to march out of the room if he challenged my decision.

He spent ages lighting his pipe, observing me over the top of the bowl. 'You'll be a long way from home and South America is going to be very foreign to you.'

This was good. He had accepted the inevitable.

'I hope you'll be careful.'

'Careful? About what?'

'About girls.'

That got me thinking. A continent of dangerous girls, but what did he mean by 'be careful'? Was he referring to contraception, or was it an instruction to avoid girls altogether? I waited for him to continue, but he refilled his pipe, struck match after match and tried to puff it alight. After what seemed like minutes, he removed it, still unlit, and looked at it as if it were a naughty child. He nodded towards the door.

This was hardly parental approval for my decision, but it was the first recognition on the part of my parents that I was now in charge of my life.

I booked myself on the 20,000-ton Royal Mail Lines' *Arlanza*. My ticket arrived with information about the journey to Buenos Aires and a postcard photo of the ship approaching Rio de Janeiro. Painted ice-cream white, this was, for me, an ocean liner from the movies, churning a foamy wake on a blue sea.[1] I imagined a palm court orchestra and women with cigarette holders, tripping over their pearl necklaces. Gentlemen in blue blazers. The captain's table. Deck quoits by day, love affairs by night.

The *Arlanza* was one of Royal Mail Lines' three ships on the London–Buenos Aires route. The other almost identical ships were the *Amazon* and *Aragon*. They were all passenger ships with refrigerated holds. On the outward journey, cork was loaded in Lisbon. On the return to London, the massive fridges were filled with beef for Vesteys who were ranchers, meat importers and owners of Dewhurst, a chain of butcher shops. Vesteys had their own shipping company, Blue Star Lines, but there was plenty of Pampas beef to transport.

We set sail in mid-January. My family piled into the Morris to see me off from King George V Dock which, along with the Victoria and Royal Albert, were the largest in London.[2]

My sisters were allowed on board and taken to meet the Captain on the bridge. I think they were almost as excited as me and would have joined me if they could. I walked down the gangplank with them and, as they and my mother hugged me, my father stood on the quayside, looking anxiously at his watch. I went back on deck and blew kisses to them as my mother dabbed her eyes with her handkerchief. This was a repeat of Waterloo station four long years earlier.

It took ages for the ship to manoeuvre into the river and by the time we had exited the lock gates, my waving family had long gone.

We moved down the Thames and out through its estuary, the islands of Sheppey and Thanet and the massive oil depot at Thurrock receding into the damp winter mist.

We passed the mouth of the Medway and I looked back at Rochester where my father belonged to the sailing club. I could see the familiar sights of anchored naval reserve ships which he and I had sailed round in his Enterprise dinghy. I hoped I would be a better sailor than he'd been. I remembered the day he had steered our boat through the telephone and electric lines connecting the *Arethusa*, a Royal Navy training ship, to the shore. The Ministry of Defence had sent him a large bill.

Soaring birds followed us out into the North Sea. That month the water had frozen one mile from shore at Herne Bay and as far out as four miles at Dunkirk. Before I left, the BBC had expressed a fear that the Straits of Dover would freeze over. By now, it was too cold to come back on deck and check this out, but we got through.

After a brief stop in Cherbourg, we headed south into the grey mist of Biscay, the sea surprisingly calm for this time of year. I'd never been further from home than Brittany, so setting off to the other end of the world was both scary and exciting. I stood on the deck staring at the horizon, wondering if I'd made the right decision. The nervousness I felt was calmed by the ship's engines which are the marine equivalent of a mother's heartbeat to an embryonic child, a comforting throb.

The trip was to take three weeks via Vigo, Lisbon, Las Palmas, Rio de Janeiro, Santos and Montevideo. Off the coast of Spain, the weather brightened. By the time we reached Lisbon, the sun was out and the city was sparkling white. After loading cork, the next stop was the Canaries. Winter was over. At Las Palmas the officers and crew changed into their tropical whites.

The South Atlantic was calm the whole way and I spent a lot of my time at the stern, looking back at the wake and thinking of all I'd left behind. If I felt any sadness, that emotion soon disappeared when I considered the alternative: a new term at Canford.

Crossing the Equator, we had the Neptune party with the purser dressed up in a white sheet and carrying a trident. Traditionally, this involves a harsh initiation ceremony for those 'crossing the line' for the first time, but not for us. We were given certificates that allowed us two free drinks at the bar.

I've always liked Cuba Libre and associate this cocktail with my first sexual experience. An indirect one. I had a single cabin on the inside of the ship. It had no porthole and was claustrophobic, but I soon discovered that it had its uses.

A young couple who were in four-berth cabins started a shipboard romance. When they found out about my cabin, they asked if they could use it in the afternoons. I was paid with a rum and Coke in the bar each evening. The vicarious reward was that I went to bed each night savouring the woman's Chanel No. 5, presumably the only thing she wore in my bunk.

Eight Cuba Libres later, the *Arlanza* arrived in Rio where I swam off Copacabana Beach. Looking up at Sugar Loaf with its enormous Christ, I couldn't believe I had now arrived in South America.

I'd become friends with the only other young passenger, Joseph Moreno, a Jewish communist who could trace his family back to Spain and Morocco. He was returning home after completing an engineering degree at Manchester University. We would sit on the deck for hours talking politics, and he told me of his fears that the Argentine elections due that July might result in a military coup. Joseph was out by 13 years.

I told him I wanted to see Buenos Aires before heading for the Boyer's *estancia* and Joseph invited me to spend a couple of nights at his parents' home in Calle Tucumán. On the first evening there was a family gathering. His mother cooked fried fish with cilantro and parsley, rice-stuffed peppers, couscous, lentils and chickpeas, followed by date-filled pastries. After the meal, Joseph and I headed for the bars in Puerto Madero. He persuaded me to try *fernet* and Coke, a bitter, syrupy liquor mixed with herbs.

The next day I set off for the Boyers'. I had trouble finding my way to the bus station as I spoke no Spanish. It was pouring with rain. Clutching a disintegrating map of the city Joseph's mother had given me, I decided to walk there. Many of Buenos Aires's pavements were being replaced and I kept tripping into large muddy puddles. I missed the early evening bus and finally set off at midnight.

After the sprawling suburbs, we were on an empty highway heading towards Córdoba province with occasional stops in darkened, dusty towns that looked like film sets for *Gunfight at the OK Corral*. I expected to see Kirk Douglas and Burt Lancaster riding out of the gloom toward the night-stop cafés from which I bought *choripán*, a spicy sausage sandwich, and tepid coffees.

After ten hours we arrived in Rosario in the centre of the Pampas, the town where Che Guevara had been born. Norman and his father, Bernard, met me at the bus station and drove me to their home in the family's 1942 Ford V8.

Four hundred and fifty kilometres north-west of Buenos Aires, the ranch was set in the middle of a copse of white cedars, Osage oranges, figs, native walnuts and ash trees. At the end of a dirt-track avenue lined with eucalyptus, we arrived at their house. Its garden had lawns and shrubs and was full of roses, wall flowers, petunias and begonia creepers. At a distance from the house was the dormitory for the farm workers, cattle dips, corrals and a 14-metre-tall wind pump that drew brackish water from 20 metres down.

This *estancia* was an oasis in the middle of the Pampas grasslands. The lush island of vegetation and woodland encircling the farm house and its outbuildings giving way to the plains. In the distance you could see the next island, the next oasis.

On the first morning, Norman woke me at 5.30am. At six the cook rang the 'bell', a steel bar and a bit of railway iron. I was introduced to the foreman, Juan Gómez, and the other eleven *peons*: six cattlemen, three tractor men, a blacksmith and the cook.

The men were gathered around a half-side of barbequed beef, slicing large cuts off with their *facones*, a knife they kept tucked into the back of their *rastras*, wide belts decorated with silver coins. I was handed a knife and joined in. I was conscious that they were all looking at me as I copied them. There were no plates, and you had to cut into an upended slab of meat to slice away each mouthful. I was frightened that I was going to cut my nose as I leaned forward to feed myself.

Norman gave me a piece of *galleta*, unleavened bread, and the cook came over and offered me a dried gourd with a metal straw. Inside was *mate cocido*, a tea made from the yerba plant. '*Bienvenido*,' the cook said and the others nodded their welcome.

Norman took me to the paddock and called Hilacha over. Hilacha means 'frayed thread' or 'rags', but this six-year-old mare was anything but. She was a small pony with beautiful black-and-white markings. She was very gentle and lowered her head for the bridle. I was shown how to saddle up. The saddle was made of leather, a ridge at the front and rear, and covered with a thick sheepskin to make the ride comfortable.

The men rode with the reins held in the left or right hand, leaving the other arm free for work. To turn the horse, both reins were pulled across to the new direction, unlike the individual left- and right-hand pull in England. There was no raising and lowering of your bottom from hard leather. You kept it firmly on the sheepskin. The cowboy system of riding, common across the Americas, was designed for those who had to work. The English system, by contrast, is ceremonial and deliberately uncomfortable: hard, unyielding and fixed. A bit like public schools.

The horsemen still dressed like the *gauchos* of a hundred years earlier. They wore loose-fitting trousers, known as *bombachas*, belted with a sash and carried a *rebenque*, a two-foot-long leather whip with a metal handle. Some had lassos. Each of them had, of course, their knife.

I was given denim trousers, a brown cotton shirt and felt hat. Norman's father supplied me with leather riding boots.

And Norman turned out to be right. I learned to ride in a day. Left foot into the stirrup and up and over into the saddle. 'Follow me,' Norman said. 'Grip your knees into the side of the saddle and give her a little kick.'

I didn't need to do anything to Hilacha. She followed the other horses as they went from walk, to trot and then into a canter. I stayed on and was even galloping by the end of the day.

A day's work involved riding long distances. We'd move cattle to new pastures, young steers had to be brought back to the corrals to be de-horned, marked and castrated and all of them, from time to time, vaccinated and dipped. Others had to be prepared for market.

It was tough work, but I enjoyed every minute, except when herding took us close to the 380 hectares of mosquito-infested marshy lakes. We had to use our hats, themselves covered with insects, to beat them away from our faces and eyes. There was

43

hardly any point as we'd arrive back at the *estancia*, scratching at the bites.

On Sundays, we started with an enormous English breakfast made by the family's maid, Dominga Arias, a Ranquel Indian. She also cooked us Sunday roasts with Yorkshire pudding, which she called 'ocho puree'.

Between that breakfast and the ocho puree, Norman and I would drive out on hunting expeditions in an old Jeep. I can't remember what we were going to shoot, but I do remember we never killed anything.

Sometimes the Boyers would take me to visit their neighbours. The nearest oasis was an *estancia* called Fortin Las Tunas. The family there were Afrikaners who'd emigrated to Argentina from the Witwatersrand. They'd decided to be cattle farmers in a country without any *kaffirs*. They were awful and I remember the farmer's two daughters, Johanna and Lettie, looked like Cinderella's ugly sisters.

Las Tunas had an interesting history, probably not lost on its new owners. It had been a staging post for travellers going to and from Chile, and a lookout encampment for raiding Ranquel Indians. At least that is how the Boers would have described its history.

One day a lorry arrived with the six-monthly delivery of Mendoza wine. The driver asked me if I'd like to go back to Mendoza with him. He said he'd be passing through Arias in a week and would drop me home. I didn't want to abandon Hilacha and turned him down.

After he left, I realised I'd refused a once-in-a-lifetime trip to the Andes and that the farm work was becoming a comfortable option to everything else the world had to offer. It was time to leave.

I told the Boyers I was going to try and get to the USA and that I'd go to Buenos Aires for a few days to check out the possibilities of a job on one of the shipping lines that sailed from Argentina to the US. I took the bus to the capital and stayed again with Joseph and his family.

The US shipping firm, Moore-McCormack, offered me a job in the purser's office on their cruise ship, the SS *Argentina*. On the wall above the main desk I saw a photo of Tony Curtis and Vivien Leigh, standing on the deck of this ship. Two years before, in 1961, the two actors had travelled on this vessel en route to film *Taras Bulba* in Argentina.

Moore-McCormack said to come back the next day to complete the paperwork. The *Argentina* was sailing to New York in six days so I would have time to take the bus back to the *estancia* and say my goodbyes.

When I returned to their offices on the Plaza Mayor, they informed me that the US consular office wouldn't allow me to enter the USA or work on a ship. They had been given no reason as to why my visa had been refused and apologised.

I had no choice but to try and work my return back to London so I went to the Royal Mail Lines' office. Did they have a job? They did, and on the same ship I'd arrived on. One of the two laundry boys had jumped ship in the Canaries. I was warned that it would be tough work as the laundry was almost as hot as the engine room. It was in the stern which, along with the bow, is the worst place to be in bad weather.

The *Arlanza* had just docked and it was going to take seven days to load with its new cargo of chilled beef. I was to report to the office the day before departure and someone would take me to its berth at Dock Sud.

I took the overnight bus back to Rosario to spend my last few days with the Boyers. I was sad to leave them and my fellow workers. I had been warmly welcomed there and Norman's parents had treated me like a second son.

I didn't have a camera in Argentina and have no photos of my own from my time there, but I can see them all vividly in my mind. Norman's father was a small man who never lost his temper, or expressed the many worries that must have come with running such a large ranch.

Isobel was like my own mother, always concerned for me: 'I'm sure your mother would want you to have a haircut,' she'd say and Norman and I would be piled into the back of the Ford for the obligatory trip to the barber in Arias.

The cowboys were also like friends to me, even though I hardly spoke any Spanish. The *estancia* was a happy place to work and I knew that if I didn't go, I would stay.

When I arrived back in Buenos Aires, Royal Mail Lines told me they'd been unable to get me an exit visa for working on ships. If I was prepared to be smuggled on board and hidden in the hold until we reached international waters, I could still join the ship's crew. An officer escorted me through the quayside gates and told the guard I was collecting some documents for the Buenos Aires office.

I had to sit in the dark between two of those enormous refrigerated containers. At dawn the next day I was brought up on deck. The first thing I saw were the masts of the German battlecruiser the *Graff Spee*, sticking out of the mud in the middle of the Rio de la Plata. I had seen Anthony Quinn in Michael Powell's *The Battle of the River Plate* at school, but hadn't realised that the German warship had been scuttled in such shallow waters.

The *Arlanza* was now a very different ship to the one I had travelled out on. No more Cuba Libres or the smell of Chanel No. 5 as I drifted off to sleep. No more political discussions, only long, sweaty hours leaning over a steam press. I shared a cabin on the waterline with the other laundry boy, John Turner, a young man who farted a lot and was obsessed by his next sexual encounter.

After Montevideo we headed for Santos, the port town for São Paulo. The ship's engines had been faulty since we left Uruguay and we were told we'd have to berth in Santos for a few days while the ship's engineers fixed them. John and I headed for the waterside bars which doubled as brothels.

Santos was where I lost my virginity. The cantinas were full of whores of every shape and size. We sat at a table and a woman who looked about the same age as my mother came over to me and grabbed my scrotum. I don't remember it being a sensual experience at all. But after a few drinks, which must have been laced with Mickey Finns, I staggered upstairs with a young prostitute in a tight, red dress. She left me in a small room and disappeared. There was an iron bed and a small cupboard. Its cracked plaster walls were painted faeces brown. The window was partially covered with a broken wooden blind which had once been white. A bare, bright ceiling light celebrated this cheerlessness. No red lights here, no concession to the room's purpose.

After all the drinks I'd had, I was desperate for a piss. The corridor was dark and I couldn't find the toilet so I opened the drawer of the bedroom cupboard and relieved myself there.

The woman returned and we had sex. I remember that she kept her dress on and that I, and no doubt she, wanted to get it over with as quickly as possible. There was a lot of fumbling about in the light.

When I went downstairs to wait for my shipmate, the barman grabbed my arm and marched me back to the room. He opened the damp drawer. 'Is that you, *senhor*?'

I acted dumb.

He must have felt sorry for me because he let go of me and returned to the bar.

I was at the top of the stairs, ready to go down, when I heard John screaming from a nearby room. 'Help, help!'

I opened the door to see a naked woman straddling him, holding a razor to his throat.

'I don't have enough money!'

I threw 30 real onto the bed. She made a dive for it. John pulled on his trousers and we ran back to the ship.

Safely on board, he thanked me for saving him with the money. 'I owe you. Tell you what. I'll pay for your next fuck.'

'No thanks, John,' I said. 'That won't be for a long time.'

I decided to stay with the crew who had no need for those bars – the gays. Chris was a waiter who was about 40. He was short, balding and permanently cheerful. When he smiled, his face was an ear-to-ear grin.

After I told him about my adventure in the whorehouse, he took pity on me. 'Perhaps,' he said, 'you made the wrong decision.'

'What do you mean?' I said.

'It's not too late, you know.'

'Too late for what?'

'You're a handsome boy. You'd have no trouble finding yourself a partner.' A pause. 'Among us.'

I turned down his invitation to a party in his cabin. John had plucked up courage and returned to the brothels but, after another night of sitting alone on deck and listening to distant laughter and the *bossa nova*, I gave in to the next invitation. 'I'll come by for a drink tonight, but I am not—'

'Don't worry. We'll leave you alone.'

His cabin was covered with photos of his boyfriends, all of them taken on beaches and all of them wearing budgie smugglers. 'Pretty boys, aren't they? All much more handsome than me. Aren't I the lucky fellow?'

He was true to his word, that night and every other. Neither he, nor his two companions, the cooks, flirted or made advances. We drank and played poker and for the rest of the long journey, I was always welcome for a nightcap in his cabin.

He told me how he'd been married, had three children, but had had to drop the pretence and tell his wife, whom, he said, he still loved, that he was gay. She had kicked him out of their home. His children, now grown up, refused to see him. He went to sea.

With the engines at half-speed, our ship moved slowly across the Atlantic. There were storms and it was heavy going. After work, John and I would stagger out to the bow, clutching the crane davit. We attached ourselves to the bow rail with harnesses and whooped with excitement as the ship dipped beneath the waves and laughed as we rose again. Youth is fearless.

Vestey got their meat and I got home. Home, but worried and fearful. My scrotum felt itchy and I went to the STD clinic at Westminster Hospital. After an embarrassing and intimate examination, I was given the all-clear.

Norman left for Australia soon after my return to London and, for many years, ran a sheep farm at Binalong, northwest of Canberra. Isobel Boyer died of heart failure in her mid-seventies and Bernard committed suicide. He shot himself in Norman's bedroom. He had never recovered from his son's decision to emigrate to Australia and the death of his wife.

After 40 years, Norman tracked me down and, today, I am again friends with him and his artist wife, Fling. They run a small farm in north Devon.

I have no idea what happened to Joseph Moreno, but I hope he survived the years of repression and did not become one of the many thousands of *los Desaparecidos*. The Disappeared.

I have often thought about returning to Argentina, but the Pampas where I worked is no longer there. Today, most of the beef farms have gone, replaced by thousands of square miles of GM soya crops. In 1970, soya accounted for 3,000 hectares, only 400 hectares more than the Boyer *estancia*. Today GM soya covers 20 million hectares, 14 of the 20 million under the direct ownership of Monsanto.

In the years from 1990–2010, agrochemical spraying increased eightfold in Argentina – from 9 million gallons in 1990 to 84 million gallons twenty years later. Glyphosate, the key ingredient in Monsanto's sprays, is used eight to ten times more per acre than in the United States.

The result leaves people dangerously exposed to cancers. In a 2012 study, house-to-house surveys of 65,000 people in farming communities in the heart of Argentina's soya bean business, found cancer rates two to four times higher than the national average, as well as higher rates of hypothyroidism and chronic respiratory illnesses.[3]

Today, the countryside is an unhealthy corporate agro-factory, the old grasslands and crops replaced with miles and miles of soya. Massive silos stand where eucalyptus trees were once home to the burrowing owl and raptors. On the Pampas, the ostriches, iguanas, native weasels, deer and hares have all but disappeared. I can only return to the Pampas in my mind.

SPEAK MEMORY

'If a violin could ache, I would be that string.'

Vladimir Nabokov

Broken Dolls

In 1953 my parents bought a TV so that my mother and sisters could watch the Coronation of Elizabeth II.

The first time I saw my father take any interest in the 9-inch LV30 Pye screen was two months later when the BBC broadcast *The Quatermass Experiment*, the first science fiction series ever on British television. If this interested him, then maybe it interested me too.

For six knee-knocking Saturdays, I peeped from behind my mother's armchair. With its theme music of 'Mars, the Bringer of War' from Holst's *The Planets*, the series was about a rocket. Sent into space from Earth, it crash-landed in Wimbledon, containing not a tennis trophy or strawberries and cream, but an alien intent on destroying life on Earth.

As head of the space programme which had launched the rocket, Professor Bernard Quatermass had to save us all. I still shudder at the memory of him placing his hand in a pipe which contained an intelligent, 100-foot vegetable which had somehow made its way to Westminster Abbey. The brave professor succeeded in destroying the thing. Now it sounds more Monty Python than *Alien*, but at eight I was paralytic with fear. I was sent to bed as soon as each programme ended and had nightmares.

A few years later at Canford, I saw Ingmar Bergman's *The Seventh Seal*, which was shown as part of the school's annual film festival. This was the first movie I 'read'. It had an equally powerful effect. The knight, Antonius Block, played by Max von Sydow, tries to escape death in a plague-ridden country whose people see mystical omens everywhere. He is pursued by the Grim Reaper whom he challenges to a chess game, demanding, 'If I win, you let me live.'

The knight, no Bobby Fischer, joins a line of dead as they are led by the hooded Reaper across hills, silhouetted against dark and rushing clouds.

The film deals with superstition and the inevitability of death. As an impressionable schoolboy, it deeply marked me. From a young age, I was superstitious and knew that I would die. Even now, I never walk under ladders and cross myself when I take off and land in a plane.

When I spilled salt as a child, my mother would tell me to throw the grains over my left shoulder three times and make a wish. I still do this. Salt was a valuable commodity in earlier centuries and the first wages were paid in it. A mineral to respect, not squander.

Many other superstitions and religious practices also have a logic behind them. Take the Muslim and Jewish prohibition on pork. We are told that this is because pork is unhealthy, but all carcasses are unhealthy and pork is no more dangerous than lamb or fowl. In fact, the reason pork was proscribed is more interesting. The pig is a village animal and the Semitic peoples were nomads. Anyone who kept a pig was a threat to the tribe because it would mean settlement and an end to movement. So ladders can fall on you and pigs can threaten to halt communal migrations. Reasons to be wary.

In March 1964 my father returned from a tour of West Africa where he'd been researching medical services. He brought back a present for me from Nigeria: a pair of Yoruba *Ere Ibeji* wooden dolls. He told me they were always carved in twos and given a special place in the home, even fed and talked to. This custom of the double carvings and the respect afforded them is said to be because the Yoruba have the highest twin birth rate in the world. The statuettes of the *Ere Ibeji* are invested with supernatural powers and can bring bad luck if mistreated. Mine were sisters, ten inches high and coated with red sandalwood powder. They had red-and-white bead necklaces which my father told me meant they were devotees of Shango, the protector of birth.

My bedroom was now full of memorabilia collected from my time in Argentina: *bolas*, *mate* gourds and pipes, a whip and lasso. I put the *Ibeji* women on the only space left: the windowsill. One day when I opened the window, one of them fell to the street below. Her neck was broken and the beads scattered across the pavement.

I threw the damaged doll in the rubbish and felt ashamed when I looked at her surviving sister. I hid her at the back of my cupboard. I couldn't bring myself to throw the carving away as I felt uneasy about the accident and remembered what my father had told me about their powers.

The only person I talked to about the doll was Jenny Earp, a pretty 16-year-old brunette who I'd met the year before while camping in Cornwall. She thought I should return her to the windowsill. 'It's what her sister would have wanted. Not to be shoved away because you feel bad about it.'

Jenny lived with her parents and sister in a big house overlooking Dorking Golf Club. At weekends, I would borrow my parents' Ford Cortina and drive the 20 miles to see her.

We drank in local pubs with her friends and went for walks on the North Downs.

When I took Jenny home, her parents would make an excuse and leave us alone in the house. 'Just popping round to the club for a drink,' her father would say. 'Make yourselves at home.'

We did. Her bedroom was more comfortable than the Cortina.

I remember travelling with Jenny to Osterley in West London to meet a friend of mine and his girlfriend. We'd arranged to play bowls at a bowling alley near Heathrow Airport. I don't remember the bowling, but I do remember ending up in a house owned by my friend's father that was used to make porn films. Our lovemaking was like the movies made there. A lot of simulation.

In May 1964 I bought two tickets for a Chuck Berry gig at

the 100 Club on Oxford Street. I was excited. I was a big fan of rhythm and blues and was looking forward to seeing him perform 'Memphis, Tennessee' and 'Johnny B. Goode'.

Jenny had never heard of him so it was going to be a new experience for her. The club was packed out, hot and sweaty. I bought her a Babycham and myself a Double Diamond beer. She was wearing a grey lambswool sweater dress, her waist waspishly tucked in with a white belt. I remember taking off my rayon sweater because I was so hot (and a little ashamed in front of my stylish partner). It was thrilling to see Chuck Berry sliding across the stage with his guitar almost touching the ground as he got to 'Go, go, go Johnny, go, go'.

Everyone was dancing, but Jenny was clinging to me. She said she needed fresh air. As we went up the stairs, she collapsed. I thought she had fainted from the heat because she quickly recovered.

I took her to Waterloo station to put her on the train home. She apologised for ruining the evening and kissed me goodbye. I said I'd call her the next day.

I never made that call because I'd started dating another girl. Two weeks later, Jenny's mother rang to say that she had died. A brain aneurism. She apologised for not telling me about her daughter's condition earlier, but that she and her husband had wanted Jenny to live a normal life for as long as possible. So that's why they had left us alone in the house.

I wished I'd contacted Jenny, even if it had just been to say our relationship was over. She'd been the first girl who had shown love for me and I was her first boyfriend. I was certainly the first person she'd been to bed with, and she must have been distressed that I'd dumped her so brutally. I'm sorry, Jenny. The cruelty of youth.

At the time, I thought her death was the long hand of fate, stretching into my life from the broken *Ibeji* twin. But I was going to learn that our lives are not determined by spirits, ghosts or wooden carvings. Each of us are each responsible for our own destiny.

Skinny Dipping

After returning from Argentina, I worked in a lawyer's office and became friends with another clerk there, David Sprecher. He asked me if I'd join him for a holiday on the Costa Brava. When he went to book it at his local tourist office, the package holidays to Spain had sold out. Fate was going to take me somewhere else.

Instead of Spain, it was ten days on a Yugoslav island. He showed me the tickets. 'It's spelled wrong,' I said. 'It's missing a vowel.'

The island was called Krk. I hardly knew where Yugoslavia was, let alone this unpronounceable island. The cost was £35. This covered the return train journey from Victoria station to the Adriatic coast, ferry to the island and full board at the Hotel Malin in the village of Malinska.

I had been in South America, but had never travelled across Europe so the journey was exciting. After a night in Rijeka, we took the ferry across the Adriatic to Krk. We dumped our suitcases at the hotel and headed for the beach.

'Beatles, Beatles!' followed us wherever we went. It was 1964 and Beatlemania was at its peak, but our haircuts weren't that moppish so maybe it was our pale skin or because we spoke English.

We used our novelty value to attach ourselves to a group of girls, one of whom was a foxy young woman named, curiously enough, Renata. She was wearing a yellow bikini. At the beach-side café I made sure to sit as close to her as I could, but we had problems communicating because she hardly spoke any English and I didn't speak a word of Serbo-Croat.

As the son of German-Jewish refugees, I roped David in as my translator. It was all basic stuff as I hardly knew how to express myself to this pretty girl in English, let alone through a translator. *'Bist du oft hier?'* and *'Du hast schöne Augen.'* Towards the end of the ten days the romance had graduated to *'Kuss mich,'* and *'Schatzi, Ich liebe dich.'*

She taught me some words in her language and I taught her some in mine. We would sing Beatles songs and she would ask me the meaning of the words. Try translating 'A Hard Day's Night'.

Everyone swam in a small bay below the hotel. To the side of it was a water slide, six metres high with a rickety wooden ladder. Because it had missing rungs, the climb up was as hazardous as the journey down was thrilling. The metal slide would have been dangerous without the water that flowed from a pipe at the top, preventing people from burning themselves on the baking metal.

'Idemo,' Renata said. I wasn't sure what she meant, but I guessed it was 'Let's do it', as she was looking up at the top of the slide. She moved her right hand in a swooping motion and shouted, 'Whoosh. You and me, yes?'

I climbed up first and sat down at the top. It seemed a long way down. The shoot was steep. I hesitated.

'Go, go,' she said and began climbing the ladder behind me.

I closed my eyes and let go. Gravity did the rest. I was hurled a few metres into the water. As I rose to the surface, Renata landed on top of me. We were both laughing as she grabbed my arms and entangled her legs with mine.

'Again?' I asked, coughing water.

'Yes,' she said, pointing at herself. 'I first. On stomach.'

I was ready to go as soon as she had launched. This time I landed on her back.

On the last three days of our stay the water pipe wasn't working. There was a sign on the bottom of the ladder. *OPASNO.* Dangerous. No more slide, but by then it didn't matter. We were physically entangled without the need for any watery props.

We were wet with love – skinny dipping to the distant sounds of a band, *Glup Dječaci* – Silly Boys – who played each evening on a platform above the sea. When we got back to land, there were the children's swings in the pine woods behind the beach. We held hands and stared at the rocking stars.

The night before we left the island, Renata invited me to a barbeque at her home. Her parents had a small house with a vine-covered terrace. The tiny garden was full of vegetables. While her father's sea bass sizzled on the grill, I helped Renata's mother pick enormous tomatoes for the salad. After we'd finished eating, neighbours came by as her father brought out his homemade *rakija*, played his accordion and sang sad Dalmatian songs. No one was flinging themselves on the sherry and made to go home at eight o'clock. I was now in love with more than the girl in the yellow bikini.

Lighting Candles

At Victoria station, alongside platform announcements for services to Chatham and Orpington, there used to be the international routes. From 1965 until the early 1970s, I'd board the train for Dover, ferry to Belgium and then couchette train to Cologne, Munich, Salzburg, Ljubljana and Zagreb. I savoured the long journey – a feeling I've never lost, even in these EasyJet days. But more importantly, there was the anticipation of seeing Renata again.

At Ostend, I would find my six-berth third-class compartment. I always hoped to be the only passenger – not because I wanted to be alone – but because it meant that the train would fill up in Cologne, Bonn and Frankfurt with Turkish immigrant workers, *gastarbeiters*, on their way home for their annual holidays.

They would always have two suitcases, one for clothes and the other filled with food and drink which they generously shared with strangers. There were *kebabis*, spinach and cheese *borek*, hummus, pitta bread, dates and honeyed cakes. We would drink *raki* through the night.

My own suitcase was packed with gifts. The latest Beatles album for Renata, Nescafé, teas and biros for her mother, fishing hooks and nylon lines for her father.

After a short sleep, I would wake up as the train travelled through the Karawanken Alps into Yugoslavia. A five-kilometre tunnel under the Wurzen Pass marked the border. The Austrian customs officers in their smart, blue uniforms were replaced by the Yugoslavs in their drab brown when they came on board at Jesenice. The only other colour to alleviate their uniforms were the red stars on their caps.

After Ljubljana, the train arrived in Zagreb in the early evening, 30 hours after leaving Victoria station.

All cities have their unique characteristics; defined by their architecture, climate and inhabitants. What is rarely referred to are their smells. Zagreb's was the coal burned in the steam engines: lignite from Breza in Bosnia, a soft brown fuel somewhere between coal and peat. This smell characterised the Croatian capital until steam engines were replaced with electric and diesel, five years after I met the girl in the yellow bikini.

When I arrived in Zagreb for my first visit there, I took the No. 4 tram to Renata's home. The blue cars clanked and screeched their way over the bumpy rails, the driver hunched over a lever which was both accelerator and brake. Pedestrians ran when they heard the tram's bell, a double dang-dang. It was like being on the set of *The Third Man*.

The Kasuns lived close to the Sava River. Renata's father Ivan – Ivo – was a café musician and her mother, Nada, a dental nurse. Their street, *Cvjetno Naselje* or Settlement of Flowers, was a row of detached two-storey houses with pretty gardens. All except theirs. They lived in the ground floor flat of a house which, even on sunny days, was dark. The garden was overgrown with thorn and blackberry bushes and the apartment above had a balcony which jutted out, blocking the light.

The toilet was to the side of an unlit hall. It was full of Ivo's fishing rods and, in place of toilet paper, carefully-torn pieces of *Večernji List*, the Zagreb daily. You clutched a large key as you stumbled through the darkness and risked bumping into the Dostoyevskian mad woman with wild grey hair who lived in the flat above.

On my arrival at the Settlement of Flowers, I was shocked. I came from a middle-class suburb in London and this was a poor family living in a tiny flat in Zagreb. Its inhabitants were different to anything I had experienced in my London life. I think that was part of Renata's exoticism. She was so utterly unlike the girls I had dated. In contrast to my English girlfriends, she was unashamed to accentuate her figure and I was eager to help.

Yugoslavia was opening up to the West and what little money young women had was spent on the latest fashion. Every girl knew the name Carnaby Street. I remember buying a miniskirt for Renata from Biba's in Kensington, with tennis-ball-sized red, white and blue dots. She looked wonderful, but her parents were shocked. Her mother wanted to lower the hem and her father wanted her to wash off the Chanel No. 22 ('Perfume of Romance') I had bought for her with the dress.

Renata was studying dentistry. She didn't have her own room and the only surface to write on was the kitchen sideboard. There was little space and no peace as Ivo would spend the day practising his café repertoire on his accordion. Renata spent as much time as she could at the university. When I visited Zagreb during her term time, I would accompany her there and take walks in the Old Town while she went to her lectures.

We would spend evenings visiting her friends or hanging out in city centre coffee bars. In good weather we'd sit on a bench on the Strossmayer walkway which overlooked the city centre, talking and cuddling. Her Slav pronunciation and sentence structure of English words and phrases was an additional sexual thrill. 'You are loving me, yes?' 'Do you like when I paint red my finger toes?'

At night I slept in her bed, a divan in the living room that, by day, her mother kept pristine under a plastic cover. Renata slept on the floor in her parents' bedroom. Nada left for work at 7am and as soon as she'd gone, Renata would join me. She had recently finished an affair with a rock singer and was a better lover than I was. I hadn't advanced much from my tumblings and fumblings with poor Jenny.

We weren't disturbed by Ivo because he never got back from work until dawn and slept until Nada returned to make lunch. We made sure we were up and dressed before she came home.

The living-cum-bed-cum-dining room was sparsely decorated. There was one picture on the wall: a reproduction of a smiling girl clasping a bunch of marigolds. She tilted to the right in her unsteady frame. There was a wooden coffee table which doubled as the dining table. Under its glass top were postcards from relatives in the United States. The ones I remember are Detroit by night and a Chicago skyline.

Ivo said he'd had the chance to go to the US after he arrived in Trieste with the Partisans in 1945, but had stayed behind, he said, 'to build communism'.

For him, it was a lifetime's disappointment. The kitchen did double duty as a bathroom and the tub had a green plastic curtain to match the Formica of the small unit set to one side of the oven. Behind the curtain, there was just enough space for a live trussed chicken, waiting to be killed for our dinner. They didn't have room for a fridge.

When I think of that kitchen now, I think of Nada, forever shopping and cooking. She spent her life feeding her family, and anyone else who came within range. None of us, except Ivo, ever demanded food, but she demanded of us that we eat. Incessantly. That is when she wasn't foraging for ingredients at the Trešnjevka Market, which she visited daily on her way home from the surgery.

At 1pm Nada arrived from work, dropping her bulging bags into the only free space, the bath. This was accompanied with a sigh of '*Bože dragî.*' Dear God. At that moment Ivo would wake up and call from his bed, 'Give me coffee.'

Two hours later, Nada would serve the big meal of the day. It started with soup made from leftovers. Nothing was wasted. Chicken soup consisted of the bird's feet, head, heart, kidneys and liver. Vegetable soup was made from peelings. This might be followed by Wiener, Milanese or chicken schnitzel, accompanied by a salad dressed with lemon.

Then there were the stews – beef or lamb – or delicious stuffed peppers called *punjenje paprika*. The fresh vegetables were carrots, cabbage or kale. Everything she made was delicious. If you left the tiniest bit of food, a lecture followed from Ivo with its theme the war, the Nazis, the Partisans, how family and friends had died of starvation and how what we'd left on our plates would have kept them alive. It was the Kasun family's version of 'Think about the hungry babies in Africa'.

In winter there were Nada's pickled vegetables, stored in large jars in a cupboard behind the bath. In the same cupboard she kept a plastic bin with fermenting cabbages, on its top an upturned frying pan weighted with a five-kilo cast-iron doorstop. Inside the bin was the maturing sauerkraut for *sarma*, cabbage leaves stuffed with beef and pork, a dish we'd eat while watching the New Year's Day Concert from Vienna on the black-and-white television. Watched only, as the TV's speakers had long since broken and Ivo would try to tune into the concert on their Grundig radiogram.

After Ivo had finished his meal, which he always ate while reading his newspaper, he went to bed to get a few hours sleep before leaving for work in the evening.

Nada was a workhorse. She washed and cleared up, refusing any help. When she had nothing else to do, she would fold paper bags and – in later years – plastic ones, as though they were delicate items of lingerie. She then placed them carefully in the long drawer under the divan.

I cannot remember ever seeing Nada put her feet up, read a book or watch the soundless TV. When she wasn't running around for her husband or cooking meals, she was visiting family and friends who were alone, ill or needed help with their own shopping.

She was forever lighting candles in memory of someone or something. Whenever I was with her in the city centre, she'd insist we walk up to the Old Town. She would disappear into St Mark's Church, drop a dinar into the collection box, light a candle, place it on the tiered platform beneath the Virgin Mary and say a prayer. Before she placed her hands together, she'd smile at me. 'I know you don't believe, David, but it's important that I think of—' and she would name a sick relative she'd been unable to visit that week or someone who'd recently died.

One day I followed her into the church. My Croatian was poor and I couldn't make out what she was praying for, but I recognised two words: 'Renata' and 'David'.

When we got home, I asked Renata to ask her mother what she'd said. Nada repeated the words to her daughter and, as she did so, Nada started to cry.

Renata translated. 'Holy Mother, please look after my family and may my daughter Renata and David stay together, get married, have healthy children and a happy life.'

Tito Was Watching

1968: the year of street fighting from Paris to Berlin to Prague. While parts of the world were high on optimism and rebellion and other parts just high, I was getting married. In Zagreb. Married to Renata and, as it turned out, to her relatives, her country, her culture and the entire Balkans.

Instead of a train journey in the company of Turkish workers, *kebabis* and *raki*, I drove the one thousand miles from London in my minivan. Alastair Hatchett, a student friend, travelled with me. He was going to be best man. His girlfriend, Diana, and two other friends would meet us there. My parents were flying in from London. The only concession to '68 was the sticker on the back window, *FATE L'AMORE, NON LA GUERRA*. I had bought a batch of them earlier that year from the radical Milan publisher, Feltrinelli.

The night before arriving in Zagreb, Alastair and I bought a bottle of plum brandy on the outskirts of Ljubljana. Camped beside the road, we drank it all. I was getting married the next day and I was past the point of no return. When I woke up the next morning, I had to throw away my pillow.

On August 20th, 1968, Renata and I were standing in a long queue outside the Trešnjevka Registry Office. Nada and Renata's aunt, Mirijana, handed out rosemary buttonholes as we entered the building.

Because we had to have an official translator, our wedding took longer than the others. As we declared our vows, I couldn't help looking into the cold white eyes of Marshal Tito whose life-sized marble bust stood behind the Registrar. His stare seemed to be asking me if I was doing the right thing with the right person in the right place.

Behind us there were a lot of angry about-to-be-weds. As we left, some of the brides looked like they were about to throw their wedding bouquets at us, and not because of the tradition of whoever caught it would be the one to get married next.

Renata's parents treated us to a limousine while the 30 guests walked the two kilometres along the busy Slavonska Avenija to their tiny flat. Ivo and Nada made the journey on Ivo's Lambretta scooter, Nada hanging onto her hat.

The reception was crowded. Nada had one sister, but Ivo was one of 15 brothers and two sisters. To feed everyone there were four suckling pigs, chicken, and hams served with roast potatoes and cabbage. For an hors d'oeuvre, Nada had prepared smoked beef on rye bread. To finish the meal, there was chocolate ice cream scraped out of a freezer bag which had sat in the middle of the bath since early morning. For drinks there was beer, Slavonian white wine, Dalmatian red and plum brandy. An American uncle had brought two bottles of Jack Daniels.

There wasn't enough space for 30 people so we had to use the living and the bedroom. Ivo and I pushed the double bed against the window and set up a second table that had been borrowed from a neighbour. Family sat around the table in the living room and the other guests were in the bedroom.

I worried what my parents would think about it all, but they seemed fond of Renata. My mother was made to feel like a queen and my father was plied with drink. He put his fluent German to good use, helped along by the brandy. When he got up to speak he managed, 'I was drunk when I arrived in Zagreb and I'll be drunk when I leave.'

Ivo and his band set up in the hallway and there was just enough room for two couples to dance, or rather turn, in the centre of the living room. The extra table, now empty of food, had been taken into the front garden ready to be returned to the neighbours.

The last guests left at 2am. Ivo and Nada offered us their bed, but we didn't get much sleep and it wasn't for the reason you think. The new Czech president, Alexander Dubček, had been trying to shake off the country's Soviet masters and the Russians were about to invade Prague.

The Yugoslav army were moving north on the dual carriageway to the border, only metres away from our window. Military vehicles had started rumbling past when the party was still on but, by the time we went to bed, there was an endless convoy of tanks and artillery. It was audibly ominous and we were scared. We joked about whether our marriage was going to last long.

Salaam

Renata had qualified as a dentist in Yugoslavia and, on arriving in London, she had to retake her exams to practise in the UK. Two years later, she started work. Like most young couples, we wanted children and after a miscarriage, our first son, Benjamin, was born at University College Hospital on April 7th, 1973.

Fathers were allowed to be present. I remember six hours after her waters had broken the midwife saying to the nurse, 'Go get the Registrar.' She sounded distressed as she turned to me and said, 'You must leave the room.'

I left Renata crying and in pain and sat in the corridor of the maternity unit. I had no idea what was going on and was terrified.

After an hour, the nurse came over to me. 'You can go in now and see your beautiful son.'

'How is he? How is my wife?'

'They're both fine, but the doctor had problems and your wife was given an episiotomy. He had to use forceps.'

Over the coming years, I was going to think more and more about those forceps.

Ben vomited when given his first dose of powdered milk and our doctor said that when he was due for his immunisation for diphtheria, tetanus and whooping cough, he should only have the double injection, not the triple, omitting the whooping cough vaccine.

When he was three months old, I took him to the local health clinic to be immunised and reminded the receptionist about the doctor's instruction. When the nurse gave him the injection, I didn't think it was necessary to repeat myself.

A few hours after arriving home, Ben started fitting. We watched helplessly as our child writhed in pain, his body jack-knifing. We called for an ambulance and he was rushed to UCH where he was diagnosed with Salaam epilepsy, seizures that involve bowing backwards and forwards. The doctor told us that the severity of these fits kill, or leave an infant severely brain-damaged, so steroids would be used to stop them. After 24 hours, the drugs took effect and the fits stopped, but Ben was so weakened by them he contracted pneumococcal meningitis.

The consultant admitted that Ben had been given a higher dosage of steroids than they'd used with other infants. He said they'd been so pleased with the first results of the drug they had decided to increase the dosage.

When I looked down at him, Shakespeare's words came to mind: 'Misshapen chaos of well-seeming forms'. Ben looked so beautiful and I remember a nurse telling me that he was 'cute'.

But his eyes weren't. They were two little windows into his chaos. He looked dazed and confused and, worst of all, in pain.

I remember Renata and I sitting with him one weekend, desperately trying to get the nurses to check on his deteriorating condition. He had a high fever and the staff dealt with this by placing a fan at the end of his cot. We asked to see the consultant when he did his ward round on Monday, but it proved unnecessary. When we arrived at the hospital that morning, we were told that Ben had developed hydrocephalus and was being moved to Great Ormond Street Children's Hospital.

Ben needed an operation to fit a Spitz-Holter shunt inside his skull to drain cerebrospinal fluid from his brain to his heart. The first operation was a failure and had to be repeated. Renata and I were then taught how to operate the pump. Set on the right side of his skull, we had to press it five or six times, twice a day.

We were both distressed when we got home from our hospital visits. We would sit and cry over dinner.

Inside a get-well card I wrote words from William Blake and taped it to the head of Ben's cot: *It is right it should be so; Man was made for joy and woe; And when this we rightly know, Thro' the world we safely go.*

The card was for all three of us. It was going to be a long and hard search for that joy and, if I'd been this poor child and able to offer an opinion, I would have said to hell with Blake.

After six months, Ben's consultant, Dr John Wilson – no relation – asked to meet us. 'I'm afraid that your son will never lead a normal life. He will need special care and I think it unlikely that he'll live beyond the age of three.'

We both started crying.

For the next year, the hospital would take Ben back once a month for a few days so that Renata and I could get some sleep because he would projectile vomit every night. It's not called 'projectile' for nothing. This small infant would scream and cry as he hurled sick and bile across the bed and floor. The hospital supplied us with a large stock of disposable bed pads which we placed around him in the hope that they would contain the vomit. We took it in turns to spend the night with him.

After Ben came home from hospital, I started drinking. Heavily. At parties I would pass out in bedrooms, bathrooms, on summer lawns. My GP put me on anti-depressants which made me feel ill so I returned to the alcohol.

I was embarrassed to drink in front of Renata, who was also distressed, so I drank in the darkness of the cellar. It was not an easy place to get into. It was full of junk. Old bicycles, bits of chairs and tables, an old carpet, garden furniture from my parents' home in Bromley. A large metal tool kit without the tools, damp books, Renata's archived dental records. That Coronation Pye TV. Empty bottles. Dozens of them. And full ones. Whisky. I descended into this mess in the evenings. Renata never asked what I was doing.

I didn't bother with mixers, although there was a tap somewhere in that gloom. I slurped the booze directly from bottle to mouth. I would then sit on the bottom step and cry.

When I came back up to the ground floor, I was drunk and ashamed. I'd mumble something about going out for milk and stumble through the streets. This sobered me up a bit, but did nothing to lessen my misery as I'd spent my walk peering into the front rooms of family homes in Muswell Hill. No nets and many people didn't bother with drawing curtains or pulling down blinds. Families sitting watching TV together or eating around a table. A child playing the piano or violin with their parents staring adoringly at their little maestros. Why didn't they have our pain? Where was their whisky? In cut-glass decanters brought out for special occasions. I have hated Muswell Hill ever since and when I am there – not often – I am back in that cellar gloom.

Many years later, Renata ran into Dr Wilson and she told him that Ben was still alive and making progress with his life. He told her that he was surprised we hadn't sued. We thought he was hinting at the experimental steroid doses Ben had been given, but perhaps he was referring to the forceps delivery or the vaccination.

In June 2002 Anthony Barnett wrote an article in the *Observer* which said, '… Confidential records belonging to drug giant Glaxo Wellcome show three-month-old infants were potentially given faulty vaccines for preventing whooping cough, diphtheria and tetanus … Cholera vaccines are intended for adults and should not be given to children under six months … There were hundreds, possibly thousands, of doses in each batch and these were injected into babies between 1972 and 1974. Doctors at the time reported that babies inoculated from these batches had suffered convulsions.'[1]

When I think of Ben, I start with the 'what ifs'. What if he had not needed forceps delivery? What if I had been more careful in checking what they were doing at the health clinic when he was given the vaccine? What if we had reacted more strongly at UCH when Ben developed a fever? What if he had gone to a school that had been better able to help him with his disabilities? Renata had been keen for him to attend a normal school. What if we had known about the GlaxoSmithKline scandal earlier? What if we had sued? But who should we have sued? I know this is a destructive way to think because there are no 'what ifs'. There are only what was, what is and what will be.

When Ben was four, Renata became pregnant again. Because of Ben's illness, the Royal Free Hospital gave her regular checks and, after she was given an ultrasound, we knew she was carrying a boy.

We had a name for him. Elton John's 'Daniel' had been at No. 1 when Ben was born and we had agreed that, if we had another son, we would give him that name.

A few days before her estimated delivery date, Renata was worried that there was little movement and we went to the hospital. They told us that everything was fine, but that if her waters hadn't broken within the week, she would be induced.

Two days later, Renata was convinced the baby wasn't moving. We returned to the hospital where she was rushed to surgery. They induced a dead infant.

Renata was still unconscious when I was visited by the health support officer. I was asked whether we'd like to see the baby and hold him. I said no. When Renata regained consciousness, she also didn't want to.

Three years later, Renata gave birth to our third son at the Royal Free. He was a long time entering the world. Fifteen hours into labour, the midwife told me to go to the pub across the road. I had just downed my first pint when a nurse ran across the street and told me to hurry back. I was in time to see a boy dangling from the hands of the midwife, crying loudly. This was Jonny.

After Jonny's birth, Renata and I agreed that we needed to acknowledge Daniel's existence. We needed to forgive ourselves for not seeing his body, not giving him a burial. It had been difficult to listen to Elton John's song on the radio or enter a pub and hear it on the juke box. *Daniel, you're a star in the face of the sky*.

He had been buried in Finchley Cemetery. The hospital told

us where he was and we found a metal stick with his number on it. It was spring so we placed daffodils on his grave, stood back and cried. Tears of sadness, regret, shame.

I was learning not to turn away from suffering, but to walk through the fire and hope to come out the other side.

Ben is now 42 and bravely faces his difficulties. He regularly picks up common illnesses and, in recent years, has had a recurrence of epilepsy. He lives in Cornwall, has many friends, a great knowledge of music and does occasional DJing. Jonny lives in Barcelona. He works under the banner of Eclectic Method and is a successful video and music remixer. U2, Snoop Dogg, Monty Python, Fatboy Slim and the BBC have all sought out Jonny's services to create video remixes and he has played the after-parties at the Sundance and Cannes Film Festivals. He and his Mexican-American wife have recently made me a grandfather with their son, Rhys Matteo.

THE IDIOT

'You can be sincere and still be stupid.'

Fyodor Dostoyevsky

Naïve

One August morning in 1987 I came out of W H Smiths in the London suburb of Muswell Hill. Parked outside was a Peugeot with Zagreb number plates. I knew that because the first two letters of the registration were ZG, Renata's city. A tall man was getting out.

'*Dobro jutro,*' I said.

Surprised to be greeted in his own language, he introduced himself and I invited him home for coffee. He was Ivan Prpić, a professional violinist, in London taking master classes from Yifrah Neaman. In the course of the next few months we became friends and, before his return to Zagreb, he mentioned that he was looking for someone in the UK to help him represent his father-in-law, the artist Ivan Rabuzin.

His off-hand remark excited me. Perhaps this would be a way out of my depression over Ben and, in any case, I had been teaching for 16 years and was burnt out. The classes I taught were developed to offer a bit of culture to apprentices at college on day release. At Kilburn Polytechnic these courses had been given the title of Liberal Studies. Neither I, nor the students, took this seriously and whenever I could, I'd organise ghost trips to galleries and museums which neither they, nor I, had any intention of visiting.

When in college, I was supposed to show them slides of Renaissance art or hire in cultural films – like *The Seventh Seal* – ones you had to read.

Then there was music. In one class we were playing the Rolling Stones and they wanted 'Street Fighting Man' at full volume. As I bent down to turn the knob, I was kicked in the arse by Suggs, later the lead singer in the band Madness, who was an electrical apprentice at Smith's Industries.

At the door stood the Principal. 'What's going on here?'

I said, 'This week we're listening to contemporary music. Next week it'll be back to Mozart.'

He looked unconvinced. 'I see,' he said and left the room.

It was all a con and I had had enough.

The two Ivans might have needed a dogsbody in London, but I saw their offer quite differently. It was my escape route. I said I'd love to help them as I knew Rabuzin's naïve style of painting, spoke Serbo-Croat and spent every summer in Yugoslavia. The truth was that I had no background in art and the only original Rabuzin I had seen was owned by Dr Kruzić, a gynaecologist friend of my wife. I didn't even speak Serbo-Croatian that well, but Ivan agreed to let me help him promote Rabuzin and so started my career in the art world.

Naïve artists work without formal technical qualifications and with a remarkable indifference to perspective. Uninfluenced by art traditions, they paint pictures mirroring their memories, desires and dreams.

When most people think of naïve art, the names that come to mind are Henri Rousseau and Grandma Moses, but southeast Europe has produced many primitive painters: the peasant Ivan Generalić, the postman Ivan Lacković and the carpenter Ivan Rabuzin, among the most well known.

Rabuzin had buyers such as Yul Brynner and Woody Allen, whose Rabuzin paintings can be seen in *Annie Hall*.

Rabuzin's pastel-coloured silk screen prints sold well in the Far East and he was known in Germany, France, Italy and Japan, but his reputation had never been established in Britain. My job was to find a London gallery that would represent him and try and get his work onto quality products such as Rosenthal vases and Halcyon Days miniature boxes.

I bought a copy of the trade journal *Galleries* to see if there might be a London venue specialising in primitive and naïve art. The only ones I could find were the Portal Gallery, who represented Beryl Cook, and the Rona Gallery which was located in Weighhouse Street, off Bond Street. The Portal was not interested, but Stanley Harries, the director of the Rona, was.

At that time, Stanley was representing the naïve artist Dora Holzhandler and British figurative painters. He knew of Rabuzin and had sold a work of his some years before. He thought it would be difficult establishing a market for him in London, but said he'd give it a try. If I was prepared to help in his gallery, I could work from a small room on the first floor and Ivan Prpić would have an office when he was in London.

Stanley was a lovely man. Every morning when I arrived, he would greet me with 'Hello, old chap. So good to see you.' His assistant, Sheldon Williams, was an authority on Caribbean naïve art. The author of *Voodoo and the Art of Haiti*, he looked like a Fifties dandy with swept-back hair and a constantly changing parade of floral bow ties. Clients would come to the Rona to ask about a Holzhandler and Sheldon would enthuse them with a long talk on voodoo art. This didn't endear him to Stanley who didn't have any Hector Hyppolites or Wilson Bigauds for sale. When Sheldon was manning the gallery alone and someone knocked on the door to ask how to get to Bond Street station, he would show them the way and leave the front door wide open. Though he never said so, I think Stanley was happy to have me there to keep an eye on him.

There were many interesting visitors. George Melly often dropped by. Known as 'the jazz musician with the big personality and the big hat', few people know he was an authority on primitive art and the author of *The Tribe of One*, an outstanding book about British naïve art.

Then there was Gustav Delbanco, then over ninety years old and living alone in a huge house in Hampstead. He came from a German-Jewish family who could trace their roots back to Venice. His expertise was the art of the seventeenth and eighteenth centuries and his evaluations were respected by the British Museum, among others. He and I got on well and I used to visit him for tea. The house was dark, there was no central heating and the place had that musty smell I associate with houses inhabited by the elderly. He always had a cake on the table, and we used to talk about everything from art to politics.

After the Second World War, he and his two partners, Henry Roland and Lillian Browse, opened a contemporary art gallery in Cork Street. Though never one of London's richest galleries, it became one of its most prestigious. Their first exhibition was of Rodin, whose work had been neglected in Britain. They exhibited Josef Herman, a Jewish socialist, who fled Eastern Europe and ended up living in south Wales. He was nicknamed Joe Bach by the miners he painted. Other artists included Philip Sutton, famous for his bright canvases and expansive drawing style, and the American Alfred Cohen, with his vibrant flower compositions, portraits and English countryside scenes.

Gallery gossip had it that Gustav and Henry Roland adopted a double act with female clients. Roland would seduce them and Gustav would then move in and strike the deals. Perhaps it was the other way round. Gustav was a man of extraordinary charm and wit. I asked him why he'd never written a book and he replied, 'Who cares what I think?'

In his house there were wonderful Rodin figurines and a Degas sculpture of a dancer. 'Compare it to a Rodin,' he would say. 'Do you see that the Degas is cold and lifeless. Degas didn't like women. Rodin did.'

The walls were full of artists he'd represented and, every time I visited him, he would walk me round the house and tell me stories about them.

A third gallery visitor was Mervyn Levy: writer, artist and art critic who'd had his own BBC TV series in the 1960s, *Painting for Housewives*. He'd been a childhood friend of Dylan Thomas and they'd shared a flat together in the thirties. Mervyn was a small, dapper man with a moustache and neatly clipped white beard. He wore pink shirts and never less than two Swatch watches. He always had an attractive young girlfriend in tow. We planned to write a play about Dylan together, based on Mervyn's memories, and he would invite me to the Chelsea Arts Club to discuss our project. We never got far after the first three bottles of wine.

Ivan Prpić, Stanley and myself planned a London launch for Rabuzin but, before we did that, we needed an English-language book about the artist. We invited Mervyn to write it. Ivan told him that funding was available from the Rabuzin family and a fee of £4,000 was agreed.

The book, published in 1990, is full of phrases such as 'light is what Rabuzin seeks, and light is what he finds. His art is born of light … The marvellous mature landscapes are bathed in pure radiance; as though there had never been any darkness.' Mervyn told me he couldn't stand Rabuzin's work, but 'he who pays the piper gets his tune'.[1]

Rabuzin was a man who took himself seriously. He always wore a suit and tie and spoke slowly, seeming to weigh his words before he let them escape from his mouth. When I first met him, he couldn't quite understand what I was doing in his village, and I knew I had to earn his respect. He had no such problems with Mervyn who was known in the art world and had been paid to be appreciative of his work. The two of them had an impressive natural cunning, each using the other for their own purposes.

Rabuzin lived in Ključ in a large modern house on the site of his childhood home. The windows offered magnificent views across the valley to the hills which were the source of his inspiration. The rooms were oak-panelled, oak-floored and doored. However, the result was like taking a Beverly Hills villa and depositing it in the middle of the Croatian countryside. The rest of the village remained medieval with unpaved roads, clucking chickens and peasants driving horse-drawn carts. I doubt whether the local priest appreciated it when Rabuzin constructed a ten-metre totem pole in his front garden which looked like it had been shipped from the Tlingit Indian Reservation.

NAÏVE

His paintings represent an idealised countryside with a deliberate symmetry linking nature and man. His pastel colours contain landscapes with puffy clouds, small doorless houses and oversized flowers. The world as it isn't. Beautiful fakes.

Café Slavia

We are surrounded by fakes. There are fake pearls, fake fur, fake blood, fake signatures. Some fakes are not just meant to deceive, but to impress as well, like fake books that fill the shelves of people who wish to appear more learned than they are, or fake aristocrats who purchase their fake titles. Fakes can be used negatively, such as documents created to justify the attack on Iraq. Or positively, inflatable tanks placed on the cliffs above Dover before D-Day.

The art world is rife with fakes, where they are called forgeries. They are as old as the Old Masters and often the Old Masters were the greatest forgers of all. Michelangelo produced replicas of Domenico Ghirlandaio's drawings that were so good, Ghirlandaio thought they were his own.

I spent a lot of time in Ključ, helping catalogue Rabuzin's prodigious output. After one visit in October 1990, I returned to Zagreb a few days before my flight to London. I arrived on a Friday and my plane had been booked for the following Tuesday. I had planned to spend my three free days with my friend Darko Glavan, a rock critic. Unfortunately, when I got there, Darko said he had to go to Paris that weekend to visit Jim Morrison's grave and write an article on The Doors.

I went to a bar on Tkalčićeva Street that was frequented by artists. There I bumped into Marko Tomić, a wheeler-dealer who was always introducing me to ex-communist party 'bizinessmen', all of whom knew someone who knew someone who had a Picasso they wanted to get out of the country. It was less than a year since the fall of the Berlin Wall. Eastern

Europe was full of art works migrating westward, lured by the promise of insanely high prices.

Over a beer, Marko said, 'There is interesting painting in Prague. I'm going there to authenticate it. Come with me, David. It will be, as you English say, jolly good fun.'

I shook my head. 'I have to go back to London.'

'When do you leave?'

'Tuesday.'

'We have time.'

'But it's Friday afternoon.'

'We go now.'

Marko had many crazy qualities, one of which I shared: impetuousness. Two hours later, we set off in the pouring rain in his beat-up, unheated Citroën *deux chevaux*. There was a leak above my head. Cold and wet, I climbed into the back seat for the rest of the journey.

The tin snail's windscreen wipers were worn and their scritch-scratch was tortuous to listen to. The car's signal lights were broken and when Marko overtook lorries, I shut my eyes and prayed. I didn't think we'd make it but, 650 kilometres later, at three in the morning, we arrived in Prague.

Marko drew up outside a large house in the leafy suburb of Karlin. An old man answered the door and led us into a cellar. At its centre was a one and a half metre circular wooden castle, complete with battlements and flag.

I stared at it.

The old man smiled at me. 'Prague Castle. I make.' He walked to the side of the room and turned on a tap. There was a large wheel with yoghurt cartons attached to its outside rim. As each carton filled with water, the wheel started to turn. Like a large clock, the wheel had cogs connected to the rim of the castle which began to revolve.

'I see you like,' the old man said. 'Turn off after you enjoy.'

He pointed to a camp bed in the cellar's far corner. 'There you sleep.'

The old man and Marko disappeared and I was left alone in

the basement. When I tried to turn off the tap, it came away in my hand. The castle cranked and groaned. What could I do? I had no idea where Marko or the old man were. The noisy castle kept me awake.

In the morning, Marko brought me a coffee. 'So you like this,' he said, nodding towards the turning contraption.

'Like it? It kept me awake and I couldn't turn the water off. Find a way to stop the damn thing.'

He shrugged. 'That not matter. We go now to Café Slavia and wait Maja. You will like her. She very beautiful.'

Located on the banks of the Vltava River, the Slavia was typical of the cafés you find throughout the former Austro-Hungarian Empire: varnished wood panels, sturdy chairs and tables and newspapers slung over wooden dowels. Old men sip their coffees while playing chess and fur-coated women gossip in low voices and eat éclairs and chocolate gateaux.

Marko and I sat drinking foul *kavas*. In those days of *glasnost*, but before the arrival of Starbucks, Czech coffee was dark, strong and served in mugs. Oily, gritty coffee grains floated on the top of the cup and stuck to your lips.

Marko kept getting up to make phone calls, returning each time to say, 'Maja is on her way.'

I trusted his word as much as I did his driving, but we were a long way from Zagreb and there was nowhere else for me to go.

After three hours, Maja finally arrived. Marko was right; she looked like she belonged on a catwalk. Tall, leggy and sultry, she had the appearance of a tigress who would eat her own cubs if necessity demanded it. She was poured into her Levis and over her white silk blouse was an expensive black-leather jacket zipped to just below the last button.

She took us to a waiting car. As we drove through the town, I felt like the castle, going around in circles. We were. After a 15-minute journey, I could see the Café Slavia two hundred metres down the road.

'We get out now,' Maja said.

She led us into a small gallery. As the door was closed, so

were the curtains. A jacketed guard appeared from nowhere. He revealed an Uzi sub-machine gun.

Marko whispered, 'I have told them you are English lord. Expert on Renaissance art.'

I was shaking with a mixture of fear over the gun and anger with Marko. 'You've done what?'

Another man came up from the cellar with a large painting covered in linen. He placed it on a table. 'I am Karol. This is my gallery.' He lifted the cloth. 'Please look. We think this is Jacopo Bassano. It is going to Munich, but first we need authentication. Your fee will be two per cent of sale price.'

Not knowing what the hell I was doing, my instincts told me to play for time. I pretended to examine the picture and concentrated on two or three parts of the painting, as though I had noticed something that would attract the attention of an expert. The fish on the kitchen floor, the figure of Judas Iscariot slumped in a chair, the haloed Christ sitting at the dining table, talking to his disciples.

I then turned my attention to the scratchings on the back, the woodworm holes in the frame. I took a notebook from my pocket and wrote a lot of gobbledegook. Hoping my voice wouldn't shake, I told Karol that I must have professional photos of the painting and that, after studying them, I would give him my answer from London.

Karol snapped his fingers and Maja stepped forward with a camera. 'She will take them and bring them to your hotel.'

I couldn't tell him that I was staying in a cellar in the suburbs with a pirouetting castle. I left it to Marko to sort that one out. After he'd said something to them in Czech, I asked Karol, 'Does this painting have any provenance?'

'It does, but the paperwork is unreliable. That is why you are here.'

After we left the gallery, I said to Marko. 'You bastard! We're going back to Zagreb tonight.'

'We can't do that,' he said. 'We have to wait for the photographs.'

'Oh yes. And which five-star hotel is this lord staying at?'

'Don't worry,' Marko said, waving a soothing hand. 'I told them you travel incognito and I would pick up the photos from Maja at the Slavia.'

I was in the shit now, up to my knees. I had to get away from Marko to think things through. I told him I'd get myself back to the house that night. I headed across the Charles Bridge on foot. I wanted to see that damn castle for real.

When I landed at Heathrow, I rang Mervyn and told him what had happened. He said he would make an appointment for me at a major London auction house with the person who dealt with seventeenth-century Renaissance art. I felt better when he said he would come with me.

In the meantime, the calls from Prague and Zagreb continued. Every time the phone rang, my legs buckled. It was Karol, Maja or Marko wanting to know if the painting had been authenticated.

A few knee-knocking days later I met Mervyn at the auction house and the two of us were introduced to the expert. He was, in fact, a young aristocrat, someone I will call 'Charles'.

'Where did you see this picture?' he asked.

'In Prague.'

'In a gallery or someone's home?'

I gave him the name of the gallery and told him about Karol. I didn't mention the machine gun.

Charles looked briefly at the photos, then at Mervyn. He waved his hand. 'A fake,' he said authoritatively. 'There's a lot of this stuff about these days.'

I felt relieved. If the painting had been genuine, I would have been implicated in what was possibly an art crime. Now I could extricate myself from a situation I had foolishly stumbled into.

Back at the Rona gallery, I told Stanley the whole story. He listened and smiled wryly. 'Why didn't you tell me earlier?'

I explained that I had felt too ashamed. Then Stanley told me about an incident he'd had some years before.

'I was in Los Angeles where I was asked to visit the home

of a millionaire who said he owned a Picasso. When I saw it, I told him it was a fake. That evening his bodyguard came to my hotel. Fortunately for me, we had become drinking buddies. "Get out of town," he said. "You have given him information he doesn't want repeated." I left on the next plane.'

Stanley laughed. 'Do you know what the French say about Corot? That in his lifetime he painted one thousand canvases and that three thousand are in America.'

That evening the phone rang. It was Karol again. I told him that I needed more time. There was some confusion between the picture he had shown me and another of Bassano's paintings. 'Ring me next week,' I said.

To my relief, there were no more calls.

Six months later, I was at a party and met a lecturer in the Art Department at University College, London. He was an expert in late Renaissance paintings. I told him about my misadventure in Prague. He asked me if I still had the transparencies of the fake Bassano. I said that I did.

'Could I see them?'

'Of course,' I said.

I sent them to him.

A few days later he called me. 'That's no fake. It's one of Bassano's kitchen paintings. This one has been lost for years. It's worth millions.'

What a fool I'd been. A fake art expert and a fake lord.

Now as I look at the transparency of this painting, I see a cook scrubbing a copper pot. There is a hole sunk into the stone floor where a half dozen still-alive fish have been netted. Surrounded by cats and cooks, they know their fate has been sealed. My eye is drawn back to the central character in the foreground, Judas Iscariot, who sits in a pose of regret and shame. He is dressed sumptuously in fur-lined robes, a glint of an earring below his crimson turban. He is staring at a goblet of red wine and a loaf of bread.

Like all Renaissance paintings, it is an allegory. The more you study it, the more you see. The long white towel draped over a hook could be the swaddling used for Christ on the cross and the shine of silver in Judas' ear could represent the shekels he received for his greed.

I share his emotions of regret and shame brought about not, as in his case, by the betrayal of another person, but the betrayal of myself. I had been the real fake.

The Artists' War

I was lucky to have known the actor Bob Hoskins because he'd married a friend of mine, Linda Banwell. I had been a fan of Bob since seeing the 1978 Dennis Potter BBC series *Pennies from Heaven* and, two years later, the movie *The Long Good Friday*. It remains one of the best British gangster films with Bob playing the menacing Kray character.

When I first met him, he'd written a song, 'Whirligig', and recorded it with our then nine-year-old Ben singing the chorus. Of course, Renata and I were hoping the recording would be released and make a child star of our son. It was not to be, as the record company wanted Bob to complete a whole album, but he was too busy with his film and theatre career.

It's often forgotten that Bob was a great stage actor. I saw him at the National Theatre as Nathan Detroit in *Guys and Dolls* and opposite Antony Sher in Sam Shepard's two-hander *True West* at the Donmar Warehouse. Shepard's play was unforgettable, and not just because of these two great actors. At one point in the evening Bob had to open a door, and it wouldn't budge. He laughed and turned to the audience. 'The fucking door won't open so I'll have to walk around it.'

In 1986, while working on Neil Jordan's *Mona Lisa*, Bob, Linda and their then two-year-old daughter, Rosa, came on holiday to Krk. We helped find them a villa to rent in our street. I remember them coming by for a barbeque on their first evening there. He was worried that there didn't seem to be a spare set of sheets. 'Do you think you can ask the owners for some more? It's very hot and I sweat a lot. And things might get seriously romantic.'

The next day things got seriously dangerous. I took them out in our small fibreglass boat. Six of us in a three-metre dinghy and no lifebelts, which were unknown in Yugoslavia.

Rosa's hat fell into the sea and Bob stood up and leaned over to retrieve it. As water poured over the side, we nearly capsized. I didn't need to shout at him to sit down. We were that close to disaster.

Sitting in Bob and Linda's kitchen one Saturday evening in 1987, and after a bottle or two of wine, I showed him some Rabuzin images and told him about my idea for a film about the artist. Bob was off to Czechoslovakia to finish directing and acting in *The Raggedy Rawney*. His next big project was to star in *Roger Rabbit*. He said he'd be willing to take part in the documentary if it could be made and that he knew a film director who made art movies. He gave me the telephone number for Bill Leeson of Waveband Films.

'Yeh, Dave,' Bob said. 'Can't you see it? Me walking across those hills, surrounded by all those fucking flowers. Bloody marvellous. Ring my agent on Monday.'

I did, but his agent was less enthusiastic. He told me that Bob had left a book with him about some Polish artist.

'No,' I corrected him. 'Yugoslav.'

'Geography was never Bob's strong point,' he said. The phone went dead.

I contacted Bill and he and his editor, Larry Boulting, visited Rabuzin in Croatia. Together, we made plans for a film about the artist. Nothing came of it, but four years later, war broke out in Yugoslavia. While Rabuzin and his wife remained at home in Ključ, Ivan Prpić and most of the Rabuzin family had left Croatia and were living in Lausanne. I wrote a treatment which involved the naïve artist painting his fluffy clouds and mountain-sized flowers while war raged around him. The contrast between his images of a rural idyll and the actuality of what was going on would, I thought, make a strong story.

Bill suggested we go to Chrysalis TV who'd made their reputation with the World Snooker Championships. He'd heard they were looking for a foothold in the arts slots. He was right and they agreed to take us to Anthony Wall and Nigel Finch at BBC *Arena*.

I was nervous. Although the treatment was mine and Bill had made films before, I had no idea where to start. I had been working from Benjamin Lucitti's *Student Film-maker's Handbook*. With a combination of Lucitti, Bill and Chrysalis, we got funding from *Arena* to go to Croatia and start filming.

We arrived in Zagreb and recruited a camera crew from Croatian TV. It was the first time I'd been in a war zone and I felt a mixture of fear and excitement. I invited Darko Glavan to be the narrator and we set off for Ključ. The film crew travelled in their van and I drove a hire car with Bill and Darko as passengers. We were playing The Pogues *Rum, Sodomy and the Lash* at such a high volume we never heard the shelling. Then I saw a soldier waving at us from a bridge across the road. 'Why's he doing that?' I asked.

Darko turned the volume down. 'Fuck it, David. This is the front line. Turn around.'

We arrived at Ključ a little later than the others and not much further away from the fighting. The Yugoslav People's Army (JNA) were being driven out of their base at Varaždin, ten kilometres east of Ključ.

We stayed in the town at Hotel Varaždin. The first evening there a soldier ran into the lobby shouting that the Serbs were dropping chemical bombs. They weren't, but we joined a crowd of women and children in the casino basement and spent the evening on the roulette wheel, using a conker I kept as a lucky charm for the ball. That night I smoked my first cigarette since Canford Heath.

The next day at Rabuzin's house we filmed the artist at work in front of a window. Outside, we'd set up a blue screen so that we could later show scenes of war over his shoulder as he continued to paint his utopian visions. Rabuzin was nervous about the screen, expecting it to attract the interest of the Yugoslav air force.

When filming a family meal, Rabuzin ate his food like a bourgeois, conscious every action was being recorded. But when he was alone, I'd seen him pick up his soup bowl and dispense with the spoon. As the meal continued, we left the camera running and told him we were going outside to smoke. He tucked a napkin under his chin and slurped his soup. The shot was included in our film. I doubt he found it in his heart to forgive me.

Before we returned to London, we had a chance encounter in Zagreb. We came across the *Umjetnička Brigada* – the Art Brigade – a group of singers, actors, dancers, directors and artists. They had set up their own unit in the Croatian army. We took photos and interviewed some of them on camera.

When we got back to London, Nigel and Anthony were lukewarm about our Rabuzin footage, but they liked what we showed them of the Brigade and we were given further funds to return to Croatia to bring these two disparate subjects together.

We weren't happy to go back as the war there was getting worse, but Bill and I knew we didn't have a complete film with only Rabuzin's involvement.

We filmed the Art Brigade performing cabaret on the front line near Karlovac and invited Rabuzin to Zagreb while we tried to find a way to link the two themes. Our solution was to use the town's funicular railway which connects the city centre with the Old Town. We put two members of the Art Brigade in the car going up, and Rabuzin was filmed coming down. They passed each other halfway and Rabuzin did a voiceover, reflecting on the role of the artist in war: how the fighting had to be done by those younger than himself. The end result wasn't Spielberg, but it was a way out of a tricky problem.

Three days before the scheduled broadcast, I was contacted by our executive producer and asked to meet the Head of BBC2, Michael Jackson, in his office. He was unhappy about the film. We had too many dead bodies. 'Thirteen,' he said. Could we cut it back to five or six? He asked his assistant to fast forward the film to a sequence of corpses which he then proceeded to count.

I asked him if he'd watched the whole film. He said no. I asked him if he was aware of the context in which we'd shown the dead. He said no. I asked him whether he knew of any wars when people didn't get killed. He said nothing. I explained that we had panned across a Rabuzin mural on the wall of a school, filming a line of children in front of it. When the camera reached the end, it panned back, this time soldiers replacing the children. The camera returned a third time, showing a row of empty graves, then closed in on the mural as a child turned cartwheels under it. This was then followed by the footage of the dead.

While this was going on, Rabuzin was speaking, 'When a man looks at something, he just sees half of it. At every moment, half the world is missing to us. So we must turn in order to see the second half. Everything depends on what we see and how long we see it; that's how long we live. Unfortunately, for most of us, even when we are alive, we live only half a life.'

I said all those involved with the film would disassociate themselves from it if there were any cuts. It was shown complete. I was told later that the BBC had a policy that film-makers can show as many dead bodies as they want if the wars are in Africa or Asia but that, with Europeans, there had to be greater circumspection.

Giles Smith reviewed our film in the *Independent*. After disparaging comments about the Art Brigade, he continued: 'Strangely, in a programme so questioning about art and its roles, there was little enquiry into the merits of Rabuzin's actual work – mostly pictures of skies filled with fluffy clouds and landscapes done up as puffballs. Rabuzin, it was said, "regards himself as a God in the sky of his paintings". Even so, most of them looked like the kind of get-well card you might buy for someone you didn't know that closely.'[1]

After what happened later in Bosnia, I am embarrassed

by how strongly pro-Croat the film is but, at that time, they were the victims of urbanicide at Vukovar and other towns and villages. And groups such as the *Umjetnička Brigada* had characteristics of the citizens' militias from the Spanish Civil War.

Not long after the film was made, Zagreb's liberalism was replaced by the racist nationalism that was never far below the surface in Croatia. Even my old friend, rock'n'roller Darko Glavan, moved to the right. I was to end up working in Mostar, the Herzegovinian town that was to become the worst victim of this revanchist Croat nationalism. My experiences there make it difficult for me today to watch more than a few minutes of the film.

Historical change can be witnessed by observing the use of symbols. The most obvious example is the swastika. Originally it was a Hindu symbol for eternity, but Hitler hijacked it as the sign for Nazism. In the case of the wars in former Yugoslavia, the cross was the symbol to watch. When making our film in Croatia, it was everywhere. Militiamen had rosaries wound around their necks with huge crucifixes hanging from them. It seemed to me a fashion accessory, rather like the GIs in Vietnam and their bandanas.

By the time the war reached Bosnia, the cross had become synonymous with Croat fascism because the first thing the Croatians would do after occupying a former 'Muslim' town or village would be to erect a huge wooden cross, often on the site of a destroyed mosque.

Wiser observers than I foresaw all this. Misha Glenny, in his book *The Balkans*, refers to the Zagreb and Belgrade Springs of the early 1970s when liberal reformers in both the Serb and Croat League of Communists were denounced and driven underground by Tito. This ensured that a future revival of nationalism would be anything but liberal.

In Ted Hughes' powerful version of Aeschylus's *The Orestia*, he writes about the attack on Troy:

But now let them take care
To respect the gods of that city,
So long as they violate nothing sacred,
Violate no temple, shrine, priest
Or priestess,
Perhaps these destroyers of a city
Will escape destruction.

The next ten years of my life were going to take me very close to the destroyers of cities.

Charity Virgins

When making the *Arena* film, Bill and I had visited the Klaićeva Children's Hospital in Zagreb where we were appalled to find that they were short of vital equipment. Croatia's capital city had hardly been touched by the war, but this was an example of how quickly the infrastructures of all societies are disrupted by conflict and, as in all wars, children are most at risk. We decided to donate a ventilator to the mother-and-baby unit and to fund this from the income we'd made from our film. We then had to find ways to raise money for further aid.

I suggested we restage my play *Simple Writings*, as it was about a child victim of war. I contacted Michael Walling who had directed it when it first appeared on the London Fringe in 1989. He was willing to get involved and said he'd contact Susannah York and ask her if she'd support the project. She liked the script and agreed to perform.

On the strength of her commitment, we booked the Mermaid Theatre. Bill suggested we change the title to *War Child* and that we should register ourselves as a charity with those two words.

Bill was good at getting himself invited to events where we might meet those with sympathy for our work. At a music launch party in Belgravia we were introduced to Bob Geldof. When we told him about our idea he said, 'If you want to raise money, don't put on a fucking play. Nobody goes to see plays.' With Geldof's words ringing in our ears and the Mermaid now asking for a deposit, we cancelled our theatre plans and decided to organise a music event.

Bill knew the Bhundu Boys so we had something to start

with. And he didn't want to stop there. 'What about a classical night, contemporary music, a rock night and let's throw in comedy as well.'

Bill lacked fear and I lacked caution. Why not?

We booked the Royal Festival Hall for four nights, from Saturday, February 27th, 1993. The RFH didn't want any money until after the booking so we took the plunge.

I wrote a letter to promote the evenings which was published in the *Guardian* on November 12th, 1992.[1] Among the signatories were Bob Hoskins, Maureen Lipmann, Peter Gabriel, Krist Novoselic of Nirvana, Richard Branson, The Pogues and Max Stafford-Clark.

With contacts like these we were able to recruit the BBC Symphony Orchestra, Julian Lloyd Webber, Stephen Kovacevich, Peter Donohoe and the Phoenix Dance Company for the classical night. For the contemporary night, Tom Stoppard, John Mortimer, Stephen Isserlis, Joanna MacGregor and the Smith Quartet. Jo Brand, Lee Evans, Jonathan Ross, John Sessions and the Tiller Girls for the comedy night. The Bhundu Boys, The Blues Band, Denny Laine and Krist Novoselic for the rock night.

We told them they didn't have to do much, just be there and contribute something, drawing on their particular skills. All the artists did much more than just turn up, contributing performances that made it difficult for us to squash them all into each evening's timings. The Tiller Girls were a big hit, reformed from the 1960s dancers and most of them now in their 70s and 80s.

After the show on the last night, we organised an all-night vigil at nearby Gabriel's Wharf. We set up a rudimentary stage and sound system and invited the Bishop of Barking, Michael Meacher MP, Ken Livingstone, Maureen Lipmann and Susannah York to speak about the plight of Bosnian children. We distributed candles with War Child logo holders which proved useful as hand warmers, since it was a bitterly cold night. Most of the audience tried to get into the small tent we'd set up for the performers.

It was a financial failure with barely a third of the RFH filled on each of the evenings. It was one of those times in life when you lie awake at night thinking, How the hell do I get out of this? Of course, there was no escape. It was like crawling through a long tunnel without room to turn back and hoping that there was an exit at the end. I would wake every morning, turn over and wish myself back to sleep to avoid having to face the day.

As we negotiated with the RFH to accept staged payments of our massive debt, Bill and I considered the possibility of remortgaging my house in Muswell Hill. I couldn't have done this without the agreement of Renata, but the fact that I was even willing to consider it shows to what extent my life was in crisis.

With no money and the Festival Hall chasing us, we had no alternative but to press on with our plans for the new charity. The event had given us access to the music world – promoters, managers and artists. Bill decided he would travel to Sarajevo and take music with him. We made contact with Brent Hansen, head of MTV Europe and one of War Child's early patrons, and with Sue Lloyd-Roberts at the BBC. With their support, both broadcasters supplied us with hundreds of CDs and tapes. Bill started a series of trips, first to Sarajevo and later to Mostar. He visited youth centres and radio stations and distributed the music recordings. Without his willingness to make these dangerous journeys, we would not have survived. Thanks to him, War Child was seen to be doing something, and that something was original and captured the attention of the media.

In the run-up to the Festival Hall, we'd tried to get free advertisements in the papers. Much to our surprise, the European edition of *Time Magazine* offered us three weeks of free full-page ads. We later found out that the European Manager had confused the name of War Child with another charity which had been set up by an ex-employee of *Time*. He had wanted to help her and, in trying to do so, unintentionally played a leading role in raising the profile of our charity.

David Warner, ex-Bermondsey paperboy, with a business

empire stretching from Canada to South East Asia, was on a flight to New York when he read the ad. As Managing Director of Regent Export, one of the largest procuring agents for the British Government, he asked himself: why hadn't he heard of War Child?

Soon after his return from the US, David rang and introduced himself. He told us that he thought he might be able to help with our aid work and invited us to visit him at his office in Salisbury. Two days later, a black Mercedes was waiting for us outside our office in Camden Town with the registration, *WAR 1*.

We told David that, despite our Festival Hall debut, we were struggling. We had supplied that ventilator and now Bill was visiting Sarajevo with music aid. We told him that we shared an office in Camden Town with the Serious Road Trip, young Australians and New Zealanders who went to Bosnia as musicians, jugglers, stilt-walkers and clowns. Travelling in brightly-painted trucks decorated with cartoon characters, these humorous and brave Aussies and Kiwis were bringing a lot of happiness to children. They now wanted to take in a mobile bakery to feed hungry refugees and we wanted to help them with this project.

David thought it was a good idea and arranged for us to meet Andy Bearpark, Head of Emergency Aid at the Overseas Development Agency.[2]

I went to the first meeting with Christopher Watt of the SRT. A few days later, David Warner rang to say that the ODA were prepared to put up £250,000 to purchase a mothballed military bakery from the Ministry of Defence. There was a condition: they were only willing to give the money if it was a War Child project. I guess the SRT were too left field for them. David's company were contracted to source additional equipment and vehicles. He was clearly a man of influence in government circles as War Child had no track record whatsoever, and the ODA had nothing to go on except his word.

I went to Andy Bearpark's office to sign the agreement for the quarter of a million pounds. 'It had better work,' he said, 'or we'll have that bakery out of there faster than your balls shrink in cold water.' His rough Yorkshire threat was a long way from *Yes, Minister*. I left the meeting grateful that War Child's immediate future was secured, but scared at the sheer scale of what we were taking on.

I need not have worried. In addition to our contacts at MTV and the BBC, we now had the attention of the government and behind, or alongside, them, David and Regent Export plc. Bill and I started receiving invitations to radio and TV shows which resulted in War Child receiving donations from across the country. Children sent us their pocket money and pensioners sent us stamps. One widow even sent her wedding ring because that was all she could give.

Money poured in from schools, and some of them adopted War Child as their charity of choice. Supporters ran races, baked cakes, swam lengths and organised concerts to raise money for us. We did our best to link these schools with children in Bosnia and, when travelling there, took with us letters and paintings from British schools. When we returned, we had bundles of drawings from Bosnian children who wanted these sent back in thanks. They were stark images of war with titles such as 'The Day they Killed My House', 'My Lost Street', 'Wounded Children'. I remember one of a tank firing red flowers at a line of children reaching out to catch them.

As the ex-teacher in War Child, I visited schools around the country. I found a humane concern for the children of war, sadly missing among our political leaders. One of these visits was to Maidstone Grammar School for Boys where I was invited to address morning assembly. I arrived at 8.30am, in time for coffee with the Headmaster.

I hadn't been told that it was Speech Day. I was dressed in jeans and leather jacket and found myself among senior staff in dark suits and academic gowns, local dignitaries and the town's mayor, glittering with his chain.

We filed onto the dais in front of 500 uniformed boys. Behind us was the school choir and orchestra. A religious service followed that brought back appalling memories of my own school days.

My turn came to speak.

I stuttered my way through a talk on music in war, its role as an antidote to racism and fascism. I ended with an appeal to my young audience that they appreciate the music that unites humanity and reject the music that divides, like military marches and nationalist hymns.

As I sat down to polite applause, the Headmaster announced that they would sing the school hymn, which was in Latin, and then conclude with 'God Save the Queen'. After the hymn, the orchestra behind me began to play and the line of mortar-boarded teachers and their scruffy guest stood stiffly to attention and sang to Her Majesty. Standing mid-stage, I had no alternative but to mouth the words for the first and last time in my life as I watched smirking smiles light across the faces of the more intelligent boys.

The Museum of Broken Relationships

In my ex-wife's home town of Zagreb there are the usual museums and galleries found in most capital cities. But there is one which is unique – the Museum of Broken Relationships. Set up by former lovers, Olinka Vištica and Dražen Grubišić, it is a place 'to store all the painful triggers of memory around us, creating a safe place for both tangible and intangible heritage of past love'.

In 2014 I returned to Zagreb. I wanted to see the house where Renata had spent her childhood and where we had first made love. The cafés we had sat in, the walks we had made together on Sljeme, the mountain that rises above the city. I wanted to cross town on the blue trams we had travelled on together. Of course, I wanted to visit this museum as I had something to give them.

I spent a morning looking at the cathartic displays. They included an axe donated by one woman. 'I used it to break up the furniture of the girlfriend who left me. Each day I smashed a bit more. When she returned for her furniture all she had were bits of wood.' A Virgin Mary holy water bottle has the accompanying words: 'My lover gave me this as his "special" present. He didn't know I'd opened his bag and found it was full of them.' There is a stuffed toy caterpillar: 'Every time we met, we tore off one of the caterpillar's legs. When all the legs were gone, we would live together. As you see, the caterpillar never became a complete invalid.' Most sadly, a suicide note from a mother to her daughter: 'To write a letter under these circumstances is impossible … Lots of love and happiness, Your mama.'

The museum welcomes donations. Before leaving, I gave them a ceramic beer stein I had brought with me with these words: 'After my wife and I separated, she was reluctant to let me return to collect my possessions. Eventually, she allowed me to take a few of my books. As I left the house, I picked up this imitation Bavarian mug. Apart from my books, it is the only thing I was able to remove from the house. It therefore has great value and should be in a museum.'

I was married to Renata for a quarter of a century, but in the last few years of our relationship, we couldn't remain in the same room without fighting. Working for Rabuzin, the BBC film and starting War Child hadn't helped. Renata knew as well as I did that I preferred to be in a war zone rather than be at home with her. Whatever love there had once been between us was disappearing.

One Saturday evening in March 1992 an argument broke out over dinner. Ben sat at the table shouting, 'Stop it, stop it.' I heard Jonny crying upstairs and went to his room to find him trying to climb out of his window onto the roof below. I pulled him back, hugged him and told him that all the arguing would stop.

I immediately packed a small suitcase and left the house. I walked to friends who offered me a bed. It was the first of many refuges.

We divorced when Jonny was twelve and, four years later, he came to live with Anne and me. The break-up of the marriage had affected him deeply and had disrupted the careful nurturing of his early childhood.

At the time of our separation, I was advised to fight my corner in court, but I ceded the house to Renata rather than have my children dragged through a messy divorce.

A marriage which comes to an end should be like a treasured book. You occasionally bring it down from the shelf to glance at its pages, discuss its contents with others who have read it, then put it back. I wish this had been the case with ours.

The memories of our marriage are overwhelmed with sadness. I would guess that is true for both of us. Too many years of suffering get in the way. For me, I can recall only the anger and the bitterness. Lust and Biba mini-skirts don't last long. Love, too, can be dead before it dies.

I'm sure Renata had expected better things from me. When we met, I was studying law and she saw a future for herself quite different to her upbringing in Zagreb. When she first visited me in London, she found herself in my parents' house with people who shook her hand and said, 'From Yugoslavia? How interesting. You have communism there. Do you have television?'

During the years of our marriage, Renata suffered a lot. An ill child, a stillbirth, my collapse. She must have felt like the surviving *Ibeji* doll – confined to the back of the cupboard.

Unable to guarantee her material security, she convinced herself that I was also unable to guarantee her emotional security. In retrospect, she was right on both counts. When I left a salaried teaching job for the uncertainty of the art world, and then the greater uncertainty of setting up a charity in a war zone, that justifiably enraged her.

Today I spend summer holidays on Mljet, an island near Dubrovnik. When I hear Croatian spoken, my memories take me back to that other island with no vowels. I am not sure whether I like the language; whether I ever did. Perhaps that is why, after spending so much time in the region – holidays, working in Zagreb, living in Bosnia – I have never spoken Croatian fluently. Just enough to understand what people are talking about. Just enough to get by. *Just enough* are two words that sum up not only my language skills, but my marriage. Everything was just enough – but not quite enough.

Ivo's Boat

When I married Renata, my father-in-law gave me a black melanite ring. He told me that, with the arrival of the German army in 1941, he and Nada had hidden it with other jewellery inside the stove of their flat in Zagreb. If I ever left Renata, he wanted it back.

As a young man in the 1930s, Ivo demonstrated against the Ustashe whose leader, Ante Pavelić, became President of a Quisling Nazi Croatian regime in 1941. Their slaughter of Jews, Serbs, Gypsies and anti-fascist Croats was enough to shock even the Wehrmacht. General Edmund von Glaise-Horstenau reported to the German Army Command on June 28th, 1941: 'According to reliable reports from countless German military and civil observers during the last few weeks, the Ustashe have gone roaring mad.' Their militia literally hacked their victims to death and specialised in burning women and children inside barns and churches.

Ivo joined Tito's Partisans and ran messages in Zagreb. One day the Ustashe came looking for him and he hid in the cellar. Nada answered the door and a militiaman asked her for her husband's first name. When she said Ivan and that he wasn't at home the man said, 'Don't worry. I wanted to check as I know he has many brothers. Ivan saved my life when I was a child. He pulled me out of the Sava River. I know he's here, but will tell my comrades he's not.'

Ivo took his Marxism seriously and believed in 'from each according to their abilities, to each according to their needs'. Unfortunately, Tito's government didn't share this enthusiasm and, after the war, Ivo was imprisoned. On his release, he was offered a party job. Disgusted by what he considered Tito's betrayal of communism, he turned it down, went to work as a vet's assistant and taught himself the accordion. In the mid-fifties he set up a café band.

There were three of them. Ivo played accordion, Franjo the violin and Boris, drums. Boris and Franjo were always drunk and Franjo loved women as much as he loved the bottle. I always knew who Franjo had been to bed with the night before because his latest lover would sit at the band's table and he would dedicate every piece of music to her. It was touching because, in the years I knew him, he was elderly and so were his rouge-cheeked amours in their faded sundresses.

The three musicians retained their youthful exuberance well into the later years of their partnership. Not only for women, but also with their looks. Franjo was small and suave with his immaculately pressed trousers, waistcoat, and endless supply of bow ties. Boris was short and fat with a moustache that drooped over the sides of his mouth like a Montenegrin hill bandit. When he talked, he'd caress it as though stroking a cat.

Ivo was tall, clean-shaven and hairless as an American Indian. He wore white shirts and changed them twice a day. When he played his accordion, he looked as though he was telling himself a joke.

Ivo and Nada dreamed of building a summer vacation house on a small plot of land they owned on Krk. He hoped to earn money playing in local bars and hotels and spend his spare time fishing. Nada looked forward to watching her future grandchildren swimming in the nearby cove.

The house in Malinska was ten years in the making. Whenever he had money and a little time, he would travel from Zagreb to the coast on his Lambretta, with Nada riding pillion. They would take the ferry to the island and camp on their land. The foundations took four years, the walls another three, the window frames, two. The roof had to wait for paid professionals.

Ivo made most of the furniture, but he wasn't as competent a carpenter as he was a musician. The dinner table had uneven legs and wobbled precariously when bread was sliced and dishes laid out. Fortunately, the chairs were solid. I remember they had *DUBROVNIK* stamped on them and were cast-offs from a Zagreb hotel he had once worked in.

Ivo found seasonal work for the band at a hotel in Punat, ten kilometres away. Every afternoon he would sleep until five o'clock, when he would demand a coffee from Nada or his visiting daughter. He would then get dressed for work: crisp white shirt, gabardine trousers and polished leather shoes.

After the band finished playing at midnight, he always went fishing. So, before setting off from home, he would inspect the old metal box that contained everything he needed for the second of his nocturnal passions.

He then packed his accordion, rods, lines, floats, hooks, torch and a knife in the back of his Wartburg, which I rechristened 'Fartburg'. This East German car was a tank, running on a mixture of petrol and oil, belching out a gaseous smoke. Neighbours covered their faces as he headed down the narrow lane.

Fishermen can often be seen standing side by side on harbour walls looking as though they are pissing into the sea, but Ivo wasn't one of them. He had respect for the intelligence of fish. He would say, 'Fish have ears as well as eyes.'

When most fishermen get a bite, they wrestle with their prey in a look-at-me way, but you wouldn't know when Ivo had caught something. He would continue to smoke his cigarette and let the fish run until it was exhausted. He would then reel it gently in to shore and, without a splash or sound, slip it into his bag.

Ivo had other secrets. He had invented a float which could be thrown far out to sea. The simplicity of its design was astonishing. He'd cut three inches off the bottom of a candle, tapering one end so it would float upright in the water. After removing the wick, he'd run a line through the centre, keeping it in place with a lead pincher.

If anyone came too close when he was preparing his bait or throwing his line, he would mouth a silent curse at them. If that didn't work, he'd pretend to throw out the line and whack the offender on the shoulder with his rod.

On his drives to work in the evening, he would look out for a quiet spot where he would stop. Not to fish, but to feed the water. He had a catapult and, like an old Viking, used it to fire balls of wet bread out to sea. When he finished work, this was where he was going to fish on his way home.

One day I went with him and we both fished at a spot he had been 'feeding'. He caught four large mullet and left me there to go to work. 'It's only a kilometre so come along later, David, and have a drink.'

He picked up the plastic bag containing the fish. 'I'll take these with me,' he said. He'd only brought one bag so I asked him to leave it with me in case I caught something.

'Okay,' he said, 'but if anyone passes, don't let them see the fish. If you do, half the island will be here tomorrow.'

An hour later, a car stopped and a small boy clambered down to where I was fishing. Without asking, he opened the bag and shouted to his father, 'Dad, look at these.'

I did catch one more mullet, a small one, and at the hotel, Ivo asked if anyone had seen the fish. When I told him what had happened, he was angry, but when he got home the following night, he was laughing. 'I was right. There were four people fishing at that place when I passed by this evening. I stopped and asked why they were there and one of them said, "Last night an Englishman was here and he caught several large mullet."'

On his nights off, he would go fishing with his brother, Joža, and sometimes me as well. One morning, the two brothers were drinking coffee on our balcony. Nada asked if they'd caught anything.

'No,' Joža said.

Ivo smiled, got up from the table and opened the fridge. He returned holding a plate of several large mullet.

Joža said, 'But we didn't catch anything last night!'

'You didn't,' Ivo said, winking at us. 'Would you like to take one home?'

Later that day, his wife, Mirijana, came to see Nada and told her Joža had caught a large fish. 'Did Ivo have any luck?' she asked smugly.

Nada laughed. 'We're barbequing tonight.'

One year Ivo's band did well with their bookings and he decided to buy a second-hand, fibreglass boat. He found it advertised in the local paper and it was delivered on the back of an old truck, together with its trailer. The boat was in good condition, but the trailer's wheels were rusted to the chassis. Renovating it took a week, and we waited impatiently for the launch. Ben and Jonny would climb inside and plead, 'Can we go on the sea, *Deda*. Please, can we?'

'Not yet,' said Ivo. 'I'm not ready.'

'We are.'

But they had to wait and wait.

He wasn't going to waste money on a mooring rope. He had a cheaper solution. At the back of the house he kept a pile of bicycle tyres. He peeled them like apples and connected the pieces of rubber to both ends of an old piece of rope. The result: a flexible mooring rope. His invention meant that, when the wind blew, the boat would stay in one place. As one bright idea led to another, staying in one place was just what the boat did. It was to be another year before its launch.

When we arrived for our holiday the next year, the boat was on its trailer and parked at the side of the road. We were finally going to make it to the sea. I suggested we moor the boat in the harbour.

Ivo looked at me angrily. 'The first storm will throw it against the harbour wall. It must come home every night. Why do you think I bought a trailer?'

The motor to power the boat was Ivo's pride and joy. Everyone in Yugoslavia had a Slovenian-made Tomas outboard engine that had cheap and easily replaced parts, but he had a second-hand, 9-horsepower Swedish Penta motor which weighed as much as most 20-horsepower engines. Ivo insisted that the motor and fuel tank would have to be carried by hand because he refused to allow it to be placed on the boat on dry land as it would 'damage the hull'.

We were also not going to be allowed to run the boat into the sea on its trailer so it gently floated off. 'Sea water will rust the trailer again. We'll wedge it above the water line and carry the boat to the sea.'

The two boys sat on the wall beside the boat, waiting impatiently for Nada to prepare the picnic and for Ivo to give a last inspection to every screw on the motor. Meanwhile, neighbours and family gathered in the street to help. Two hours later, we were on our way. It was like one of those Feast of Assumption ceremonies on the Amalfi Coast where the Virgin Mary is waded, slowly and elaborately, into the sea.

Waved off by the laughing crowd, our first trip was to a bay four miles from the village. There were picnicking families with their boats pulled out of the water. Ivo would have none of that. His boat must not touch the shore: food, drink and children had to be waded to the beach.

He dropped anchor and spent half an hour instructing me on how to tie his elasticated rope to one of the rocks on the pebbled beach. Splashed by laughing children and sniggered at by their parents, I was a reluctant and embarrassed shipmate.

When we finally sat down to eat, Ivo proudly pointed at his bobbing boat. 'You see,' he said. 'It's not moving.'

Ivo's dedication to his boat didn't last long. When we returned the following year, he handed over command to me. He said he was too old for boat trips. The reality was that he no longer had the energy to act the fastidious skipper.

I made a concrete block and sunk it ten metres out into the sea, just below our house. I connected this with a line to a buoy and tied the boat up there at night. Now we only had to drag the boat to and from the water at the beginning and end of our holiday. This made life easier for me, but for Ivo everything was getting more difficult.

He was finding his accordion heavy to play. He bought an electric keyboard, but that had its problems as it needed to be transported to and from his venues. At the age of 75, he had decided to retire. Boris had already left the band after a long illness. The last straw had been when Franjo persuaded Ivo that they didn't need to replace him and that they would make more money if they bought a drum machine. When they used it for the first time, Franjo kicked it off its stand. 'The bloody thing won't keep time with me.'

Ivo and Nada started coming to London every Christmas. He didn't like leaving his home, but he would not have survived on his own in Zagreb as Nada was his domestic slave, cooking, cleaning and dealing with his many needs.

Because their visits were always in winter, much of the time was spent at home. We were held together by the house and the weather. As soon as Ivo woke, he would switch on the TV. His hearing wasn't good so the volume was set at maximum – all day.

He missed his own language and didn't speak a word of English so, one year, he fixed up a complicated aerial that was strung across our kitchen and which allowed him to tune into Radio Zagreb. The reception was weak so the crackling voices were at full volume. The living room for TV and the kitchen for Radio Zagreb. Renata and I were working and looking after the boys. We had three people who had a lot of needs and I was tolerant of only two of them.

I would leave the house as early as possible and stay at work as long as I could. But there were the weekends to get through and the long Christmas holiday. Ivo was now proud of being a Croat, declaring to us all that his youthful radicalism had been stupid. He told me how, in the mid-sixties, his band had performed at Hotel Lav in Split as Tito and his cronies dined off gold plates. I told him that Tito was as close to communism as the Pope to the teachings of Jesus Christ. That in 1946 the Yugoslav army returned Greek Partisans to British firing squads in Athens when they tried to cross into Macedonia. He ignored remarks that confused and challenged his new prejudices and loyalties.

If he saw Margaret Thatcher on TV, and she was on it a lot, he would shake his fist at me. 'She is a great leader. You will learn.' During the miners' strike he cursed the picket lines on the TV news. 'Fuck communism.'

When I tried to explain that Thatcher was importing coal from communist Poland, that the hated communists were the strike breakers in this struggle, he was silent.

In 1989 Nada died suddenly from a brain tumour after six months of terrible suffering and Ivo came alone to London. He would sit for hours at the kitchen table, looking at the candle he kept alight for her. It was depressing, and I would have preferred it if he'd found the time and energy to set up his radio antennae.

Three years later, and with the conflict now raging in Bosnia, I was driving down the Adriatic en route to Mostar. I stopped at the Hotel Lav where he had played that night for Tito. The whole family had stayed with him when he was working there one season. I remembered the pool, the bars, the tennis and Ivo and his band playing beside the sea. I could see him, clambering over the rocks for night fishing, Dalmatian music drifting from the camp site across the bay.

The hotel was now a centre for women and children from Srebrenica. No gold plates here. And instead of white-coated waiters serving tourists, lines of refugees queuing for food.

Hoping to see Ivo again, I decided to make a detour to the island. I arrived in the evening, parked the car near the harbour and walked along the coast road to the house. It was shuttered and the garden overgrown. The boat was upturned, covered in leaves, looking dark and oily. I felt that sadness which is a mix of regret and the passing of time.

'David.'

I looked around. It was Aunt Mirijana. I asked about Uncle

Jože and she told me he had died.

'I'm so sorry,' I said, hugging her. 'How is Ivo?'

'He's okay,' she said. 'With Nada dead, he can't bear to come here.'

'Does he still fish?'

She shook her head. 'His eyesight's too bad. He can't tie hooks.'

I looked at the motorless boat. 'I'd like to see him again.'

'He wouldn't want to meet you.'

I touched the ring. I would have to return it to Renata when I got back to London.

WAR AND PIECES

'Life did not stop and one had to live.'

Leo Tolstoy

Ned of the Hill

Sarajevo was under siege from Bosnian Serb forces from April 1992 until the end of the war in November 1995. During that time, an average of 320 shells landed on the city each day, destroying homes, government buildings, hospitals, communication and cultural centres. Approximately 5,000 civilians were killed and the same number of soldiers.

The city had been under attack for nearly two years when I decided to join Bill on a visit there in January 1994. We were taking in a batch of BBC and MTV CDs for the independent radio station, Radio Zid.

A week before we left we were at a Ron Kavana gig at the Stags Head in Camden Town. Ron is a folk/rock singer and a friend of Bill's.

After he had sung 'Young Ned of the Hill', composed with The Pogues, he told us that he had enjoyed performing this on tour with them to enthusiastic British audiences who seemed to appreciate its sentiments – that Oliver Cromwell rot in hell.

When Bill said we would add his albums to our Sarajevo collection, he asked if he could join us.

'Why do you want to come?' said Bill.

'My grandma was a fiddle player in Limerick.' That didn't seem to answer the question. There was a long pause. 'She was killed by the Brits in 1921. What you tell me about Sarajevo reminds me of her. She used to perform in cellars, out of sight of the Black and Tans.'

He didn't need to say more about them. They were British ex-First World War soldiers and released prisoners with a reputation for murderous brutality. They were recruited to support the Royal Irish Police in suppressing the War of Independence.

'One night they heard her playing, took her away and shot her. If I come to Sarajevo I will play music and will be honouring her memory.'

We flew from Zagreb on a UN Russian Ilyushin cargo plane. Arriving in Sarajevo, we found that airport security was in the hands of the French and we ran from the aircraft into a maze of sandbagged alleyways. They were signposted *BOUL'VD ST MICHEL, CHAMPS-ELYSÉES, AVENUE FOCH.* Border control was under the Danes, who stamped our passports with 'Maybe Airlines, Sarajevo'. Then a lift into town in an APC driven by Egyptians.

The soldier who stamped my passport told me that the French had little contact with the Danish and the Danes even less with the Egyptians. 'Watch their drivers,' he said. 'As soon as they start the engine, jump in the back. They won't tell you when they're about to leave.' The road into town passed through Dobrinja which was Serb-controlled, so this was the only way to get into the city.

The Egyptians dropped us off at the UN Headquarters in Džemala Bijedića Ulica which was some distance from our destination, the Holiday Inn. We had to hire a taxi to go any further.

Our driver said he was unable to drop us at the hotel, and we were left to run there from the main road, nicknamed 'Sniper's Alley'. I was carrying Ron's guitar which I dropped. I went back for it as Bill shouted, 'Don't get killed for a guitar.'

The Holiday Inn was a bubble set within an inferno. The cavernous eight-storey lobby set at its centre was the only safe place apart from the basement restaurant, where waiters in bow ties put on the pretence of normality, serving the only proper food in the city. Their sunken cheeks and sallow complexions gave the lie to that, as did the continuous sound of urban war. The bedrooms, those not gutted by shell fire, had no glass in the windows, and the only protection from the cold and wind was UNHCR plastic sheeting. When the shelling and gunfire seemed to be too close, I spent a lot of time in the bathroom.

The hotel was full of journalists and aid workers. At breakfast (a boiled egg, bread and Nescafé) I sat beside someone from the International Committee of the Red Cross. He already had on his flak jacket and asked me where mine was. I told him we had left ours at the airport, along with the helmets. You were not allowed to land without wearing them. He was shocked and accused us of being irresponsible. I answered that since the people we worked and met with didn't have this protection, why should we?

Sarajevo was a city of Kalashnikovs, armoured personnel carriers (APCs), rocket-propelled grenades and people who'd been pushed back into the Dark Ages: horse-drawn carts, backs bent to the weight of firewood and water containers. A Hieronymus Bosch landscape.

After not getting shot, its citizens expended their remaining energy on trying to keep warm and finding food, yet the people seemed intent on creating a sense of normality.

That normality applies to fear. In her book, *Zlata's Diary – A Child's Life in Sarajevo*, Zlata Filipović describes how her mother coped well with the war. She would risk her life to get the family food and water, but when a mouse entered a room she would jump on chairs and beds.[1]

Ivana Maček talks about how she found the city full of '"magical thinking", "macabre humour", artistic expression, and other survival mechanisms aimed at helping civilians regain a sense of control over their lives.'[2]

On our first night, we went to the Obala Bar near the Miljacka River which was practically on the front line. Bob Marley's 'War, No More Trouble' was playing as we entered: *Everywhere is war, me say war.*

The city was without mains electricity supply. The more ingenious managed to rig up car batteries, telephone jacks or bicycle dynamos. For the very lucky, there were generators.

I can't remember what they were using that night at Obala, except that the power didn't last long. Bob Marley gave way to unplugged live music supplied by Ron and some local musicians. One of them told me that his sister had recently killed herself because she'd had enough. He said this matter-of-factly, as though her death was what had become expected of life in Sarajevo.

There was a young actor there whose mother lived on the Serb side of the lines. He'd not seen her since the start of the war two years before. He said that unless he moved to the hills, joined the Serb forces and bombarded his friends, there would be no chance of meeting her.

The next day we went to Radio Zid so that Ron could perform live on air and we could hand over our CDs. We were told that these broadcasts were listened to in the hills above, but the guys up there obviously didn't appreciate 'Young Ned of the Hill'. The shelling was heavy that day.

Radio Zid was a 24-hour independent radio station determined to promote Sarajevo's non-nationalist urban culture. Over the three-year siege, there were 185 theatre productions in the city, 170 exhibitions and 48 concerts, much of this supported and promoted by Radio Zid. When children couldn't go to school because their schools were too dangerous or too cold, Zid organised *Zimska Škola* – Winter School – educational broadcasts. In blocks of flats parents would gather the children together and they would listen to Radio Zid. If they were lucky, a teacher would be there to give the semblance of a real school.

At the radio station we met Jasmina, a 16-year-old who asked us to correct her boyfriend's love poems which he'd written for her in English. They were in an exercise book at home. 'Please, will you come with me?'

We drove her there, but she didn't want us to come inside with her. She said her parents would be ashamed because they were all living in the basement. She retrieved the poems and we sat with her in the back of the taxi.

They were sad, wistful words of love, life and death. After discussing prepositions and possessive pronouns, Hussein, our driver, got edgy and pointed at a sign on a nearby wall, *PAZITE SNAIPER* – Beware of Snipers – and said that we were parked in direct line of fire from the hills and needed to back into a side street. Jasmina shrugged. She didn't think it mattered.

When we took pathetically small gifts of food and drink into homes, we were stroked, wept over and offered back what we had brought them. The dregs of whisky in my almost-empty hip flask created such excitement with an old man that he called his wife over. They put the flask to their noses, before sharing what was left. This couple lived on the hillside above Baščaršija, the oldest part of town. They considered themselves lucky because they were able to grow some food in their small garden: onions, beans, chard and squash.

The human spirit finds expression in extremes, the barbarism above the city matched by a civilisation below. An actor from the National Theatre had both legs shattered by shrapnel and they had to be amputated. On the day of the operation he and his wife were in the same hospital, she to give birth. 'I've lost half my body,' he said, 'but my wife has given birth to a whole one.' He joked that he was a big drinker and said that now he would have to be carried into bars rather than out of them.

The women of Sarajevo kept up their appearance with whatever cosmetics they could lay their hands on. Many were smartly dressed and wore high heels in the streets as a message of defiance. Getting water involved great risk because the Serbs targeted water taps. An elderly woman told us that she washed her hair every week which involved a two-kilometre walk. 'I am,' she said, 'a resident of Sarajevo.'

Sarajevo has always been proud of its cosmopolitanism, its ethnic mix and strong cultural traditions. Before the break-up of Yugoslavia, thirteen per cent of marriages in Bosnia-Herzegovina were mixed, but in Sarajevo the figure was above thirty per cent. One street had a mosque, Catholic and

Orthodox churches and a synagogue. All four buildings were destroyed or damaged by mortars.

Back at Radio Zid, director Zdravko Grebo told us that his diabetic daughter and many others like her didn't have any insulin. He'd gone to the UN medical agencies, but they'd told him that the problem was too small for them to deal with. He showed us a list with the names of the young diabetics he had compiled with help from one of the doctors at the city's Kosevo Hospital.

It was this chance encounter that was to result in War Child's diabetic project: taking insulin and diabetic equipment to Sarajevo and later, Mostar and other towns. Small NGOs such as War Child ended up being major players in bringing in vital medicines.

On our last day in the city we visited the Markale market because there were no shops left in Sarajevo. Cooking oil was 40 Deutschmarks a litre (£16), sugar 70DM a kilo and coffee 150. The monthly salary for a doctor in the hospital was 5DM.

After four days, we were on the same Russian plane flying back to Zagreb. Ron had already left and Bill and I were its only passengers, sitting strapped to the side of the cargo hold. At the front, there was a hissing samovar. The navigator came over with hot mugs of Russian tea. I think he saw how worried I looked and invited me to sit beside him in the glass bubble directly under the pilot.

Before take off, he opened a wooden drawer and took out a map. He then used a compass to work out a flight route. If he hadn't been wearing a Russian air force helmet, I would have mistaken him for Vasco da Gama. Above the noise of the engines, he threw aside his broken intercom and shouted directions to the pilot above. And we thought the Russians threatened the West with World War III.

We arrived back in London on the evening of February 5th, 1994 to find out that that morning 68 people had been killed in a mortar attack on the Markale market and 144 had been wounded. We had walked through it only the day before.

Watching the news on TV my partner, Anne, asked me if I had been frightened. I thought of the young people at Obala, of Jasmina and her poems, of the old couple and my whisky. 'How could I be? The people there are under permanent siege. I was just a visitor.'

Five Hens

In 1975 I travelled through Bosnia with Renata and two-year-old Ben. The first night we camped at Jajce beside one of the town's six picture-postcard lakes which fall from one to the next. Between these lakes are a series of small watermills. I remember waking to the sounds of falling water, the clop-clopping of a horse getting closer and the heart-stopping voice of an old man singing 'Na Klepeći Nanulama'.

After Sarajevo, we drove to Mostar along a mountainous alpine road, except that mosques, with their elegant, stone-needle minarets, stood in place of churches.

The town took its name from the bridge which spans the turquoise waters of the Neretva River. 'Most' means bridge, and 'star', old. Rebecca West was there in 1936 and wrote in *Black Lamb and Grey Falcon*, 'It is one of the most beautiful bridges in the world. A slender arch lies between two round towers, its parapet bent in a shallow angle in the centre. To look at it is good; to stand on it is as good. Over the grey-green river swoop hundreds of swallows, and on the banks, mosques and white houses stand among glades of trees and bushes.'

Constructed in the sixteenth century by order of Suleiman the Magnificent and designed by his architect, Hajrudin, the stones were held together with horsehair and manure. When the scaffolding was removed, the architect had disappeared. The Sultan had threatened to cut off Hajrudin's head if his bridge fell into the river. For many centuries, and despite earthquakes and wars, it didn't.

We spent a boiling afternoon walking through the narrow streets of the Old Town, trying to keep in the shade. After drinking at a riverside café, we walked onto the bridge and it was pleasant to stand at its centre, as Rebecca West had done, and feel the breeze from the mountains.

The tourist office had told us there was a campsite west of the town on the road to the Adriatic coast. We couldn't find it and, as it was getting dark, we drove off the highway down to the river. In the middle of this wilderness we met a family from Tuzla. They had pitched an old canvas tent and beside it was a chicken coop with five scrawny hens. The father told us that they holidayed at this spot every year.

I asked how long they had been there, and he looked at the hens. 'We came with ten,' he said, 'and eat one a day.'

'Are there wild animals in the woods?' I asked.

'Yes,' he said, 'wild boar and some say there are wolves. But it's the people you should watch out for.'

I thought it was an odd thing to say, but I would have good reason to remember his words.

Eighteen years later I came back. War Child had recruited an ex-army officer as field director for the mobile bakery. I can't remember how he came to us. Perhaps he was recommended by the ODA.

He and I made plans to travel to Bosnia to check out where the bakery would be of most use. We arrived in Split on the Croatian coast and spent a few days there, planning our recce.

He had a soldier's routine and carried on him military field equipment. His blue-twill trousers were a fiesta of pockets and zippers in which he kept his Swiss Army knife, fork and spoon, tea bags, compass, maps, a miniature radio tuned to BBC World Service, Elastoplasts and bandages, calamine, various pills and much more I didn't get to see. I asked him where he kept the cyanide tablet. 'It's up my arse, you bloody fool.'

'Pockets' would wake each morning at 0700 hours, turn on the radio, set his tiny kettle over an even tinier Primus stove and make tea. When I asked on the first morning if I could have any he said, 'Sorry, old chap, not enough for two. You should be better prepared in a war zone.'

One evening in Split, after sharing a bottle of wine, I asked him if he had any idea about my politics.

'Of course,' he answered. 'If we left this bar now, Wilson, you would shamble off to the left and I would march smartly to the right.'

Pockets clearly knew more about me than I did of him.

We went to the daily UN briefings and it became clear that East Mostar was where we should place the mobile bakery. The town was split between the Croat 'West' side and the Bosniak 'East'. Those with Muslim names had been driven across the river into the old Ottoman part of town, one of the most heavily bombarded communities in Bosnia-Herzegovina, pounded first by the Serbs and then by the Croats. People were living in basements and caves and were without food.

Split was full of NGOs, working in and on the fringes of this war zone. One of these was Marie Stopes and Pockets told me they had three spanking new Land Rovers in the UN parking lot. He said he had persuaded them to lend us one for a day.

On a hot August Sunday morning, he and I removed the brand new plastic covers from the seats and set off along the road to Mostar, the Stopes' logo on each side.

At Počitelj, almost precisely at the spot where Renata and I had camped all those years before, we came across a long line of refugees. We could hear gunfire and explosions and saw smoke rising from houses on the hillside.

With support from the Croatian government of Franjo Tuđman in Zagreb, the Bosnian Croats were busy emulating the Serbs and attempting to carve out a purely Croat segment from Bosnia-Herzegovina. They had turned on anyone with a Muslim name, never mind whether or not the name represented a mixed marriage. In the areas between Mostar and the Croatian border, villages and towns were being emptied of these 'Muslims'. In Mostar itself they were being driven into the old city, turning that part of East Mostar into a ghetto which could then be grenaded, besieged and starved.

'A spot of bother, Wilson,' said Pockets.

It was a scary sight. I felt fear for myself and sorrow for the plight of these people. When I looked at them, they could have been refugees in any war: suitcases tied with string, a live animal if they were lucky. No one carrying a TV. No one driving a car. Only the old, young women and children. The young men were fighting, had been taken prisoner or killed.

Accompanying them were soldiers from the HVO, the Bosnian Croat army. They looked as if they'd been watching too many Rambo movies with their multi-coloured bandanas and AK 47s, cartridges held together with masking tape.

We showed our UN passes and told them we were heading to Mostar. They laughed. 'No chance of that,' said one. 'We're moving these *Muslimani* up there today.'

Pockets told me to turn left off the main road. There was rubble all over the asphalt and, in the shimmering heat of midday, I could see what looked like a blown bridge in the distance.

'Stop!' Pockets banged his fist on the dashboard. 'Reverse on your tracks, Wilson. This road may be mined.'

'You're the military man,' I said, climbing into the back.

At the junction, Pockets turned east on the Mostar road.

'But we won't get there,' I said. 'Remember what those bastards told us.'

He sensed my alarm. 'Čapljina is only a few more kilometres. We'll go into town and have a coffee before we return to the coast.'

We found ourselves in the middle of deserted streets. The only people around were militia standing on the street corners, laughing and smoking.

'I don't think we're going to find any coffee,' I said.

Pockets didn't reply, but parked close to the church. I could hear singing. Was it possible that Mass was taking place at a time like this?

An old woman wearing a hijab was standing outside the vestibule door, crying. Pockets asked me to find out what she was doing there.

'I am waiting for the priest to come out,' she said. 'He is a family friend. My husband and sons have been taken away and only he can help. Please tell the world. They are being held at Dretelj.'

There was nothing I could do except remember the name of the camp.

We set off back to Split, overtaken by speeding cars with no number plates.

'The fruits of war,' said Pockets as they hooted their way past us.

These were the weekend soldiers, returning home to Croatia on this sunny Sunday afternoon after a couple of days shooting in the hills. I hoped that their marksmanship was as erratic as their driving.

It was a silent journey. This had been my first experience of ethnic cleansing. For my partner, I think it was all in a day's work.

Del Boy

Jimmy Kennedy looked like someone out of *Guys and Dolls* with his Brylcreemed quiff, dark suits and black ties. His collarless jackets and shirts were made especially for his almost non-existent neck. He was the victim of a rare disease; his spinal column threatening to grow into his brain. He had spent much of his life at the bookies and as a guest of Her Majesty in Wormwood Scrubs. He'd been convicted of GBH after putting a man who'd insulted his looks into a wheelchair.

I came to know Jim well. He was an old friend of Bill's, had been employed by him as a gaffer on his art films and was godfather to Bill's son.

After I left Renata, I moved from friend to friend until Bill and Jim offered me a room in a large flat they had rented off the Archway Road in north London. With all of us approaching, or leaving, middle age, they had nicknamed it Menopause Towers. I was happy to move in with them as it was close to my sons.

Whenever I hear Van Morrison's *Poetic Champions*, I am reminded of Jim. He played it all the time. He was a chain-smoker – Marlborough Lights – but he hardly touched alcohol. His addiction was tea. Lots of it.

My parents were living in a retirement apartment in north London and most Sundays Jim would come with me and supply my mother with cigarettes. When he wasn't accompanying me, my mother would notice and she noticed little. 'Where's that nice man?' she would ask. 'That small man with the cigarettes.'

'Jim,' I would say.

'I don't know his name, but I like him. I like him, don't I, Ian?'

'Yes, Betty, you do.'

'When is he coming again?'

'I'm sure he'll come next Sunday, Mum.'

'Oh good. Ask him to bring his cigarettes.'

Jim often told me, 'I wish I'd had a mum like yours, Dave.'

He'd learned to bake bread in prison and, as the mobile bakery was being prepared for Bosnia, Jim volunteered to join the team. The convoy of five six-metre ovens, two mixers, two water-bowsers and eight Bedford vans left its Bermondsey depot in July 1993, painted UN white and with a police escort, Jim drove the War Child Land Rover at the front. Pockets was beside him, waving at us with his swagger stick.

They were an incongruous pair. 'If I found myself in a sticky situation behind enemy lines,' Pockets would say, 'Jim is the sort of chap I'd need.'

Jim would smile and wink at us as if to say, he doesn't know much about me.

I'd had the bright idea that the lorries should be stencilled with a sheaf of wheat and the words BREAD FOR THE CHILDREN on each side of the vehicles, in both Croatian and Serbian. Practically the same language, the word for bread is one of the few that are different. The Croats say *kruh* and the Serbs and Bosnians *hleb*. A week after leaving Bermondsey, I received a call from Jim in Zagreb.

'Dave,' he said, 'we've had to paint over the word *hleb*. We were threatened last night with a gun.'

It was not going to be easy getting the bakery into East Mostar and would take time and negotiations with the Croatian forces who controlled the outlying roads.

Međugorje, the Lourdes of south-east Europe, is a small town in Herzegovina. In 1981, six children claimed to have seen the Virgin Mary on a hillside above the town. They described her as a beautiful woman in her early thirties, wearing a blue dress and white veil. She had a pale face, blue eyes, dark hair and was crowned with stars. She spoke to them in Croatian. Despite bearing an uncanny resemblance to the wax statuette in Svetog Jakova church, the town's Franciscans, hoteliers and other local wide boys saw it as a business opportunity. Catholic pilgrims poured in, hoping to see the Holy Mother.

Unfortunately, the visitors from Italy, Ireland, the US, Mexico and the Philippines were not given a local history lesson during their stay. In August 1941 the then-Bishop of Mostar described how the Ustashe had brought 'six wagons full of mothers, girls and children under eight to Šurmanci, where they were taken out of the wagons, brought into the hills and thrown alive, mothers and children, into deep ravines'. They joined the 650 bodies from Prebilovci, a neighbouring village. All of them were Serbs. It is on these hills that Mary appeared.

Alongside the busloads of visiting believers, there were refugees in Međugorje from central Bosnia who, although expelled from their homes, were not desperate for food. But for us, this was the perfect 'staging post'.

After two months operating there, Pockets and Jim managed to get the bakery into Mostar, negotiating through the UNHCR. It was set up at HEPOK, an industrial estate bombed to pieces and mostly deserted. It had contained storehouses for the food industry and distilleries for *rakia* and *Žilavka* (white) and *Blatina* (red) wines. The one remaining roofed warehouse had been chosen for the War Child bakery.

The UN Spanish Battalion was based close by, and there were soldiers from the Bosnian Republican Army to protect the operation. A few attacks took place close to the bakery, probably to do with the thousands of gallons of alcohol which were still stored on the estate. Although close to the frontline and despite occasional gunfire, it felt relatively safe because of its proximity to SPANBAT. And perhaps the UN had an agreement with the Croats to leave the bakery alone.

SPANBAT were a part of the farce that was the UN 'intervention' in this war. They intervened very little, supposedly patrolling the streets of shattered houses, flats and shops as some sort of protection for the people.

A sure sign of an impending bombardment was when the

Spanish were nowhere to be seen. They had advance warnings of attacks and always left the streets and returned to base. The attitude of the local people towards this international 'peacekeeping' force is illustrated by a local joke at the time: 'First we had UNPROFOR (United Nations Protection Force), then came IFOR (International Protection Force) and today we've got SFOR (Security Force). Tomorrow, we'll have WHATFOR.'

The bakery's drivers and volunteers were mostly young Australians, some of them from the Serious Road Trip. They found it hard to put up with Pockets' regimental ways, and Bill and I were already starting to have our doubts about his military abilities.

On the way into Mostar, he'd led the bakery convoy of eight Bedford trucks, ovens and water bowsers, up a cul-de-sac in a Croat-controlled town. With no room for the vehicles to reverse, they had to stop in front of a church. Bosnian Croat soldiers came out from Mass with their guns. Jim told me afterwards that Pockets looked at his map, then at the threatening crowd, wound down his window and, with no concession to the local language, said, 'Minor blip, chaps. Minor blip.'

He wouldn't go anywhere without his bicycle, which was odd because he kept falling off it. The cause of most of these accidents was alcohol. He fell off his bike in Split. He fell off his bike in Mostar. He fell off his bike in London. One day he arrived at our office in Camden Town, smiling broadly and bleeding profusely from his head.

'By any chance, did you come here by bike?' I asked.

'Of course, I did.' Pulling bandages from one of his pockets, he added, 'Now go and get some water and help me clean up.'

When I was in Sarajevo, I met someone working at the UN who knew Pockets from their army days. He told me that Pockets had once visited his regiment and arrived in the mess for breakfast. He asked a fellow officer to pass the salt. There was no response so he asked again.

The officer turned to Pockets and said, 'In this regiment, if a chap sits down to breakfast with his cap on, he is not to be spoken to.'

Pockets pushed his chair back, lifted his foot above the table and slammed it into the officer's cornflakes. 'In my regiment, chaps who don't pass the salt get boot in cereal.'[1]

Soon after the bakery's arrival in Mostar we parted with him and Jim took over as manager. Other aid workers in Mostar called Jim 'Del Boy', because he reminded them of David Jason's wheeler-dealer character in the BBC comedy *Only Fools and Horses*. Jim took this as a compliment because he was able to keep the bakery running through his inspired ducking and diving when others would have failed.

I arrived at the London office one morning to find a fax from him. 'Sorry, David. Delivered bread to Blagaj today. They needed it. Shrapnel came in roof of bakery van. Don't worry. Will repair myself. I'm OK.'

Jim was part-manager, part-teacher, part-cook, part-odds-and-sods man. One moment he was instructing a worker on how to operate the mixer, the next running over to the ovens to help get the loaves out, then checking the deliveries. In quieter moments, he would be working out on scraps of paper what supplies he'd need and where he might get them from.

After the team had completed its bake at midday, Jim would drive out of Mostar to do his shopping: everything from diesel to coffee. East Mostar had been gutted with the shelling and there were no shops. Nothing could be purchased in town, and only Jim could get through the Croat lines that held East Mostar in a vice-like grip.

Jim told me proudly how he'd once fooled the Croat border guards who were forever trying to hold up his supplies. One day he went to Čapljina in the bakery's battered Toyota truck to refuel and buy food and drink. The Croats wouldn't let him take his supplies back up the road to East Mostar, so he turned around and circled the checkpoint by taking a mountain track into town. He unloaded the vehicle at the bakery, then drove down the main road to Čapljina from the opposite direction in the empty truck. The border guards were astonished when he told them he was going back to the store because he'd forgotten the toilet paper.

One of the things I loved about Jim was his disdain for the wastage and high living found in some of the bigger NGOs. Attending a meeting at the UNHCR office about medical aid, someone complained about their inability to provide sufficient help because of the lack of funds. Taking his Marlborough from the side of his mouth, Jim pointed through the window at the fleet of pristine Land Cruisers. 'There's money over there,' he said. 'You could flog them off for a start.'

War Child's always unpredictable finances meant that no one at that time was drawing a regular salary. We often had no operational money to send him for the bakery, but Jim's reputation in Mostar was such that UN agencies stepped in to help. He was good friends with the head of the UNHCR in Mostar, Brigadier Jerrie Hulme, who ensured that War Child was supplied with flour when the charity had no money to buy it.

One day Jerrie brought Baroness Chalker, the Minister for Overseas Development, to visit HEPOK. Jim used to call her 'Mumsie' to her face. He sent us a photo of the two of them, Mumsie standing with Jim and holding a tray full of bread. He didn't tell her that the Kingsmill tray she had in her hands had been nicked off the streets of Camden Town.

I made my first visit to the bakery in June 1994. My memories of Mostar were from that summer afternoon 19 years before on my way to the chicken campers. I dreaded what I was going to see.

With 90 per cent of its buildings mortared, East Mostar still managed to retain its beauty. I took my first walk through the streets with Jim. An old man shouted out.

Jim looked worried because he was no linguist and had never bothered with more than the rudiments of what he called the '*dobar dan*' language. 'What's he on about, Dave?'

'He's saying that this is Jim's town.'

He smiled and shrugged his shoulders, or as far as I could tell since he had hardly any neck.

We were on our way to a meeting to check up on a delay in some essential paperwork. In Bosnia, there is always essential paperwork and essential stamps without which neither bakeries, nor anything else, can function.

The Bosnian official told Jim that it would be done *sutra* (tomorrow). Jim replied, 'Are we talking Bosnian *sutra* or English *sutra*?'

There was nothing *sutra* about the bakery. In the 18 months of its operation there, Jim and his team fed 14,000 people a day under difficult conditions.

The 'bakers' – men and women – earned almost nothing but had daily bread for their families. They worked from 5am to 3pm, mixing the dough which was then cut into loaves and placed on shelves for the bread to rise. After baking, using large wooden ladles to place the dough in the ovens, and then stacking the finished loaves in the Kingsmill trays, the ovens and mixers were cleaned.

Bread was distributed to the war hospital, emergency food centres and outlying villages. The team didn't lose one day's bake and much of this was due to Jim's commitment and leadership. He took me out on deliveries and at each drop-off crowds were gathered in queues waiting for the only food in town. I felt proud that War Child was feeding so many, that we were quite literally lifesavers.

We ate a lot of bread and whatever tinned food Jim managed to bring in from his daily visits to Čapljina. It was hot and sweaty and a splash-down at one of the bowsers became a daily treat.

I stayed with Jim in the attic of a house which had just been rebuilt. The owners were jumping the gun in their optimism that the war was winding down. One night a shell whizzed over the roof and exploded behind the house. There was no point in getting out of bed; it was unlikely to be followed by a second. Then I heard Jim putting the kettle on in the kitchen and went downstairs to join him.

'Don't worry, Dave. They missed. Fancy a fag and a cuppa?'

Unnerved by almost being blown up and with a week's gap before a meeting I had to attend, I decided to go to the Adriatic coast. I headed to Hvar Town on the beautiful island of the same name.

I found a room at the top of an old stone house. It was very hot, but a breeze blew through the open window. I watched the squealing swallows, listened to the quarter-hour chimes of the church clock, heard children laughing and smelt fish barbequing somewhere below.

I spent five days there and celebrated my last night before returning to Mostar by sitting under the sail-white awning of a harbourside café. I drank my way through a bottle of green-tinged Malvazia wine, looking at the terracotta-roofed houses. Beyond them hazy islands were slowly disappearing into the dark.

Mostar was only half a day's drive from Hvar and yet a place as far removed as the Moon is from Mars. On the first morning back, I walked across town to my meeting. I didn't hear any laughing children here.

I noticed a young woman behind me. She was singing. A dog growled as I passed his den in a bombed-out building. I turned a corner. Behind me, there was a loud explosion.

There was only one death that day in Mostar. It could only have been that woman.

The people of this town were under constant threat of sharing her fate. I realise that I was the lucky one in many ways. I had not been killed and I could come and go.

I wanted to leave, but I still had three days before returning to London. Jim told me that they were going to start using some of the bakery vehicles to take aid to Sarajevo. I agreed to join him on the first run the following day.

A few kilometres out of Mostar, a SPANBAT armoured personnel carrier travelling in front of us was hit by a shell fired from the hills. As we passed it at speed, it was ablaze. We were the last vehicle that day allowed up the Sarajevo road.

It was scary to look back and see no one following in our path. We didn't speak. It was as if we needed to remain alert. As if, by so doing, we'd have a better chance against a shell or bullet.

We dropped off our supplies at Tarčin, 30 kilometres south-west of Sarajevo, from where the boxes would be backpacked across Mount Igman and then into Sarajevo through the tunnel which had been constructed under the airport.

By the time we drove home, it was night time and slow going on the war-racked roads. As we approached Konjic, Jim asked if I'd like a curry.

'A curry?' I said. 'In the middle of the Bosnian mountains? You're joking.'

'Wanna bet?'

'Not with you, Jim.'

A few minutes later we drove into the UN Nepalese battalion base. Though it was now 10pm, food was still being served in the mess.

Our stomachs full of diced lamb and *chatamari* rice, we set off on the final stretch to Mostar. As we drove out of the Neretva canyon into the Mostar plain, we were nervous. The last ten kilometres was across open ground and along the most shelled road in the area. We sped past the still-burning Spanish APC. The UN later reported that no one had been killed or injured. I doubted the truth of that.[2]

Little Pieces and Big Stars

War Child today still emphasises the charity's historical connections with the music world, but one of the first money-raisers for our work involved animals. Over the 1993 August Bank Holiday we organised a three-day event at London Zoo. There were *sitar* and *sarangi* players near the elephants, Peruvian pipers serenaded the llamas and didgeridoo players the kangaroos. There were African drummers and giraffes, *gamalan* players entertaining the Indonesian rhinoceros, Brazilian *berimbau* players and the squirrel monkeys. The Chinese percussionists were kept well away from the giant panda, Ming Ming, because she needed all her concentration to breed.

The most amazing sights for me were a string quartet playing Bach in the Butterfly Grotto and a lone cellist in the shadowy depths of the Aquarium entertaining the circling sharks.

On the lawns, pathways and courtyards there were clowns, jugglers, stilt walkers, magicians, dancers and acrobats, storytellers, poets and pavement artists. Inside the monkey house we held children's workshops, art and photo exhibitions. The promotional brochure said that 'during these three days, London Zoo, with the help of its animals, will come to the rescue of another endangered species – children threatened by the 30 wars raging across our planet.'

One of War Child's first money-making fundraisers was not with Pavarotti, Bono or Brian Eno, but thanks to Sue Lloyd-Roberts.

As a BBC investigative journalist, Sue travelled to Mostar several times to report on War Child. On her first visit, she was travelling with a War Child convoy when it got shot up. I was in London and was rung up by the BBC to be told that their correspondent had been forced to take refuge in a ditch. She said of her experience, 'the part of my brain that recognised fear doesn't exist. In such situations people scream or pray, but I picked up my camera'.

This didn't stop her organising a fundraiser for War Child, 'Bop for Bosnia', which took place at the BBC TV Centre in February 1994. Sue recruited Chris Jagger as the musical director and Dave Gilmour, Leo Sayers and Ron Kavana were among the performers. As well as live music, there was a dinner and auction and she helped raise a few thousand pounds for the charity.

It was early 1994 when Nigel Osborne arrived in Mostar carrying a large bag full of percussion instruments. A big, bearded bear of a man, Nigel was Professor of Music at Edinburgh University. He'd heard that we were co-operating with MTV and taking music tapes into Sarajevo where he'd been organising music workshops with the Sarajevo String Quartet and collaborating with the poet Goran Simić on two children's operas.

He said he would like to run workshops in East Mostar in what was to be the start of a long association between Nigel and War Child.

It was no problem gathering interest. I had been amazed how quickly news travelled across this bombed-out ghetto and, in such a desperate place, anything out of the ordinary was news.

After two years of shelling, the upper floors of the UNHCR building had been blown away. The lower floors, housing the UN office, were as secure as it got in East Mostar. By the time Nigel arrived, there were 20 children and their parents. They sat very quietly and few of the children smiled. They looked as though they were about to be told bad news, not be offered the chance to bang drums and blow whistles. I looked around the room and realised most of them would have had no memory of anything but fear.

One mother sat with her blind, impassive, six-year-old daughter. I watched while Nigel tried to get the girl to play a triangle. She refused to hold it. This went on for some time until, finally, she grabbed the triangle with one hand, the metal stick with the other and struck it over and over. Her face lit up. Her mother told us that it was the first time she had seen her daughter smile in over two years.

War Child were able to develop and extend Nigel's work because an unannounced visitor turned up at our Camden Town office a few weeks before this workshop. Brian Eno's manager and wife, Anthea, heard Juliet Stevenson talking about War Child on the radio and turned up at our office with a cheque for £2,000. She asked if the money could be used for music aid for the children of Bosnia.

Her arrival was a turning point. We had our first funding for music workshops and a door had been opened that led us to Brian and other major figures in the music business.

Bill and I wanted to let the Enos know what their support could achieve. They took us out to dinner in Notting Hill and we told them about the workshop and the little girl. That evening Brian and Anthea suggested we should think about raising money and support for a permanent music centre in Mostar.

Brian had never been involved with charities. Ten years before, he had scorned Band Aid, admitting that he had been cynical about 'egocentric compassionates' who made themselves feel better by helping people about whom they knew nothing. I asked him why he had changed his mind with his support for War Child and he told me that Anthea had influenced him.[1] She had been involved with the Nordoff Robbins music therapy charity and was keen to reroute money flowing there from the music business to help the children of Bosnia. Brian said he'd been as unclear as everyone else about the issues involved in the wars in former Yugoslavia, but liked what he'd been told about our work: a charity, Anthea told him, which operated by the 'seat of their pants'. Under these circumstances, helping children seemed pretty uncontroversial.

Brian agreed to join Brent Hansen, Head of MTV Europe, Tom Stoppard and Juliet Stevenson as a patron. He didn't come alone, persuading David Bowie to join him. And he and Anthea didn't come without a plan.

Anthea set up a think tank to generate ideas as to how funds could be raised for War Child and our Mostar plans. We had fortnightly meetings at her Roland Gardens flat. There were Anthea and I, Brian's assistant Lin Barkass, Paul Gorman, Jeremy Silver and Rob Partridge. They all came with excellent pedigrees. Paul wrote for *Music Week* and *Mojo*, Jeremy was head of A&R at Virgin Records and Rob had set up his own music PR company after managing Bob Marley and U2.

The team got to work on the first fundraiser which we decided to call 'Little Pieces from Big Stars'. Music and art celebrities were asked to contribute something, the only condition being that they had to make it themselves and it had to be small.

In September 1994 the exhibition of 150 works opened at the Flowers East Gallery in Hackney. It included contributions from the two McCartneys: Paul's 2" x 2" driftwood carving and four of Linda's photographs. David Bowie exhibited 17 computer-generated prints. Bono, a music box containing sunglasses. Charlie Watts, a drawing of a hotel telephone. Billy Bragg, a brass rubbing of a manhole cover. Pete Townsend, a 2.5" x 2" model of a Rickenbacker guitar.

Brian surpassed them all with six contributions, including four sculptures made from plaster and nails: 'Ancient Head', 'Nude in Light Victorian Snowstorm', 'Siren' and 'Fruit Prison', and a Japanese forest ambient recording played on a camouflaged cassette player.[2]

After a two-week exhibition the pieces were auctioned at

the Royal College of Art. Paul McCartney's contribution alone sold for over £12,000. The evening resulted in a £70,000 donation to War Child.

In less than a year, we'd come from wondering how to pay our office overheads and trips to Sarajevo and Mostar to a situation where we were feeding thousands of people a day and a piece of driftwood could make the charity £12,000.

It didn't stop there.

Nine months later, Anthea and Brian's office organised 'Pagan Fun Wear', described by Brian as being one of the 'all-time weird events in London's recent cultural history'. The idea was to model costumes designed by pop stars which would then be sold at auction to benefit War Child.

As with 'Little Pieces', Anthea and Brian's small staff at Opal co-ordinated the event. They recruited 35 big names from the music and design worlds, 45 garment and shoemakers and 30 models, organised the catering, music, permissions from 17 recording companies, ticket sales, production and publicity.

I wondered how Brian was coping with his life as a musician and producer. Everything seemed to have been put on hold to cope with these extraordinary events.

Iggy Pop designed penis sheaths; Jarvis Cocker modelled his own shoes; David Bowie contributed 'Victim Fashion', which consisted of a model wrapped up in bandages; John Squire designed his own underwear; Brian, his coat and pants; Dave Stewart, a bikini and mac. Other contributors included Bono, Adam Clayton, Michael Stipe, Phil Collins, Bryan Ferry, Anton Corbijn, Laurie Anderson, Joan Armatrading and Jaron Lanier, one of the pioneers of virtual reality.

Getting everything together was a nightmare. Iggy Pop's design for his penis sheaths came by fax with scrawled and difficult-to-decipher graphics. They were to be three feet in length and made of multi-coloured papier mâché. All these ideas were then manufactured by students from the London School of Art and Design.

Last, but not least, everything had to be modelled on the

big night which concluded with an auction of the designs. Paul Gambaccini and Janet Street-Porter hosted the evening. The event raised more than £200,000.

'Pagan Fun Wear' was held at the Saatchi Gallery in St John's Wood. They didn't normally let this out for non-gallery events, but Brian had promised them there would be no damage. As he walked around at the end of the evening, he saw that the floor and walls had been squirted with jets of black poster paint. They had been taken from a room being used by Damien Hirst for his spin paintings. Brian spent the rest of the night scraping this off.

When he told me later about the paint, I was horrified. Being Brian, he didn't tell any of us at War Child. If I'd known, I would have helped.[3]

I thought that we would be very lucky to benefit from further Opal money-raisers, but I need not have worried. Thanks to the Enos, we'd hardly started. They had opened a door to the music world that was to result, not only in further funding, but to the dream of the music centre being built.

In August 1995 I was asked to speak at a demonstration in Trafalgar Square in support of the right of Bosnians to defend themselves. Other speakers included Michael Foot and Brian. As a director of War Child, I was breaking British charity law by speaking politically. I said: 'I would like to speak on behalf of the young people of Bosnia. They are like young people everywhere. They take pleasure in music. They party, they study and are interested in all that is happening beyond the prison of their war. They have the anger of youth and they can love like only youth can love. Something I will never forget is the sight of young girls watering the flowers on the graves of their dead boyfriends in Mostar. Where indeed have all the flowers gone? They are covering thousands of graves of young people in south-east Europe. It is the young who die when they are the ones who should live. It is the teenage soldiers who die on the front line, rarely their older commanders. In this war, it is the child who is killed because it is the child who plays in the street. This is a war of the calculated and deliberate targeting of children.'

Tony Crean of Go Discs!, the record company that represented Paul Weller and had recently launched the band Beautiful South, happened to be walking through the square. He had been recovering from flu and later told *The Times*, 'For once, I was getting further into the papers than just the sports pages – watching more television than normal too – I was reading about ethnic cleansing and mass graves, seeing genocide on the tea-time news – I realised that I didn't really understand what was going on.'

A few days later, we got a call from Andy Macdonald, the head of Go Discs!, to come and see him and Tony. They had an idea for helping War Child: to bring together musicians and record an album on one day, a Monday, and release it the following Saturday.

What was to become the *Help* album had more than 20 artists, including Oasis, Blur, Radiohead, Orbital, Massive Attack, The Stone Roses, Neneh Cherry, Sinéad O'Connor, Paul Weller, Paul McCartney and Portishead. It was recorded on Monday, September 4th, 1995, in studios across Europe and released, on target, five days later.

Help sold over 70,000 copies on the day of release, becoming the fastest-selling album in British music history. The artists and Go Discs! waived royalties and *Help* raised more than £1.5 million. Brian produced the album and was responsible for making sure the recordings were ready for pressing in time for the Saturday release. Racing against the clock, he said of the experience, 'Enjoyable panic, but I went into Hitler mode in the last few minutes.'

The income from the album was used to provide artificial limbs for wounded children, food and clothing to orphanages, the purchase of a refrigerated truck to supply insulin, funding for school meals in central Bosnia, support for a mobile medical clinic in Bihać, the supply of premature baby units to Banja Luka, as well as baby milk, contraceptives and even funding for mine clearance programmes. Linda McCartney supplied 22 tonnes of her veggie burgers which we delivered to three Bosnian cities. *Help* monies were also used towards the running of the War Child bakery and to expand the charity's music programmes.

That summer, Brian had been working with U2 in Dublin when the phone rang. It was Luciano Pavarotti inviting Bono to perform with him at the 'Pavarotti and Friends Concert' that September. When Brian told Anthea about the call, she persuaded him to get Bono to take part and do it for War Child. Pavarotti's partner, Nicoletta Mantovani, then came to London and met with Anthea. Nicoletta was soon to marry Pavarotti and was to prove instrumental in winning and retaining the Maestro's support for War Child.

Anthea told Nicoletta about War Child's music work in Sarajevo and Mostar and said that she and Brian had been discussing the construction of a music centre for children in war-shattered East Mostar.

Nicoletta said that Pavarotti had been looking for a project to support in Bosnia and that the suggestion might appeal to him. It did and the result was that he became a patron of War Child and the next 'Pavarotti and Friends' concert would be held to make the idea into a reality.

The concert took place at Modena's Parco Novi Sad on September 12th, 1995. Pavarotti, Bono, The Edge and Brian performed 'Miss Sarajevo', a song Bono had written for the event and which became a hit single. The words were about the young women of Sarajevo who had staged a beauty contest at the height of the war. Lined up in swimsuits with the crowned Miss Sarajevo in the middle, they carried a banner. *DON'T LET THEM KILL US*.

When I heard Pavarotti come in over Bono's voice singing, 'Is there a time for high street shopping, to find the right dress to wear, here she comes with her crown,' there was a lump in my throat. I remembered Jasmina and her boyfriend's poems, resigned to being killed, but not willing to be defeated.

Other performers at that concert included Meat Loaf, the Chieftains, Dolores O'Riordan of the Cranberries, Zucchero, Jovanotti and Simon Le Bon. I sat one row behind Princess Diana and watched him flash his eyes at her the whole time he was on stage.

Afterwards, I walked backstage to find Pavarotti holding Anthea's hand and singing 'Happy Birthday' to her. There were three tenors serenading her, but the other two were not Plácido Domingo and José Carreras. They were The Edge's and Bono's dads.

The following year Pavarotti held the second concert in aid of the music centre. In June 1996 the musicians included Eric Clapton, Joan Osborne, Elton John, Liza Minnelli, Sheryl Crow and Zucchero. Clapton sang 'Holy Mother', and Liza Minnelli, in a War Child T-shirt, joined Pavarotti for 'New York, New York'.

In the finale, Elton John and Pavarotti sang 'Live Like Horses' and were joined by the other artists from the show. The audience of many thousands waved banners declaring *PEACE, NOT BOMBS.*

As the TV boom camera swung over our heads, I had the feeling that music can make a difference to the world. The last time I had felt this was when I was standing in cellars in Mostar during the war, with children singing and drumming to the background sound of shelling.

After the concert Anthea said, 'We've had an idea for another fundraiser. We want to get music stars to make art works on the theme of a musician or band inspirational to their own work.'

'Milestones', which was held in February 1997, involved, as Brian put it, 'the usual suspects'. Pavarotti sent a handkerchief on which he'd drawn Enrico Caruso. Graham Cox of Blur did an homage to Syd Barrett of Pink Floyd. Paul McCartney, a drawing of Buddy Holly, aged 60. Bono's inspiration was Frank Sinatra – a music box containing Jack Daniels, shot glasses and a blue napkin. It was signed 'To Frank, Love, Bono'.

Yoko Ono contributed her bronzed 'Lennon eyeglasses'. Bob Geldof celebrated the Rolling Stones with a wall-size London map that included a River Thames with moving water. Bowie's tribute was to the Walker Brothers. Sinéad O'Connor's was to Bob Marley. Brian contributed his musical dedication to the Velvet Underground, which sold for £40,000.[4]

With more than 20 contributors, the exhibition was held at the Patrick Litchfield Gallery and the private view and auction at the Royal College of Art.

Lin Barkass, from Brian's office, summed up her feelings about these fundraisers. 'Bloody hard work, bloody brilliant, best things I have ever been involved in. People did it all for free, designing, printing, staff at the *Daily Mirror* running off posters after work, designers from Warner Brothers. Too many good people to name here, like Jenny Ross, Paul Gorman, Greg Jakobek. People had caught the spirit of War Child, that they could all make a difference. If they think they can, then they will.'[5]

Writing this now, I feel stunned at what we'd been able to achieve. We had received not only significant funding, but also enormous encouragement to use music as a new form of aid to children and young people in conflict situations. We now had the chance to place music at the centre of our aid work.

Rainbows

'Towering above his escorts, he was the freest man
on earth, freer, certainly, than his captors who'd
have to wrestle with their souls as cat's paws of
unjust power.'
Mandla Langa, *The Texture of Shadows*

The day after the 1996 Modena concert I flew to Johannesburg.
I had been invited there by the Nelson Mandela Children's
Fund who told me that a meeting was being arranged with
the President.

I had Luciano Pavarotti to thank for this invitation. He
was raising millions to help War Child and I think the NMCF
wanted to find out how we had won his support in the hope
that his generosity might extend to their work. With Eric
Clapton and Elton John's music ringing in my ears, I flew from
Rome on Alitalia, hoping this new connection with Mandela
would be a major part of internationalising our music work.

As we approached Johannesburg the steward announced,
'We will soon be landing at Jan Smuts Airport. Do not enter
the Republic of South Africa with any material defaming
the Republic.' A moment later came an apology. 'We are not
landing at Jan Smuts, but at Johannesburg International.
The restrictions on entry no longer apply under the
new constitution.'

In the arrivals terminal, I watched an elderly white couple
reject the offer of a taxi from a black cabbie. The husband
insulted him while his wife tried to hit him with her handbag.
Could this be, I asked myself, the new South Africa?

While I was in Johannesburg, I stayed with a businessman who had been trying to get War Child involved in a project of his. He and his wife lived in the exclusive suburb of Waverley. The only black faces I saw there were sweeping the roads, guarding gates or clipping hedges.

I was told not to make my bed in the morning and to give their maid any dirty laundry. I made sure to tidy my room and had brought enough clothes to see me through the week.

I had arrived at the weekend and my hosts took me to their country club. The buffet was set up on the lawn and we were served by turbaned waiters dressed like sepoys. Only the red bishop birds in the trees and the ibis standing on the side of the lake hinted at Africa.

On Monday morning I had a meeting with Jeremy Ratcliffe, the CEO of the Mandela Fund. He told me the President was ill, but that he was coming to London the following month so he would arrange a meeting with him there.

I decided to visit a street children project in Soweto. After driving through a 'suburb' of small brick buildings, I arrived in an area of densely packed shacks and barrack blocks. The shacks had canvas, plastic or tin roofs and were made in an attempt to recreate a long-lost village. Many homes had no proper sanitation and no access to drinking water.

I then flew to Durban to meet Edmund Mhlongo. I'd promised to visit him when we'd met in London. A member of the local Peace Council, he ran a children's arts centre in KwaMashu. As we entered the township, we passed squatter camps: rows and rows of barracks which, Edmund told me, housed recent arrivals from Mozambique and Angola. We then drove past four-storey hostels where migrant Zulu workers lived. It was apparent to me that the conditions of the people here were even worse than in Soweto.

We arrived at a derelict and roofless shopping centre where Edmund ran his workshops. I was introduced to the caretaker, a woman who looked 60 but told me she was 35.

As we drove out of KwaMashu, a voice on the radio was

talking about the need for reconciliation and quoting Mahatma Gandhi: 'An eye for an eye and the whole world is blind.'

Back in Durban, I took Edmund and his colleague, Makhuscheke, for a meal at the Blue Water Hotel on the sea front. The restaurant was full of white businessmen and their wives who looked blissfully unaware of the new South Africa.

I couldn't help thinking that Gandhi's reconciliation seemed far off and that it had to come from the residents of Waverley and the diners at this hotel. It had to come from the people I'd met at that country club who'd travelled to London, Paris and New York, but had never visited Soweto.

On my return to London, an invitation was waiting for me. 'Mr and Mrs Nicky Oppenheimer request the pleasure of your company at Apsley House on Friday, 12th July 1996, at a dinner to celebrate the work of the Nelson Mandela Children's Fund.' The guest speaker – Mandela himself.

There were 36 guests, including the Duke and Duchess of Westminster, Lord and Lady Montagu, Lord and Lady Sainsbury, bankers Rupert Hambro, Bruno Schroder and Oliver Baring, as well as prisoner-in-waiting Conrad Black.

I arrived with my War Child co-director in Bill's ancient Volvo. The epauletted valet tried to hide his disgust as he steered the banger away to join the Mercedes, Daimlers and Rollers in the underground parking lot. I noticed that he took off his white gloves to drive.

My partner, Anne, stepped out of our battered coach wearing a hired gown from Angels, the costumiers. I had borrowed a tie and hoped that no one would see that moths had made a meal of my suit.

The Oppenheimers welcomed us into the chandeliered lobby. After delicate canapés and two flutes of champagne, we were ushered into the Duke of Wellington's dining room. Mandela was sitting at the far end as we settled down to enjoy the food and wine.

I am not someone who is star-struck, but here I was in the same room as one of my political icons, a man who'd endured so much in the struggle for freedom and never given up hope, even during his long imprisonment.

I was talking to Ken Follett's wife when I felt a tap on my shoulder. I turned my head to see Mandela smiling down at me. 'I'm so sorry,' I mumbled and started to get up.

'Stay there. I can talk to you from here.'

The conversation continued, with me awkwardly looking up at him over my shoulder. 'Very good to meet you, Mr Wilson.'

'It's an honour to meet you, sir.'

'No, it's an honour for me to meet you. I am sorry I was unwell when you were in my country. I hear you are doing great work with the children of Bosnia.'

I was stunned that he knew about me and War Child's work. I realised that he'd been walking around the table, introducing himself, presumably well briefed on everyone there, though I never imagined that he would speak to me. I mumbled that we were planning to open a centre for young people to try and bring the communities together through music.

'I know. I have heard. You must keep us informed. We need similar projects in Africa. Music is a great healer.'

I told Mandela I'd been one of the protestors arrested for running onto the rugby pitch at Twickenham in 1969 to stop the Springboks' match.

'Thank you,' he said.

Nineteen years after this dinner party and my visit to South Africa, 19,000 homes in Soweto still have no access to drinking water and 72,000 don't even have minimal sanitation. The water company has, of course, been privatised.

Jeremy Ratcliffe had to resign as President of the Children's Fund after accepting, for 'safe-keeping', diamonds Liberia's ex-President Charles Taylor had given to Naomi Campbell.[1] Edmund Mhlongo is today at the centre of what I hope are unfair allegations of abuse of charity funds.[2]

When Nelson Mandela died, politicians fell over themselves to claim him as their hero. George W. Bush said, 'Mandela was one of the great forces for freedom and equality of our time.'

Tony Blair claimed that Mandela 'was one of those people who was absolutely as good as you hoped he would be.'

David Cameron said, 'Mandela's dignity and triumph inspired millions.'

Israeli Prime Minister Benjamin Netanyahu said, 'He will be remembered as a moral leader of the first order.'

As late as 2008, Mandela was on the US terrorism watch list. He said this of George W. Bush: 'A president who has no foresight, who cannot think properly, is now wanting to plunge the world into a holocaust.'

Of Tony Blair he said, 'He is the foreign minister of the United States. He is no longer Prime Minister of Britain.'

Did Cameron mention Mandela's 'dignity' when he visited South Africa while Mandela was on Robben Island, there as a guest of a lobby group set up to oppose sanctions on apartheid South Africa?

And Netanyahu must have forgotten that Mandela said, 'Palestinians are struggling for freedom, liberation and equality, just like we were struggling for freedom in South Africa.'

As we left Apsley House, I stood on the steps, watching the guests leave in their limousines. I remembered an old woman I'd met in Soweto and what she'd said to me. She'd been the organiser of a day centre for the elderly where they were given meals and encouraged to sing and play musical instruments as a way to ease the difficulties in their lives. She described herself as being religious because it was the only way to guarantee the work she did was for the good of the people and not to satisfy her own vanity. 'God is a wall,' she said, 'and I have to throw the ball well to make sure I can catch it when He returns it to me.'

I asked her if she received any government funding. 'Goodness no,' she answered. 'The politicians used to be a bunch of white clowns. Now they have been joined by the black clowns.'

Mandela was no clown. When he tapped me on the shoulder that night, I looked up at this tall man who, to the end of his long life, was a political and moral giant.

Darkness and Light

After the first 'Pavarotti and Friends' concert, we started to plan the Mostar Music Centre. The bulk of income from the Modena concerts and the Eno fundraisers would be spent on construction, but we had to make sure our finances covered equipping, staffing and operating programmes. We'd have to find architects willing to charge us a charity rate.

The Enos introduced us to Nicholas Lacey, who had a reputation for a radical approach to design. Bill and I went to meet him at his office close to London Bridge. He was keen to take the job and, working with his engineer, Bryn Bird, was responsible for the first designs of the centre.

Even with Nicholas's very reasonable costings, the maths wasn't working. With no hard feelings, he passed the project over to Mike Lawless of LA Architects.

The initials 'LA' are not a reference to 'Los Angeles', but to 'Lawless & Adams'. Based in Lewes, Sussex, Mike and his team had experience designing hospitals, community and sports buildings. He agreed to work without fee in the early stages of the project. At their own expense, his firm supported an associate office in Mostar run by Nedjad Cupino and sponsored the fitting out of the social areas at the centre: the apartments, bar and kitchen. Mike told me that it was one of the toughest projects in his career, but that it was 'one of the best and most rewarding times of my life'.

Construction started in early 1996 and Bill and I took it in turns to oversee the early stages. Mike and his local team were working against the clock as the building had to be completed in a year. The Bosnian construction company Hydrogradnja were sub-contracting much of the work and progress was slow. Mike was spending more and more of his time in Mostar and I think his UK work must have suffered. In retrospect, he and his partner, Elizabeth Adams, and Nedjad Cupino deserved a plaque alongside the one you can find today at the centre celebrating the name of 'Luciano Pavarotti'.

With the centre far from completed, I moved to Mostar in July 1997 to take up my post as Director. Working from a small shop that had once been a butcher's, we started some of our projects. The schools' music team were able to begin their programme of school visits and workshops were held at the local orphanage and at the school for the disadvantaged.

In the months leading up to the December opening of what had now been named the Pavarotti Music Centre, we had numerous visits from local, and not so local, politicians. I remember stumbling across ex-Tory minister Michael – 'something of the night' – Howard in the reception area. He was being shown the nearly completed building by an official from the EU Administration offices. I asked him what he was doing in Bosnia-Herzegovina.

'I'm on a fact-finding mission,' he said.

'Who are you meeting to do that?' I asked.

'Politicians.'

I answered, 'Mr Howard, you should know better than anyone. You don't go to them for facts.' To his credit, he did laugh.

In July I had watched Steve Biko's ex-driver, the percussionist Eugene Skeef, run workshops in the town. He had been invited to Mostar by Nigel Osborne and had recently worked with Edmund Mhlongo in KwaMashu. I had heard about the success of his *djembe* classes with children in the UK. Remembering Mandela's words that our music centre was a project needed in Africa, I realised that Eugene was a key to internationalising the Pavarotti Music Centre.

His first workshops were so successful I offered him the job of Director of Music Development. He agreed to start work when the building opened.

A few days before Eugene returned to London, we went to Dubrovnik. There we met two German doctors who were interested to hear about our work in Mostar. Eugene had their eyes popping with his words about the importance of music and rhythm in our lives. One of the doctors said he spoke like a poet. Eugene laughed and rewarded them with, 'Listen for the cadence of the sun in its journey that never ends. When night falls and the song fades, follow the rhythm of the moon when your voice disappears like a bird.'

Those words got us a bed for the night. When we told them we were going to sleep on the beach, they invited us to stay at their hotel, Villa Dubrovnik. Much to our surprise, there, at the bar, was a politician I was delighted to meet: Michael Foot and his wife, Jill Craigie. They told us they stayed there every summer.

Sitting on the hotel balcony overlooking the old city walls, we discussed the war and the film he and Jill had made about it, *Two Hours from London*. I told them what a good documentary it was, but that it was a bit light on the Bosnian–Croatian war and that they should visit Mostar. Michael agreed to come with us the next day. Jill opted out because she didn't want to travel on the serpentine coastal and mountain roads.

Eugene and I showed Michael round Mostar's Old Town. He was already 84 and walked very slowly. It was impossible to use a car in Mostar's narrow streets, but he was determined to see as much as he could. We ended our walk at the Centre where he sat down in the uncompleted courtyard. 'This is very impressive, David. I am sure you will be doing wonderful work in this building.'

That afternoon I drove him back to Dubrovnik and we spent the three-hour drive discussing politics and poetry. I told him I'd enjoyed Paul Foot's *Red Shelley*, his nephew's book about the poet. Michael laughed and broke into:

Rise like Lions after slumber
In unvanquishable number,
Shake your chains to earth like dew
Which in sleep had fallen on you –
Ye are many – they are few

After a pause he added, 'But you know, Paul is wrong. Byron was the greater poet and greater revolutionary. Have you read "Darkness"?'

I shook my head.

'Stuck on Shelley, are you?' Another pause and then he recited:

They slept on the abyss without a surge –
The waves were dead; the tides were in their grave,
The moon, their mistress, had expir'd before;
The winds were wither'd in the stagnant air,
And the clouds perish'd; Darkness had no need
Of aid from them – She was the Universe.

Michael smiled at me. 'Byron goes further than Shelley. You must read him.'

When I got back to Mostar later that evening, Eugene and I went to a café close to the suspension bridge which had replaced the destroyed stone bridge. We watched in horror as a young man climbed over the rope handrail and threw himself backwards, like a scuba diver, into the Neretva, 20 metres below.

We rushed down to the river and Eugene and I managed to grab hold of his arms. We thought he should go to hospital, but he said he was okay and got up to walk away. I persuaded him to come to my flat which was close to the bridge in Marshal Tito street.

He was soaking wet and Eugene gave him one of his T-shirts and a pair of his trousers. Over coffee, he told us his name was

Hamid and that he'd come from Kiseljak in central Bosnia. He had never recovered from the loss of his mother, father and two sisters in the war. He had an aunt who had been living in Mostar and had come to look for her.

She, too, had been killed. In despair, he had spent the last of his money on drink and had then decided to end his life. He had been disappointed to find the suspension bridge was four metres lower than the old bridge which had been 24 metres high at its apex. But he still thought he would die if he fell backwards into the water. While he was talking, Eugene played soothing rhythms on his *djembe.*

When he left us, we felt guilty we hadn't been more persistent in insisting he go to the hospital.

Two months later, a package arrived at my London address. It was a collection of Byron's poems with a dedication on the inside cover: 'Byronic greetings from Michael Foot, with many thanks for a most instructive visit to Mostar, Sept 1997. Read especially "Don Juan", right through non-stop, as I did again. See also "Darkness". It has reflections of Mostar.'

I don't remember giving him my address so I assume he must have contacted the War Child office. All these years later, Michael's 'Byron' is on my shelf. I dip into the book frequently and always start by reading the dedication.

Eugene is still working his magic with his *djembe.*

Mike Lawless is still designing buildings.

I don't know what happened to Hamid and what he did with his darkness.

THE UNBEARABLE
LIGHTNESS OF BEING

'… for there is nothing heavier than
compassion. Not even one's own pain weighs
so heavy as the pain one feels with someone, for
someone, a pain intensified by the imagination
and prolonged by a hundred echoes.'

Milan Kundera

The Opening

Ivan Prskalo's office was full of bleeding Christs and weeping Marys. Chequered Croatian flags were on each side of the door. The mayor of 'Croat' West Mostar greeted me wearing a shiny blue suit. This divided town had two mayors: Prskalo on the west side and Safet Oručević on the east. I was there to invite Prskalo to the opening of the Pavarotti Centre. This was an important political act, as the centre would only work if it had support from both of Mostar's communities.

His secretary placed a tray of coffee and biscuits on a side table. Before leaving the room, she turned down the volume on the Spice Girls. Unsurprisingly, the brand of biscuits were Paprenjaci whose wrappers said, 'These cookies reflect Croatia's history, combining the nation's suffering – pepper, with its natural beauties – honey.'

Prskalo told me it was offensive to be invited to the east side of his home town by an Englishman. I wanted to answer that people didn't normally bomb their homes, but I felt that it was better to be diplomatic. I said that I was English, but I was of Scottish and Welsh ancestry with a Jewish first name and a Christian family name, but that I was neither Jewish nor Christian nor, strictly speaking, English. Instead, I told him that my ex-wife was Croatian, that my children were half-Croatian, that I had made a film for the BBC and Croatian TV about the war there and that my association with the country stretched back more than a quarter of a century.

It was a short meeting. As I walked down the corridor, I could hear the volume being turned up on the Spice Girls' 'Who Do You Think You Are'.

A week later, Safet Oručević's office rang to say that both mayors would attend the opening and that they'd visit the centre together the next day.

I gave them a tour of the building and invited them to my office. I had placed a large plate of baklava on my desk and, as we sat down, Hamid, the bar manager, came in carrying a tray with a Bosnian copper coffee jug and three small porcelain cups. All very Ottoman.

Prskalo turned to Oručević. 'Doesn't Mr Wilson look young for his fifty-two years? That is because he is married to a Croatian woman.'

'No,' I answered. 'It is because I divorced one.'

Oručević laughed.

Prskalo said he had another meeting to go to.

After he left the room, Oručević smiled. 'Don't worry. He'll be at the opening.'

Ivan Prskalo was never going to be my friend. We had already been criticised for calling the centre 'Muzički Centar Pavarotti' because the Croats had recently discovered an ancient Croat word for music, *glazba*. They were offended that we were not using that in place of a word recognised from Beijing to Buenos Aires.

Soon after the wars in former Yugoslavia, politicians from all sides actively 'xenophobised' their languages. Antun Vrdoljak, Croatian TV chief in the 1990s, declared that,'Language preserves the nation's history and culture … language is the womb.' At its worst, the Croatian Education Minister, Jasna Gotovac, said, 'The fight for our language and culture is a part of the war.' Alija Isakovic, a linguist who published a Bosnian language dictionary in besieged Sarajevo warned against a purge of Turkish words. 'If they do,' he said, 'none of them will have a kidney.' The common word for kidney being *bubreg*.

This might all seem to be archaic thinking, but this process applied to contemporary words as well. In Croatia, 'helikopter' was to be *zrakomlat*, 'telefon' – *brzoglas*, 'aeroport' – *zračna luka*; making the internationally comprehensible into a jumble of incomprehension.

Behind arguments over words, there was something much darker. The radio station on the west side questioned why we'd built the centre on the 'Muslim' side of town, an accusation repeated when my old friend Darko Glavan visited me and said, 'There are too many Muslims here.'

'Yes,' I replied, 'and there were too many Jews in the Warsaw ghetto.'

Oslobođenje, the Sarajevo daily newspaper, asked me to contribute an article on the situation in Mostar. I decided to deliver my piece in person. I was eager to visit them and meet their staff. I had briefly visited their office after it had been shelled and they were operating from a bomb shelter. I hoped to see they now had better circumstances.

When there, I told them of my experiences in Mostar. One of the journalists told me, 'Only three things grow there: snakes, stones and fascists.'[1]

The atmosphere at the Pavarotti Music Centre in the days leading up to the opening was documented by Pay-Uun Hiu, writing in the Dutch newspaper *de Volkskrant*:

'Director David Wilson does not waste time on greetings and formal chit-chat. Six days before the official festive opening on December 21 ... time is running out ... "Just follow me," says Wilson, while running on the shiny-tiled floor through the courtyard to one of the performing areas, "we're just unpacking a grand piano". At the same time, he explains about the building: the central courtyard where a fountain still has to be placed, a section for music education, a special section for music therapy, rehearsal areas, concert areas and a professional recording studio in the basement. Finally, there are two apartments in the semi-circled towers on the top-floor. These are meant mainly for guests, but Wilson also wants to use one of them as a healing and meditation area ... "It sounds romantic," Wilson says, "but Mostar lost its bridge and the Music Centre could well be a new bridge, a bridge to the future, a bridge between music cultures, a bridge to the peace.'"[2]

Six weeks before the opening, Nicoletta Mantovani visited us. She wanted to check on progress with the building. I took her inside where the floors of the reception area and bar were still being laid.

'Are you sure it will be ready, David?' she asked.

'Of course it will be,' I said as I stumbled over a pile of bricks.

In fact, I was as worried as she was. We'd had endless delays and problems with the construction company, Hydrogradnja. But I had put my faith in Mike Lawless who seemed to be practically living in Mostar. He and the local team were doing their best to make sure the building would be completed to the contract schedule.

Mostar does not have the snows of Sarajevo and central Bosnia, but it does have rains and vicious winds which sweep down from the east into the Mediterranean plain of the Neretva Valley. The forecast was bad for December 21st, the day of the opening.

Pavarotti, Bono, Eno, Zucchero, Paddy Malone of the Chieftains, Bianca Jagger and half the Italian press were to arrive in Split on a chartered plane that had set off late from Stansted. It was to pick up Pavarotti and his party from Bologna for its flight across the Adriatic to Split in Croatia. There, the British military had arranged for two Chinook helicopters to bring them all to Mostar.

Until the last minute, we were unsure whether Pavarotti would agree to fly. A few years before, he'd been in a helicopter crash in South America. He was understandably nervous, but he'd told Nicoletta that he would not let the children down and nothing would stop him from opening the centre that carried his name.

The weather closed in. Rumours spread through the building that the Chinooks were unable to make the journey. We later found out that the pilots had been so concerned they almost didn't make the journey. They finally decided to fly the long way into Mostar. Instead of taking the direct route over the mountains, they followed the coastline south and headed inland up the Neretva Valley.

By mid-afternoon, the streets were packed with children and young people waiting for the Maestro's arrival. The building was full to bursting. When I stepped out into the street to see if Pavarotti had arrived, I saw Spanish APCs and thought this must be one of the few occasions in history when the opening of a cultural centre was protected by soldiers.

The delayed flights meant that it was going to be a long wait and that Pavarotti and his party would only have time for a quick visit. The chartered plane had a 7pm deadline for its return from Split to London, via Italy. Meanwhile, my job was to keep the guests of honour happy as they sat waiting in a draughty hall. In the front rows were Bosnian politicians, diplomats and military brass and I was horrified to see that there were not enough chairs. Mohamed Sacirbey, Bosnia's UN Ambassador, and Safet Oručević made light of it and stood at the back in good humour. Ivan Prskalo decided that he was not to be outdone in this display of civic populism. Unsmiling, he stood up and offered his chair to someone else.

As rain fell diagonally against the windows, young people had formed a conga line in the courtyard, dancing to Eugene Skeef's drummers. Quite a few of the notables looked as if they wished they weren't Minister of this or that for a day so they could join in.

The plan was for Pavarotti to visit the Special School on the road into town, but with the delays, the children there were told they would have to walk up a muddy path to the main road since he only had time for a brief stop. As the entourage approached, they started to sing. His car came to a halt and so did the singing as they watched him open his door and embrace them with a laugh and a huge smile.[3]

Two hours late, Pavarotti entered the building, one arm around Nicoletta, the other over Bono's shoulder. I greeted him at the door and he kissed me. There were tears in his eyes. His only words were a whispered, 'Thank you, thank you.' As he entered the hall, even the politicians' faces lit up as the cheering started.

The children danced and sang. Adin Omerovič, aged nine, remembers this:

'I, together with my classmates, practised a song to perform for the opening of the Pavarotti Music Centre. I had heard of plans for the Centre, but I could not dream that I would be there or near to Pavarotti. At the end of the song, "Big Bam Boo", I gave Luciano Pavarotti a flower. I still remember that day when we waited for him so long and I cannot forget how strong my heart was beating after his speech. He said, '*Grazie, grazie,*' I still remember that. I got a toy from him which I still have. I would like to have more memories like this one. Thank you very much, Pavarotti.'

Weeks earlier, children had decorated the art room with their hand prints. This gave us the idea to have Pavarotti and the other guests place theirs under the tablet we had had made to commemorate the opening. We arranged for trays of paint to be prepared for this. When Pavarotti's head of security saw two children standing at the side with the paint, he told me that the last time this had happened was at an Italian school and paint had ended up on Pavarotti's clothes. I was about to order the graffiti exercise cancelled when, to my horror, the children stepped through the crowd just as Pavarotti, Bono and Brian Eno were unveiling the memorial. Pavarotti gleefully covered his hands with poster paint, followed by the others. Luckily, no one's clothes were splashed.

I then had to get Pavarotti upstairs for the press conference. I pushed my way through the crowd to arrange for the lift to take him up. It was full. Its occupants included the Swiss Ambassador and a German army general. Unceremoniously, I ordered them out to let the Maestro enter.

Before the conference, I'd made sure that there were spaces on the dais reserved for Pavarotti, Bono and a child.

As I entered the hall, I saw there were not enough chairs. Tom Stoppard saw my face and vacated his. Bono picked up the child and sat him on his knee.

I was now being told that the party had to leave for the Chinooks in five minutes. There was only time for Pavarotti to say, 'My message is peace. You saw the horror of war – you see today the peace. The future now is in the hands of the children who will soon be grown up. Try to live in peace. That is the reason why we are here today.'

It was then a dash back to the lift and just enough time to give Pavarotti and Bono a quick visit to the studio in the basement.

'*Ciao*,' Luciano called out as he was pushed into the street by an increasingly nervous military escort. He was gone.

Some months later, I asked Pavarotti if he would send his memories of the day to us and he wrote this:

'It is no exaggeration to say that visiting Mostar that day was truly one of the most beautiful moments of my life. For two years, we had been raising funds through concerts and albums to build the Music Centre and to eventually see its completion, and to witness some of the beautiful and talented children of Mostar performing for us on their inaugural day was simply a joy. The children that day were so very patient. We were delayed on our journey by something beyond our control, the weather! But, when we eventually arrived in the beautiful city that was overwhelming, and the people of Mostar certainly proved that they have something very special that is their future. Those children are an example to us all and a tribute to Mostar. If music is central to a person's life, it can be something very special and life-affirming. The Music Centre was built for the children – I can only hope that making music helps in the healing process and that it will bring joy to the children of Mostar for many, many years to come.'

The next morning I spent time with Tom Stoppard before taking him to Sarajevo where he was to spend the night before his return flight to London. We walked through the town. He was silent and didn't seem happy. After he returned home, he wrote to say that he'd felt uncomfortable to be a fleeting visitor to a place of such suffering.[4]

I sat with him in the lobby of the Hotel Bosna in Sarajevo while Anne went to our room to pack. She is a militant non-smoker and I had to hide my bad habit from her. As the lift's glass doors shut on her, I asked Tom for a cigarette. I said that if I was still smoking when the lift came down with Anne, I'd pass it to him. He happily agreed and spent the time staring at the 1960s light fittings, commenting that this lobby would make an excellent stage set for a play.

As he was talking, I saw the light from the descending lift. It was Anne. I passed my half-smoked cigarette to Tom, but he'd just lit up himself. The doors opened, Tom sitting there smiling broadly, a cigarette in each hand. He stubbed one out as Anne approached.

She told me later that she'd watched it all.

Murray McCullough, Chief Administrator at the Office of the High Representative in Mostar, had been responsible for the logistics of bringing Pavarotti into town. He wrote about the opening and started with a quote from Shakespeare.

'"There is a tide in the affairs of man which, if taken at the flood, leads on to victory." On the most surreal of days, out of the mists of an extraordinary wet and cold December afternoon descended a war helicopter into the war zone that is Mostar, with cargo, to open a music centre for a charity called War Child. It was not surprising then that its famous passenger, the Maestro, should be a little nervous. Surrounded by diplomats, photographers and soldiers, he left, tense and confused, in a convoy for a tour of the city, all the time fighting with his mobile phone to reassure his mother of his safety but, like the weather, communications were bad. Still he tried, nervous, his eyes staring, his face contorted with anguish. After a while, the convoy stopped before a crowd of noisy, freezing and impatient children at the school for children with special needs. They had been there for hours, but they knew this was a special day and they had come to embrace the heart of a great man, but still the mobile took centre stage. From the steaming happy mess stepped the smallest child, blessed but free of the deferential fears that surround normal children. He climbed, as if by right, into the vehicle. Slowly, but with consummate gentleness, he ran his little toy down the cheek of the anguished face to say hello in the only way he knew. 'Mr Pavarotti,' said Bono, 'these are the children of Mostar with special needs. They have been waiting for you for a long time.' As if by a miracle, a ray of light descended, the staring and frozen eyes melted as though touched by a sunbeam. The lips parted to an immense smile, the contorted face opened the windows of the real world that is Mostar and its children. Pavarotti had at last arrived and was in full flood.'

Music and War

The Bible says, 'In the beginning was the word.'

Wrong. First there was the rhythm. From the time of the Big Bang, it is the beat that gives the cosmos its pulse. All else may be chaos, but it is there in mathematical time, something primordial.[1] In one sense, however, the Bible is right. Man's first attempt to communicate involved rhythm, movement and dance which represented the first language, the first word.

At the time of what Engels called 'primitive communism', when *Homo sapiens* were hunter-gatherers, humans signalled to each other by beating stick on stick, stone on stone. The first vocal syllables were whistles and calls based on rhythmic patterns which allowed human communication to take place.

Rhythm was there at the start of everything. It was there at the start of our species and is there at the start of our individual lives.[2] Whether or not we evolved from the sea, we all emerged from the waters of our mothers, and water is a perfect transmitter of sound. Place a waterproof watch under the surface at one end of a swimming pool. Get there early in the morning when no one else is around. Have a friend swim underwater at the far end of the pool and ask them what they can hear.

Both the heart of the foetus and that of the mother beat to a cycle of dash dash, dum dum, dum dum, dum dum. Mother and baby are in syncopated rhythm. Sounds exterior to the womb may also be heard and absorbed by the foetus. Many pregnant women will tell you that they are aware that their babies react to external sounds. So music and rhythm, or rhythm and music to be chronologically correct, are central to

167

our lives. It is a physical and emotional link, both to something in us and beyond us, linking us to the music of the spheres.

Music can move us to extremes of joy or sadness, elation or depression. Perhaps it is a piece we associate with some event in our life: when we first kissed, when we went to our first teenage party, when we first made love. This musical association is strong in all of us. Perhaps it is with Mahler's 'Adagietto', Ali Farka Touré, blues, a song sung by Ella Fitzgerald, an Indian raga, hip-hop or drum and bass. In all types of music we can be emotionally, and even physically, moved.

If you project sound waves at piles of sand, iron filings, water or mercury, you can create varied patterns, from spirals to grids. Given the sound conductivity of water and its high level in the human body, it is hardly surprising that our cells react to sound vibrations, even those at the far end of the spectrum which we are unable to hear. With this knowledge, holistic healers place vibrating forks close to the energy field of the human body and hospitals use high-pitched sound to shatter kidney and gallstones. Conversely, the negative side of the use of sound are experiments undertaken by the US military and other governments, utilising sound waves as instruments of war. Abu Ghraib and Guantanamo have shown us that music can be a weapon.

Music therapist Olivea Dewhurst-Maddock has argued that the vibrational energies of different notes affect different areas of the body. For instance, C major affects the bones, lower back, legs and feet. D major transmits energy waves to the kidneys and bladder, lymphatic and reproductive systems and skin. A major is related to pain and pain control.[3]

A few years ago, a friend of mine had major heart surgery. This is what he told me about his recuperation:

'My post-operative experience was quite disturbing. I'd brought some of my favourite music to listen to in the hospital. I have always been passionate about classical music. My mother and stepfather were professional musicians and I was brought up, from the embryo onwards, listening to Mozart,

Beethoven, Bach, Haydn and Schubert. Once I was a bit more than an embryo, I learned to play the piano, cello and guitar. During the week following the operation, I lost touch with a lot of things – my sense of taste, smell, my enjoyment of books, but the worst was being cut off from the meaning of music. Something central to my life seemed to have died inside me. I would listen to a Mozart piano concerto; I could understand the harmony and counterpoint, but found no beauty in it, nor could I appreciate its extraordinary passion and inventiveness. Listening to Mozart was like listening to Salieri. That loss and the frequent moments when I burst into tears, for no apparent reason, convinced me that lengthy and violent operations have a much deeper effect on our inner selves than medical science acknowledges. Only part of me was put to sleep. Many levels of my subconscious and my body were awake when the knife cut me open. They went into a state of shock. They switched off. They needed time to mourn. My enjoyment of music now, three years later, is even more intense than before. I don't know if that comes with age, or whether it is the result of the operation, but it is now a passion only second to my closest relationships.'

Perhaps it is for this reason that in ancient Egypt, the hieroglyph for music was also that for well-being and joy. But what about music in non-joyful situations, in war? When the lights go out and all that is left is hunger and the threat of death, you will still find music.

In 1993 and 1994 I was in cellars in Sarajevo and Mostar. Shells were exploding, the snipers were at work, but people – particularly young people – gathered together and, if they could not listen to music as there was often no power, they played it. The louder the shelling, the louder their music. It was an expression of defiance, a testament to the survival of the one thing that kept them human in an inhuman situation – the primordial language of rhythm and music which connected them to their essence.

A young soldier in Mostar visited me after his time on

the front line, a Kalashnikov on one shoulder and a guitar on the other. He tapped the guitar and told me, 'A much better weapon.'

This young man faced his former classmates across a narrow street, playing music to them when it was too dark to fight. Cigarettes were thrown into the building where he was crouching as he performed for his enemies.

Just before the war ended in 1995, I helped smuggle a Bob Marley photo exhibition into East Mostar. Sponsored by Island Records, we took in tapes and CDs with the photos. The local war radio station broadcast these non-stop for two days from their cellar studio. The exhibition opened underground on the front line. I will never forget how the town pulsed to Marley's rhythms in the middle of the thuds from incoming shells.

These are examples of overt and easily recognisable influences of music in extreme situations: music as defiance with an external enemy in mind. But what of the influence of music in relationship to the enemy within? What is its effect on the disturbed and traumatised minds of those who have been too close to the barbarism of war, who have shot and killed, have been shot at and wounded, physically and emotionally? Who have seen friends die, who have lost mothers, fathers, brothers, sisters?

The PMC was constructed in East Mostar, a part of the city that had been devastated by two consecutive wars: first in the war of the whole town against Serb forces, then in the much worse war between the Croats on the west bank of the Neretva River and the Bosniaks on the east: former allies that had once formed an alliance to defeat the Serbs. When the Croats brokered a secret deal with the Serbs, the Croats turned on the Bosniaks. Thousands of families were driven into what became a ghetto on the east side of the Neretva River.

The term is 'ethnic cleansing', but a more accurate phrase would be 'ethnic purging'.[4] The Bosniaks were forced to live in cellars for ten months, eating grass soup and emerging into the streets only to collect water and, in the case of the young men, to fight. When the Anne Frank exhibition arrived at the Centre in 1998, I was asked to say something at its opening. There was not much to say, only that the Mostar Ghetto had contained thousands of Anne Franks.[5]

The Centre allowed the healing power of music to enter this community. The young were particularly affected by the war and, from the day the PMC opened its doors, they flooded in. Some of them used music to escape their darkest memories. They would tell me that only when they played, or heard music, could they escape their nightmares.

Children and young people were brought together to make and listen to music: to sing, to beat drums, to strum guitars, to act and react together through music. These workshops took on a structured form, thanks to the work of Nigel Osborne. This was to quickly develop into our successful schools' outreach programme.

The first schools' project was called 'The Oceans'. First, our teachers started with the Neretva which flows through the centre of Mostar. They went to the schools and took with them music from the banks of that river – Croat, Serb and Bosniak songs. On the next visit, the theme became the Mediterranean because the Neretva flows into that sea: Tunisian love songs, flamenco, French, Italian and Greek music. Next, the Atlantic because that is the ocean into which the Mediterranean flows: everything from Brazilian, to blues, to Celtic and West African music. Then the Indian Ocean and, finally, the Pacific. The children became aware that they did not just live in Mostar, or more specifically in the small ghetto of East Mostar, but that their town and river had links to the world.

At the opening of the Centre, some of these children performed a Hawaiian boat dance for Pavarotti. After his long and hazardous helicopter journey across the Balkan winter skies, the Maestro looked puzzled, not knowing why these children had chosen a dance so foreign to their experience.

The Centre employed more than 30 young musicians who travelled to schools and kindergartens in Mostar and the surrounding villages to bring music into the lives of the children. Centre staff also worked in special needs' schools, the Sarajevo Blind School and in the Srpska Republika.

The Music Therapy department, staffed by the first resident music therapists in Bosnia-Herzegovina, worked with the most disturbed and distressed children. The results were amazing and a credit to a small, dedicated department who achieved so much in a damaged town with its equally damaged population. This small team were responsible for groundbreaking work. Traumatised children were treated and, on occasion, responded so well that some of them ended up joining the Centre's more mainstream activities.

For some in Bosnia-Herzegovina, much that happened at the Centre was dangerously political because music was being used to counter cultural exclusiveness – what I call cultural incest when expressed in its most extreme form. Negative and threatening music comes from this tradition: national anthems and military marching songs. To the contrary, the best music, as with the best art, architecture and whatever else expresses human creativity, comes from cultural mixing.[6] Göring once said, 'When I hear the word culture, I reach for my gun.' I would counter that with, 'When I hear the word gun, I reach for my culture.'

This attempt to universalise music and culture at the Centre was deliberate and methodical. For the first two years of our work, Eugene Skeef was responsible for setting up what became African percussion workshops. On Sunday afternoons, you could find up to 60 children and young people taking part with *djembes*, maracas, handbells, marimbas and wood blocks.

These workshops were developed, both at the Centre and, as part of the outreach work, at orphanages and hospitals. After the first half hour of drum tuition, I saw very young children express rhythmic talent as if it were latent in their essence and being.

On a recent visit to the USA, I came across an article by

Feeny Lipscomb, drummer and writer, who wrote, 'Recently, medical research has testified that drumming produces an altered state similar to meditation, thereby reducing stress. Drumming is also a right-brain activity which increases intuition, shuts down the 'rational' mind, and centers us in our hearts … I have often heard drumming compared to the high produced by endorphins. In fact, many people have taken up drumming because they've heard it's a way to get the same endorphin-produced high without running and/or doing aerobics.'[7]

For millennia, shamans have argued that drumming is 'the horse that takes you to the gods'. The state induced is a type of meditation and, in fact, the Centre offered meditation classes after an acupuncturist at the Centre was asked to teach it by her patients. Through Chinese medicine and meditation, the practitioner achieved some extraordinary results: helping the traumatised sleep for the first time in years, curing migraines, helping stroke victims and the wounded.

From the start, the ethos of the PMC had been to make a difference, not just in terms of the type of aid work that was carried out, but also the reasons why it existed. It is time that we question those aid programmes which lead to dependency and ensure the continuation of the outstretched hand. This form of aid becomes an appendage to war and does not address the larger questions of physical, spiritual and psychological reconstruction needed to minimise the possibility of future wars.

Europeans travel to Africa to teach the people how to grow their crops. One of the places they go to is in the Rift Valley, where agriculture was practised before Europe was populated. Don't get me wrong. I am not saying they should not be there doing what they do, but they should be aware of the history, economics, culture and politics of the people they have come to help. If to this is added a passion for justice and, dare I say it, an understanding of the need for political change, then their work can be more than a 'flash in the pan'.[8]

In the words of Eugene Skeef, 'The destruction visited upon the planet in the name of advancement is more than sufficient proof that those of us whose basic education and development was fired in the Western mould need to exercise a rare humility before proceeding to administer aid to others. We all know that the so-called First World (strange notion this, if we are to accept Africa as the birthplace of human civilisation) has a great deal to learn from the so-called Third World, if they can just step back, join the circle and let someone else lead the song with a different rhythmic melody.'

It was my hope that the Pavarotti Music Centre could be a resource centre for a worldwide music-based project whose purpose would be to sustain the lives of those traumatised by war and conflict. To join and widen the circle.

Here is what I wrote on the first birthday of the PMC:

'One year old, the Pavarotti Music Centre has surpassed all expectations. A schools' music programme working in more than 20 schools, kindergartens and special schools, the first music therapy department in Bosnia-Herzegovina, a hospital outreach programme, a music school, a busy recording studio, a rock school, percussion workshops, guitar classes, a youth choir, drama workshops, dance and ballet, concerts and exhibitions, even acupuncture and meditation. Above all else, a place where children and young people can find themselves and their friends. In the middle of this damaged country, this wounded town, and working from within that town's ghetto, we have done what no politician would dream of doing – produced solutions to political problems by ignoring politics altogether. We have let the music play. Of course, none of this was possible without the generosity of the many musicians who performed at the Modena concerts, none of this was possible without Brian Eno and his wife, Anthea. And none of this was possible without Luciano Pavarotti. But with them alone, we would have a building. We needed a ticking heart. That we found in the young people of Mostar who have dedicated themselves to making this place a success. And we have found it in the international workers here who seem, like me, to have fallen in love with the earth upon which the Centre stands.'

[An abridged version of this chapter was published in the *European Journal of Intercultural Studies*, Vol. 10, No. 3, 1999 and in *The Journal of Dramatic Theory and Criticism*, The University of Kansas, Fall 2000, Vol. XV, No. 8]

Mostar Sons

When I arrived in Mostar as Director of the PMC, I rented a small two-bedroom house and offered the spare room to Teo and Oha, two musicians working at the Centre. Oha's mother still lived on the west side of town which he could not visit safely and Teo's widowed mother had no space for him in her tiny flat.

Close friends, they had both been soldiers and had both realised, in Oha's words, 'that the "enemy" was bullshit. They feed you enemies.' While the war was still going on, they helped set up Apeiron, a group of young people who got together to play music.

The three of us spent most of our time outside since the house itself was damp and dark. The plumbing had given up in the kitchen and dirty dishes would pile up at the only other source of water – the bathroom. If you wanted to take a shower, you first had to do the washing-up.

The toilet was not fixed to the floor and, when you sat on the pan, there was more than one movement. There was always a puddle at the base and you could never be sure what it was. Common to all toilets in south-east Europe, the S-bend had yet to be adopted so to the smell of damp was added that of excrement. It was a mystery where it all went, if it did at all. The road bridge at the end of the street had been blown up at the start of the war and the sewerage pipes with it.

Despite the smell and discomfort, we had happy times there. We'd sit on the terrace while Teo played his guitar and sang his sad songs.

When Teo returned home from teaching in local schools,

he would smile at me and pace the living room, distractedly clicking his fingers to some inner rhythm. He would then turn and give me a second smile as he opened the fridge door to take out a beer. If there weren't any, he would tease me and offer to do me a favour: take my money and fill the fridge again. By the end of the evening we'd be out of booze, but he would consider that he'd repaid me by beating me at endless games of backgammon. The game is called *tavla* there and arrived with the Ottomans. It is as much a part of the culture in Bosnia as the ritual of serving coffee. There is always time for coffee and *tavla*. In Teo's case, most of the night.

After multiple victories, he would open the last beers and insist on a final game. 'Come on, David. You can beat me now. I'm drunk.'

Hearing him slur his words, I thought my time to win had come. It never did.

One morning, not long after he'd moved in, I woke at 4am and went to the kitchen to get a glass of water. Teo was sitting at the table, staring at the wall. I asked him what was wrong and why he wasn't sleeping.

'Sleep?' he said. 'I haven't slept for four years.'

I looked at him in shock. 'Four years? Why?'

'Let's drink some of that English tea of yours and I'll tell you.'

I knew he'd seen terrible things on the front line, but had known nothing of what he was about to tell me. How, at midnight on August 10th, 1993, Croat militia arrived at his house. 'They asked me where my father was. I was scared and so I told them he was upstairs. Then we were all ordered into the street. Me, my mother, my father, my younger brother and grandfather. They pushed us into the back of a van, but a guy was shouting at my dad, "You're staying with us." That's the last I saw of him. We were driven to the front line and told to cross over to the Bosniak side. All this time, I was thinking how I had given my dad away. We later heard he'd been shot. They said that some of the soldiers who came to our house were

177

shocked that he'd been killed. He was a well-known singer. He wasn't a soldier.'

I thought how terrifying it must have been for Teo, who'd been 15 at the time. How the guilt must be unbearable.

'How old was he?' I asked.

'Forty three.'

Nine years younger than I was when we sat in that kitchen.

That night, over the Typhoo, was the only time Teo ever spoke about the war and about his father. Despite his personal tragedies, Teo was typical of many young Bosnians, wanting nothing more than to return to pre-war days when no one took any notice of religious or ethnic differences. Knowing his history makes it more extraordinary that he was one of the first to take his guitar into the communities of his former enemies.

Many journalists who ran stories on the Centre were fascinated by Teo, but only the US writer Nancy Shalala managed to coax something out of him for the *Japan Times* when they travelled together to a schools' project in Ljubinje, a name that translates as 'place of love'.

She wrote that the presence of Teo, a former Bosnian soldier, in this Serbian village, represented a small but significant challenge to the formidable social and political lines that carved up post-war Bosnia-Herzegovina:

'… trading his Kalashnikov for an acoustic guitar, Teo now plays for an agitated mob of 60 three-year-olds in the kindergarten of his former enemy. "Three years ago I would have said that another 20 would need to pass before I would even consider entering [a Serbian village]," says the blond, burly Teo, who himself is barely 20, but already ancient in life experience.'

After I left Mostar, Teo spent much of his time looking for his father and, four years after returning to London, I got a call from him. He was laughing and I thought he was ringing from a bar or a party. He would often call me when he was drunk just to say hello and ask when I was next coming to Mostar.

'They've found my dad.'

After completing DNA tests, Teo had been told by the International Commission on Missing Persons that his father's remains had been located. His body had been part of an exchange of the dead which had taken place between the Bosniaks and the Croats. He'd been buried in a cemetery Teo had walked past every day on his way to the Centre.

Oha is a two-metre giant. You couldn't meet a gentler man. Aged 14, he had been the youngest fighter in Mostar. I once told him that, as a former soldier, he was entitled to a war pension. 'I know that, but I won't take it. I feel guilty for what I did. The money should go to the widows and the wounded.'

He would never speak about the war: what he had done and what had happened on the front line, but he carried the scars of it inside him. I would sometimes see him sitting alone, rocking back and forwards in a chair, in time to some inner anguish, yet always in time. Twenty-five years later, he still does this. I hope it's now just a habit.

Oha became a talented *djembe* player and, within weeks of the opening of the Centre, was assisting Eugene with the drumming workshops. I think he had found a way to release his distress with percussion as he pushed away his ghosts.

One of the PMC's outreach programmes was to a mental hospital in Pazarić, ten kilometres west of Sarajevo. The hospital had been caught between two front lines, the patients left unattended and starving. They were forced to bury their own dead.

The road from Mostar was mountainous and still pockmarked with war damage. In winter, snow chains were essential. Nevertheless, Oha would go there every Thursday and never missed a week.

When I first visited the place immediately after the war, it was a Bosch vision of hell. It smelled of urine and vomit because they'd had to operate with a skeleton staff. When I went there later with Eugene and Oha, I was pleased to see that it was very different.

As the two percussionists climbed out of their car, they

were treated like pop stars, mobbed and hugged. One patient, who claimed he had been President Tito's ambassador in Morocco, was pointing at Eugene's dreadlocks and shouting, 'Marley, Bobby Marley.'

It was scary to watch these deranged people getting so excited, but Oha stood there, towering above the tallest of them, beaming.

The percussion session opened with a cacophony of thuds as Oha handed each patient an instrument taken out of his old army bag. Then Eugene worked his magic and came in over it all with his *djembe*. Oha answered him with a call and response on his drum. Then a sudden stop. Eugene stood up, smiled at everyone, sat down and said, 'Follow.' They did. The room was immediately in rhythm with them.

The only person who didn't join in was the 'Ambassador', who stood by the door picking his nose, then placing the thumbs of each hand against his ears and making a waving sign at the group.

But madness doesn't mean stupid. Oha told me that one day a UNICEF Land Cruiser broke down outside the hospital. One of the wheels had fallen off and spun down a steep slope. The driver didn't know what to do. He jacked up the vehicle and fitted the spare tyre, but he needed four nuts. He sat down, lit a cigarette and started to call HQ for help on his satellite telephone.

Above him, a Pazarić patient was sitting on the hospital wall and shouted to the driver. 'Hey, you.' The driver was scared to respond to this crazy man. 'Take one nut from the three other tyres,' shouted the patient, 'Use your brain.'

Oha's enthusiasm for people was marked by equal enthusiasm for music. When he heard a performance he liked, his face would break into a smile as he grabbed the nearest person to him to hug. I have even watched while he hugged a JBL loudspeaker in appreciation.

One image of Oha remains indelibly in my memory. Michael de Toro of the Office for Security and Cooperation in Europe in Mostar, arranged for Oha to take a couple of DJs from the Centre to perform one Saturday evening at a gig in Trebinje. Like Ljubinje, this was in the Serb-controlled part of Bosnia, enemy territory for Oha. The town is in the hills behind Dubrovnik, from where the Serb bombardment of the old walled city had been organised.

The musicians travelled to Trebinje, escorted by OSCE. I was staying in Dubrovnik that weekend and met Michael in a café. He asked if I'd like to go and see this first music collaboration between Bosniaks from Mostar and Bosnian Serbs. I told him I'd left my UN card, which I needed to cross the old war borders, in Mostar.

'No worries,' he answered with a wink. 'I'll put you in the trunk.'

We set off from Dubrovnik. Halfway up the hill and a few kilometres from the border, he stopped the car. I climbed into the boot and we crossed to the Serb side without any problems. I was back in the front seat by the time we reached Trebinje.

When we arrived at the venue where the gig was supposed to be taking place, we were told it had been moved out of town to an old mill in the countryside. By the time we got there, it was 2am.

As Michael parked his car, the sounds of drum and bass could be heard in the distance. We walked along a river and, in the middle of the night, the music was in competition with thousands of croaking frogs and birds singing in the trees.

We arrived at the mill and there were hundreds of young people dancing. Oha was striding towards us, one arm around a young man and his other around a young woman. 'Hey, David,' he shouted, 'these two were at school with me.' He bent down from his tallness and planted a kiss on each of their heads. He then picked me off the ground. 'How the fuck did you get here?'

When I left the PMC in 2000, I expected Oha to leave Mostar and the country. He was too dynamic for this broken, segregated city. But Oha is no quitter. He set up a club,

Growing from Music, and was the first person to bring bands together from both sides of the city. 'Every time a project of mine collapsed,' Oha said, 'things became lighter and lighter. Nothing was going to be a catastrophe for me. The war had been that. So each project was better than the one before. I hadn't been defeated in the war and wasn't going to be defeated by a good idea involving music. And fuck them. I don't have much money, but enough to invest. I have time for everyone. The rich, the poor, the good, the naughty. War taught me not to screw up.'

Today, he manages the rock school and the recording studio at the Centre and is producer of the annual Mostar Blues and Rock Festival.

The rock school employs five teachers and an administrator. Students come there from all over the region and it is recognised as a place where division and bitter memories are parked outside.

The Blues and Rock festival is in its thirteenth year and performers have included Dr Feelgood, Snowy White, Big Brother and the Holding Company, Sugar Blue and many local groups.

When I asked Oha about his hopes for the rock school he told me, 'Mostar people lost hope. The internationals came and went. Always with a beginning and end. Too much starting and shutting down. The rock school is like a kitchen. They can learn not just music, but video making and music administration. Most important of all is, fuck it, they don't even have to be musicians. If they go home with new friendships and new hopes, they can take this into their families and communities. They will have made links which will make renewed divisions and conflicts more difficult for those bastards to organise. I have a long-term view. Fast success is not good success. It's better to be slow. Maybe in ten years I will be mayor of Mostar and finally fuck up their plans of dividing people.'

He laughed as he told me of two recent initiatives organised in Mostar. Using Facebook, emails and word of mouth, a

16-year-old created an event called Chocolate Mess. Young people were asked to come to Spanish Square on the old front line and bring chocolate to give away to strangers. Over 300 turned up with their chocolate. On another day, 200 high-school children stood outside the old Mostar music school with signs, *WILL YOU UNITE US? IF NOT, FUCK OFF.*

Oha has, of course, been at the forefront of the recent protests that broke out across the country against corruption and the political establishment. He is a powerful representative of what could be a better future for his country.

Oha and Teo now have families and both have made a success of their lives in different ways. Oha as a musician and impresario; Teo as a musician who now performs in Ljubljana cafés, but whose main task is to be a full-time father to his two sons.

Oha laughs when he tells me the story about taking Teo to the bus station in Mostar to join his Slovenian wife, Sanja, in Ljubljana. 'He was wearing an old T-shirt and was carrying two plastic bags, one with socks and pants, the other with more T-shirts. His only other possession had been his guitar which he'd left with his mother. Four months later, I was performing in Ljubljana and was told that Teo was waiting for me at the front of the hall. He was standing there in a smart black coat and behind him, a brand new Toyota.'

Oha and his wife, Maša, have two daughters named Luna and Zoe. Luna, the Roman goddess of the moon. Zoe, meaning 'life' in Greek. Teo and Sanja have named their oldest son Anej, a shortened version of Anemoi, Greek gods of the winds. Given that Teo's family name, Krilić, translates as 'wing', this name is doubly appropriate. Their second son has the name Elis, also of Greek origin. All four names make it impossible for any future nationalists to decide their children's religion and ethnicity.

Teo told me that Anej's aunt gave him a toy gun and he had no idea what to do with it. The aunt pointed it at a cartoon cat on TV and said, 'Look, I am killing the cat.' The Bosnian word for kill is *ubi*. The word for love is *ljubi*. Teo laughed when he told me that Anej went up to the TV set and kissed the cat.

When Anne and I married in April 2008, Teo and Oha couldn't be there. Teo had recently moved to Slovenia and Oha was busy preparing for that year's Blues' festival. Oha asked that their message be read to our wedding guests:

'First, we want to say hallo to everyone there and we are really sorry to be unable to come and share this special moment with all of you great people. In the case that someone don't know who we are, we are David's two sons called Teo and Oha. We would like to ask all of you good people to give Anne and David big hug and make them feel good. We want to say few words about David so you know what is the man that you are dealing with, haha, but we are sure that you already know, right? We met David in 1996 for the first time. I was 18 and homeless. And Teo was all the time with me. David invited us to his place and offer us food. He gave us jobs and introduced me to Eugene Skeef who healed me my war hurt soul and he taught me to play music. This combination of this two people in my life was sat by nature. If there is God, he sat them, or it was their assistent, I can't remember now, haha. I was feeling so close to David and I asked him one day if is ok if I take him as my father. After while I felt that David is very proud of Teo and me and he speaks of us as his sons. I cryed 100 times in front of David and I never did in front anyone else, even as a soldier with my 14 and a half. I got out all my unsolved rage from the war and all bad feelings went out. Father, thank you for being so patient listening my stories and my harmed soul. Teo and I will never forget where we come from and we come from you. We know that this is very special day for Anne and you and it is for all of us too. We wont bother you guys anymore. We want to tell you that we love you very much. And please, one more time we want to ask each of you, tonight, when you think the time is good for it, just give Anne and David a hug or at least touch them. It feels warm and we all need that. Have a good time and don't drink more then seven beers if drive ;-) Big Love, Teo and Oha.'

Dogs of War

One memory of the rapid US departure from Vietnam in 1973 is of helicopters being tipped over the edge of aircraft carriers in the Bay of Tonkin after depositing on board the last evacuees from the roof of the Saigon embassy, a rearguard of US marines pushing back men, women and children who had remained loyal to their American allies. This superpower cynicism, cruelty and wastage did not only extend to humans. What happened to the most loyal of all animals, the dogs?

I recently watched a TV documentary about dogs brought out to Vietnam from the US to sniff out mines and locate Vietcong guerrillas in their tunnels. They, too, were abandoned to their enemies and their fate. Some of these dogs were killed by their owners and others left to fend for themselves in the streets of Saigon and Da Nang.

One of the first things you noticed in Mostar after the sad evidence of physical destruction were the stray dogs, the war's canine orphans. By day, they scavenged and lay by the roadside or slept in the dark shadows of shell-gutted buildings, nibbling at their mangy sores and looking sorry for themselves. By night, they formed packs and hunted. They would attack lone walkers and to find yourself in the centre of town at 3am being chased and nipped at by animals, whose memory was longer than we might care to admit, was an unpleasant experience. Mostar's desolation was bad enough with its dark streets, crushed buildings and demoralised citizens, without having to deal with dogs who once had a sheltered, comfortable life.

When war broke out, many owners were unable to care for their animals and they ended up in the street. Other owners were killed or had fled the country, and their dogs, cats and other pets were abandoned. Those that survived best were the mongrels. In the aftermath of war, you never saw pedigree dogs: the French Poodles, Chihuahuas and Lhasa Apsos. They were war's early victims, too far away from their ancestral stock to live alone for very long, too slow and small to gain advantage in the race for scraps of food.

During and after the war, the police organised hunts to cull the survivors, but, many years later, the crafty and the hardy still roamed the streets of the towns and cities. Some of them were heroes. One of these in Mostar, Heki, was a footsore mongrel who hung about in the old town begging food from cafés and passers-by. He had four separate pieces of shrapnel in his body, one of them lodged in his brain. He limped around and somehow survived. His home was the Ruža, the shelled ruins of a tourist hotel constructed in the 1970s, across a tributary that falls into the Neretva River, close to the Old Bridge. It was completely destroyed, but you could still read the fading signs to the 'Terrace Bar', the 'Sauna' and 'Hairdresser'. Heki was its longest-standing guest and when you didn't see him there, you could hear him padding around in the rubble. Whether from brain damage, resignation or because he'd had his fill of war, Heki was a passive dog with neither bark nor bite.

Buildings don't need their ghosts. They are ghosts. I often peered inside this hotel and the many other shelled homes, offices and shops and felt a tangible memory, a feeling that if you touched the bullet holes and plaster-shattered walls, you would discover the truth of the building, its happinesses and sadnesses. The Second World War spy warning – 'walls have ears' – could have had added to it that 'walls have memories'. If that is true of buildings, how much more is it true of dogs.

Nina was no different to other young people in Mostar and, for that matter, other young people anywhere else in Europe, in appearance, dress, attitudes and interests. Except she had a special animal, Torni. He was a large black and white mountain dog from the Tornjak breed. They were used for herding sheep. Torni comes from *torn* – a sheep pen. Nina's father was on the east side of Mostar fighting in the Bosnian army and she, her mother, sister and Torni, remained at home in their apartment in the west.

Life was difficult because families were being driven out of their homes, the men killed or taken off to prison camps. Nina's mother couldn't decide whether to stay on the west side of town or join her husband in the east. Despite the dangers of life on the west, the permanent barrage of the east side didn't make it an attractive solution.

The first sign of trouble happened early one morning when two HVO soldiers forced their way into the house. Torni barked at them and one of them aimed his gun at the dog. Nina stood between them and said they would have to kill her first. Faced with having to murder a 12-year-old, they left, but a few days later the Croat militia returned and arrested the family.

They were told to walk across to the east side. She, her younger sister and mother set off across the front line, picking their way over rotting corpses which had been left where they lay. The soldiers started firing and the three of them ran forward in panic. They threw themselves into the Bosnian trenches, but there was no dog. They thought that he had been shot. A week later Torni found them in their new home, a room shared with another family. Nina heard him howling in the street outside. He rushed around the family, tail wagging, licking and jumping up with his forepaws on their shoulders.

He had arrived to share a truly terrible time with them. Shells were landing on the east side ghetto; there was little food and they were hungry. The soldiers were better fed than their families and her father would bring home leftovers from the soldier's meals.

They noticed that a few moments before the arrival of incoming shells, Torni would go to the door and cry in distress, looking at them to see if they were taking any notice. When they opened the door, he ran down the street. He was always right. Soon after his warning, shells landed nearby. Torni had become their air raid siren.

Nina's father started to take the dog with him to the front line. He and his comrades would watch Torni. When he moved, they moved. Torni saved lives. He was rewarded with military rations along with the other front-line fighters.

Nina's father wanted to get his family out of Mostar to the relative safety of Zenica in central Bosnia. Their grandmother lived there and it was far from the front lines and relatively free from bombardment.

They had to walk over the mountains to Jablanica, a mountainous journey which takes 45 minutes by car, but which took them 48 hours on foot. It was November and cold. None of them had winter clothing because the Croats had forced them from their home without allowing them to take any of their possessions. The only food they had for the journey was a small piece of lamb which their mother cooked before leaving Mostar. They set off, cold, frightened and in misery.

They could only walk at night because of the snipers. They had to travel through a narrow corridor, Serbs on one side and Croats on the other, the gap was no more than 50 metres. They were not allowed to talk and the adults couldn't smoke. The slightest noise would attract the attention of those waiting to kill them.

Torni seemed to know he mustn't bark and was treading forward carefully, watching back every few paces to make sure everyone was all right. He never stopped wagging his tail. This breed of mountain dog thrive in the cold. His owners followed him carefully. He seemed to know where the mines were.

This was the 'road' to Sarajevo and central Bosnia and the family passed soldiers, pack mules, old and young people on the move to or from greater safety.

No vehicles could use these tracks and animals were used to carry humans and their cargoes. A few weeks before Nina and her family made the journey, a horse had become so wearied by his load that it was said that he deliberately jumped over the side of a cliff to his death a 100 metres below.

After 20 hours, they reached a mounain pass where there was a large tent for refugees escaping from Mostar. On arrival they were hungry, but so tired that they decided to sleep before eating. Nina woke up to the sound of crunching. Torni had found the lamb. All they had left was a small piece of bread and some sugar. They were angry with him and he knew it. Once again he led the way, but this time, with his tail firmly between his legs, looking guiltily back at the family.

At Jablanica they waited for a helicopter to take them to Zenica. When it arrived, it was full of wounded people and the pilot refused to let Torni aboard. Nina and her sister were so distressed that the pilot relented and agreed he could travel with them if he was put in a bag. Using their father's military kit bag, they persuaded Torni to get inside, but he did not take kindly to such restrictions and, as the helicopter was about to take off, he broke lose.

Once again, they had to persuade the pilot to let him back on board and he said that was okay with him, but only if the other passengers agreed. They did. Nina remembers the noise of the engine and its blades, the cries and moaning of the wounded and Torni moving from one stretcher to the other, wagging his tail and licking faces.

On arrival at their grandmother's, her father had to return to Mostar. Torni would spend every day in the field where the helicopter had landed in expectation of its return.

Six months later, they returned to Mostar after the permanent bombardment of the city had been lifted. One day, Adi, a friend of their father's, came to visit and when he went out into the street to go home, Torni followed him, barking and jumping up with his legs on the man's shoulders. Adi couldn't move and returned to their apartment with Torni. A shell landed in the street. Three people were killed, but Adi survived. For many years, Adi visited the family every week. He always had a present for the dog.

One day Torni disappeared. Someone told them he thought there was a wounded dog on the front line. They all knew it must be Torni. Maybe he had been trying to go back to their old home. Their father and two friends rescued him at night. The bullet was still in his body when he died 15 years later.

After a few days of war
the Sarajevo streets were a catwalk for dogs:
perfumed dogs, well-groomed dogs, dogs
with cut-glass collars
and not a flea between them. Their owners
had left them as they left
the burning city.

The trash-heaps became
a battlefield where the lapdogs lost
to an army of strays, lean-limbed
and mangy with hate.
Cowering and cleansed, the back-alley refugees
retreated to the doorways
of locked apartments, barking an answer
to each unearthly whistle
as the morning shells came in.

Excerpt from 'Dogs and Bones' by Goran Simić
(Sarajevo poet)

CRIME AND PUNISHMENT

'Nothing is easier than to denounce the evildoer; nothing is more difficult than to understand him.'

Fyodor Dostoyevsky

Missing Elton

Friedrich Nietzsche said, 'There are no facts, only interpretations.' Here are my interpretations.

When the contract for the building of the Pavarotti Music Centre was agreed, the construction company offered a gift. It was accepted by two of my colleagues, Bill Leeson and Mike Terry, and they told me about it in the pub. I was shocked and informed them that, if the money was accepted, I would report this to the War Child trustees. I had to carry out my threat.

February 5th, 1997 – At the trustee meeting I argued that Bill had been under immense pressure and that this should be taken into account when making any decision about his future. I had a loyalty to him because he'd gone through a lot with me when starting War Child and had been more willing than me to risk his life in Sarajevo. As far as Mike was concerned, I argued that dismissing him at this point would delay the project that the charity's reputation was resting on.

As a condition of them staying in War Child, Bill and Mike had to write apologies for taking the money and Mike was required to produce a letter from Hydrogradnja, acknowledging return of the 'gift', a sum of £15,000.[1] Mike was also informed that his involvement in future projects would be 'restricted' and that he must cut his links with War Child after completion of the Centre.[2]

In the office, those who knew about the kickback didn't seem to have any problems with it. Bill had a charisma which I was immune to. Others weren't. And alliances are not just made over financial transactions, but over more personal and intimate relations. I was the outsider and felt more and more uncomfortable working with Bill and my colleagues. I decided that I would be better off in Mostar, looking after the future of the new Centre.

June 1997 – I arrived in Mostar to become the PMC's first Director. I was left alone. Bill never came near the place, and we didn't communicate in any way. I was told that he was claiming I was manipulative and ill. I had the support of the Centre's staff and, in the UK, the Enos remained solidly behind me.[3]

March 7th, 1999 – I received an anonymous fax informing me that Mike Terry was in breach of the trustees' instructions and was working for War Child again. When I asked the London office if this was true, I received a fax telling me that Mike 'has a part-time consultancy contract with War Child to provide project management services on the Pavarotti & Friends Children's Village programme now underway in Liberia'. I was further assured that his appointment had been 'welcomed by the Pavarotti team in Italy'. This 'team' was Luciano and Nicoletta. Four days later, I had a call from Nicoletta Mantovani which told another story.

March 11th, 1999 (Thursday) – 'David, you must come to New York. Luciano and I are very angry about the situation with War Child. We have received a letter from Bill which is offensive to us. Can you be here on Saturday?'

I booked a flight for the next day on Swissair from Sarajevo to New York, via Zurich.

March 12th, 1999 – An hour and a half before setting out on the mountain road to the airport, 130 kilometres away, I realised that the documents I would need to show to Pavarotti and Nicoletta were in London. I rang my partner, Anne, and asked her to fax them to me. She said she'd have to find the file and go to the internet café, a 15-minute walk away. I knew, from past experience, that the fax lines to Bosnia were often jammed.

'Mr Vilson, I am Nečko. I am not Formula One. Time for airplane is running out.'

Nečko, my driver, was one of my closest friends in Mostar, but he always reverted from David to 'Mr Vilson' when matters were critical.

'Nečko, we have to wait for the fax to come through.'

'I am sure United States of the Americas has fax machines.'

'We have to wait. No one but you must know where I'm going, otherwise it will get back to London. The documents can't arrive after I'm gone.'

Nečko pointed to the clock above my desk. 'You can hear that. It ticks. I am simple Bosnian, but I can tell the time. We do not have the time.'

The fax machine bleeped. 'It's coming, Nečko.'

Too slowly, it disgorged seven pages. I stapled them together and we ran to the car.

With minutes to spare, I made the Zurich flight. The transatlantic plane took off for New York at 5pm. It climbed to 7,000 metres and suddenly dropped. There were no screams. Complete silence.

The silence of fear is terrifying. After a long few minutes, the pilot told us that we'd made a rapid descent to 2,000 metres. This was, he said, because we'd lost cabin pressure. We would have to circle south Germany while he got advice from the engineers in Zurich.

I watched the TV screen as we passed over Konstanz, Ulm, Munich, Ulm, Konstanz, Ulm, Munich. Three hours later, the pilot said we were returning to Zurich and mustn't worry when we saw ambulances and fire engines on each side of the plane as we landed.

March 13th, 1999 – Transferred to another plane, we arrived at Newark Airport at 7am Eastern Standard Time – 12 hours late. I had just enough time to book into a hotel in midtown Manhattan before my appointment with the Pavarottis at their apartment overlooking Central Park.

When I got there, they told me about Bill's letter and said that they were unsure how to answer it. I explained the whole sorry history. For the next three days, we worked out a plan for the future of the PMC. Both Nicoletta and Pavarotti encouraged me to go to London as soon as I could to sort matters out at War Child. I was assured of their support.

They were both lovely and Pavarotti was fun to be with. He sang to me while I helped Nicoletta with an article she was writing in English. I was their guest for lunch and dinner. On the second day, Pavarotti told me that Elton John lived in the apartment above. 'Would you like to meet him?'

I said I would love to. Pavarotti picked up the phone. 'Elton, come and have tea with us.' He put down the receiver. 'Sorry, David, he is busy. Next time.'

As I said my goodbyes, I left the documents with them.

March 16th, 1999 – At Zurich airport I called Terri Robson, Pavarotti's manager, to tell her how well things had gone in New York.

'What have you done, David? Luciano and Nicoletta are furious with you.'

The phone went dead. I had no more Swiss Francs to continue the call.

Everything had gone so well. Why were they angry? I was in shock, but there was nothing I could do until I got back to Mostar.

It was midnight when I arrived in Sarajevo. Nečko was waiting to collect me. 'Welcome back to the beautiful Bosnia.'

'Drop me at the office,' I said.

'It will be at three o'clock. Even we Bosnians sleep at three o'clock.'

'The office, please, Nečko.'

Even though I was exhausted, I knew I would have the answer there to Terri's *What have you done, David?*

March 17th, 1999 – On my desk was a fax. It was hard to read as this was its third journey through the ethers. It was a covering note Anne had scribbled to me and which I had stapled to the documents I'd left with Pavarotti. Because of my dramatic outward flight, I'd never read it. She sent me her love for my visit to 'the fat man and his canary'.

Everyone at War Child London had a nickname: Bill's was 'God', I was 'Spreadsheet Man' and Anne was 'Madame Tongue'.[4] The disrespectful name that Bill and Mike called the Maestro was the 'Fat Man'. Anne explained to me later that she couldn't mention Pavarotti by name because I had told her no one must know where I was going.

The fat man and his canary. It was this phrase that had been underlined. Nicoletta had written at the bottom of the fax. 'Luciano and I thought we could trust you.'

Whistleblower

April 9th, 1999 – Despite that fax, Nicoletta contacted Brian
and asked him to help Terri Robson set up a meeting of the
Patrons with the War Child Trustees. Brian was there with
Tom Stoppard; Terri Robson represented Pavarotti. Tim
Spencer was there as chairman of the Board of Trustees.
Brian informed the meeting that he had a letter signed by
Pavarotti, Tom, Brent Hansen and himself. It expressed lack of
confidence in War Child London.

It was agreed that Bill be 'retired', that a new Chief
Executive be appointed and that all Pavarotti projects be
placed under the control of non-UK War Child offices which
were War Child Italy, Netherlands and Canada.

Bill and the London office ignored all this. The Trustees
were already fed up with Bill's actions and behaviour,
frustrated that he would not even attend their meetings. Most
of them resigned. The old Trustees were replaced with Kate
Buckley and Laura Johnson-Graham.

May 9th, 1999 – A month later, Brian Eno wrote to Tim
Spencer to let him know that the Patrons had been informed
of the resignations of 'nearly the entire Board' and laid the
blame on Tim's failure 'to appreciate the severity of the
current situation and to take the necessary actions agreed
upon between the Board and the Patrons at our joint meeting
of 9th April.'[1]

Bill now began to peddle the view that the charity could
dispense with its Patrons. He told *The Sunday Times*, 'I would
like to phase celebrities out of War Child completely and
let the work the charity does speak for itself. We suddenly

became fashionable with all sorts of undesirables, more interested in promoting their flagging careers than doing anything worthwhile.'[2]

Pavarotti had handed over millions to War Child. Brian not only helped plan the Centre, but visited Mostar on numerous occasions to give workshops. Tom Stoppard came to the opening and had helped publicise our diabetic aid project. When Bill and I were broke, he'd sent us both money. Brian and his wife, Anthea, had been responsible for three fundraising events in London which had raised hundreds of thousands of pounds for the charity.

I was exhausted and depressed. I was proud of our achievements and felt part of a great team in Mostar, but the Centre was now running on empty. I was having to sack staff and cut wages. I was now at the lowest point in my life. Anne was far away and my only support was the young people who were shaping the Centre and its future. I had a constant stream of visitors from the London office who seemed intent on trying to get me to resign. 'You need a rest, David', 'You are ill', 'You drink too much'. One War Child visitor took advantage of my absence in Sarajevo and went through my office files to try and 'dig the dirt' on me.

I did my best to keep the Centre going and started chasing funding possibilities. I even went to Strasbourg to visit the European Development Fund. On this visit I passed through London for a few days and had to work from home because I had been frozen out of the War Child office. These were pre-email days and I had no fax. I had to pretend that I was still in Mostar and gave out my contact details there. I could hardly tell the EU that I was working from home as an 'exile' from my own NGO. Under such difficult circumstances, and working from my attic bedroom, I am proud to say that I managed to secure a grant for the PMC.

October 10th, 1999 – I resigned as Director and returned to London. I'd been told that moves were under way to remove me altogether from the charity. My administrator, Amela Sarić, was appointed in my place and one of her first acts was to write to the charity's Trustees to defend me. In her letter she offered to come to London and speak to them.[3] She was wasting her time.

October 22nd, 1999 – The only communication that followed was not a reply to Amela, but a letter to me from Kate Buckley, the new Chair of Trustees and a partner at the large city lawyers, Allen and Overy. She invited me to attend a Trustee Meeting on November 1st to 'explore your future role within the charity'.

November 1st, 1999 – At that meeting, exploration was not on the agenda. Kate announced that, in her view, I should be sacked. Meanwhile, the Trustees had advertised and recruited a new CEO, Raymond Chevalier. Bill had resigned as War Child Director, but still remained working for the charity. I had a meeting with Raymond and, afterwards, wrote him a letter expressing my frustrations.[4] I needn't have bothered since Raymond was in the post for less than two months. He wrote to the Trustees from Thailand to inform them he'd resigned.

January 30th, 2000 – A Sunday meeting with Brian and he showed me the draft of a letter he was writing which he wanted the other Patrons to sign. In it, he expressed frustration that no fundamental changes had taken place, that funding for the PMC was in danger, and that there was 'resistance within War Child to support the Pavarotti projects and to produce answers to serious financial questions'.[5]

One of these questions related to the £140,000 royalties from the song 'Miss Sarajevo'. On behalf of the artists, U2's record company had asked for this to be sent directly to the PMC.[6] The Centre never received this money.

February 10th, 2000 – Kate Buckley called a Trustee meeting, and they were presented with Brian's letter, now co-signed by Luciano Pavarotti, Sir Tom Stoppard, David Bowie, Juliet Stevenson and Brent Hansen. There were four trustees present: Kate, Laura Johnson-Graham, John Gaydon and Anthea Eno. John and Anthea argued for respecting the wishes of the Patrons.[7]

As Chair, Kate Buckley said that I should be sacked, and that they had no other choice than 1) to organise a split in defence of the London office or 2) to close the charity down altogether. Three days later, Anthea resigned.[8]

February 23rd, 2000 – the Trustees met again and John Gaydon argued for the closure of the London office since the Trustees were unwilling to consider the terms as set out in the Patrons' letter to them.

Once again, Kate argued for my sacking. At this point, John resigned. Kate introduced a new Trustee, Peter Collins, and these three, Kate, Laura and Peter went on to agree the termination of my contract.

Brian Eno, Luciano Pavarotti, Tom Stoppard, Juliet Stevenson, David Bowie and Brent Hansen were informed that their letter had been ignored and that I had been sacked. Their resignations followed. A few days later I received a letter from Juliet Stevenson:

'Well, what a terrible story this is, really. An eye-opener for me. I feel for you so much – thinking back to the early days of the charity and all that you placed at its service, and your passion and drive … The work stands, and that is the important thing … I do feel, incidentally, that this story should be revealed at some point, though I am aware of the potential hazards … Best wishes, Juliet.'

I would be interested to know whether in legal/ethical terms a new Trustee, knowing nothing of the history of the charity and never having met me, was justified in voting for my redundancy. It seems to me to go against the laws of natural justice. Judges and juries without sight of, or sound from, the accused.

When I broached this in a phone call with Kate, she said that Peter Collins had abstained. I pointed out that his presence in the room allowed the meeting to be quorate and, therefore, his abstention was equivalent to a positive vote for my sacking.

February 29th, 2000 – I received my formal redundancy letter.[9] Kate apologised for taking so much time to write to me, but said she had wanted to hear whether Raymond thought there was a role for me in War Child. Her opinion that I should be made redundant was strengthened, she argued curiously, by Anthea's resignation as a Trustee and the reduced role of the Patrons. In addition, it was 'clear' that I had a strained relationship with the War Child office and that I should have sought 'authority' for taking the trip to meet with Pavarotti in New York.[10]

I was frustrated and angry. I had been sacked and my concerns had been ignored. I had had to leave the PMC, which was now in crisis. I had been told that I had no role in War Child by people who knew nothing about me or what I had achieved.

To add insult to injury, I had just found out that Bill and I had been given the 'Men of the Year Award' by the World Awards organisation in Vienna.[11] The first I knew of it was when a friend sent me a photo of a smiling Bill accepting the award in Vienna's Yard Castle from the President of World Awards, Mikhail Gorbachev.

I rang them and asked why I'd not been invited to Vienna with Bill. They told me that the War Child office had said I was 'unavailable'.

Dorothy Byrne of Channel 4 TV introduced me to David Hencke at the *Guardian*. He, together with Channel 4 News, set about a joint investigation into War Child.

January 10th, 2001 – After months of work, the *Guardian*'s front-page article appeared under the title, 'Stars Quit Charity in Corruption Scandal'. The opening words, 'Luciano Pavarotti has walked out of the high-profile overseas aid charity, War Child UK, with five other celebrity patrons after discovering that its co-founder had taken a bribe from contractors building a prestigious music centre named after him in Bosnia.'[12]

This was accompanied by an editorial which was critical of the Charity Commission's role.[13] That night, as the lead story on Channel 4 news, Jon Snow interviewed the new Chair of Trustees, Rosie Boycott. She broke down in tears when asked for her opinion about the problems at War Child.

She only had herself to blame. One of the Trustees who had resigned was Berry Ritchie, ex-editor of the 'Prufrock' column in the *Sunday Times*. He had phoned Rosie when he heard that she had agreed to become a Trustee and would be the new Chair. She had been dismissive of his warnings that she was about to land herself in a bed of thorns.

I am often asked whether the War Child saga has left its scars. Of course it has, but I know there is a law applying to whistleblowers that requires a formula. It goes like this. The whistleblower discovers wrongdoing in an organisation. He/she is faced with ostracism, claims that they are ill and need to rest. If that tactic isn't successful, they are informed they should retire and when that is not possible, sacked. The wrongdoers will then hide behind conventions and legalities to prevent information leaks. Finally, the whistleblower will achieve minor reforms, the wrongdoers will be exposed, but it will be too late. The wrong has been done, the wronged have been sacked, and the wrongdoers have quietly manoeuvred themselves back into positions of influence.

I only managed to get exposure because I had powerful people behind me, the front page of a national newspaper and the lead story on Channel 4 News.

Looking back, without Bill my life would have been different and not necessarily better. I could not have made the BBC *Arena* film and would never have started War Child. He was responsible for giving me the confidence to continue with the charity when it all seemed hopeless. I was grateful to him for making numerous journeys to Sarajevo and Mostar. He was a braver man than me.

I still remain puzzled as to what drove him. Was it altruism derailed by a moment's lapse? I know that he wrestled with his conscience. Just before I left for Mostar in 1997, we went for a drink. With tears in his eyes, he told me he was proud of me. I never asked him why. It was a curious moment and out of character. What roles did others play in influencing his decisions? On this I have only conjecture, rumour and hearsay.

I recently watched a documentary on the relationship between German film director Werner Herzog and the actor Klaus Kinski. Kinski was subject to violent mood swings which came close at times to murderous intent. At the other extreme, he was affable, humorous, generous, even loveable.

When Herzog was making *Aguirre, Wrath of God* in the Peruvian jungle, Kinski exploded and threatened to walk off the set. Herzog drew a gun, telling him that it contained nine bullets. Eight for Kinski and the last one for himself. The actor stayed.

Bill was my Kinski. It used to amuse me how often he used the first person when talking with people about the setting up of War Child, even when I was present.[14] As recently as a 2010 interview with Ed Vulliamy in the *Observer*, Bill said of the founding of War Child, 'I wanted to come up with something that didn't sound like your established charity.'[15]

Over the years, I got to feel like Trotsky, airbrushed out of the story.

As with most of us, Bill had good and bad in him in equal measure. It's a pity that he has to take the brunt of my criticisms because there were others close to him who did not have that equal measure. I have a self-imposed D-Notice which prevents me from saying more about them.

RESURRECTION AND RETURN

'But this is how it had to be. And you have your own life to live.'

Leo Tolstoy

Tie a Knot

When I left Mostar, I was concerned that the Centre and its work was in trouble, starved of funds and neglected by the charity which had set it up.

Although I had resigned as Director of the PMC and been sacked from War Child, I was not yet ready to abandon the project. Ringing in my ears were the words of the director of a street children's project in Soweto, telling me that he never gave up hope. 'When you get to the end of a rope,' he said, 'tie a knot and hold on.' In addition to Anne, my knots were Eugene Skeef, Jane Glitre and Hiroshi Kato.

I had found out during my visit to South Africa in 1996 that Eugene was widely respected amongst political and cultural activists. When he arrived in Mostar, he quickly replicated this reputation in Bosnia-Herzegovina.

Eugene came to London in 1980 as a political refugee from South Africa. Since that time, he'd been working at the Oval House Music School as composer, instrument maker and workshop leader. He brought these skills with him to the PMC where he was central to my dream of an international network of music centres that would seek to bring reconciliation to divided communities.

Like me, Eugene retained his connections with Mostar after he left Bosnia. He returned there with his Umoya organisation which he set up in 2003. Working with Oha, they started a production of Udu clay drums. Eugene hoped to have production stretching from Nigeria, where they originate, to Bosnia.

Today, Eugene is part of an international peace-building

initiative called Quartet of Peace. He recently composed 'Uxolo', specially commissioned for two violins, viola and cello. The title means forgiveness in Zulu and honours South Africa's four Nobel laureates: Nelson Mandela, Dr Albert Luthuli, F. W. de Klerk and Archbishop Desmond Tutu.

When we were both working in Mostar, I introduced Eugene to Jane Glitre whom I had got to know after her visits to Sarajevo in the war. She had made a number of journeys into besieged Sarajevo with a group of women who called themselves Through Heart to Peace. On one trip she walked over Mount Igman, through Serbian lines, helping to take one of Frederick Franck's steel sculptures, called 'Unkillable Human', into the besieged city. An act of solidarity.[1]

Jane had helped out at the opening of the PMC and was going to be an active collaborator of mine. From 1996 until its closure eleven years later, she ran the Spitz, a music venue at the heart of London's Old Spitalfields Market which hosted concerts featuring the best in cutting-edge music. It also had a gallery. I had brought artist Dragan Andjelic from Sarajevo there in 1999 to exhibit his 'Angels' series of paintings.[2]

She and Eugene organised an extraordinary gig there in 2003 featuring Oha and Atilla Aksoj from the PMC, performing with the multi-instrumentalist Tunde Jegede and musicians from Ghana, Jamaica and Nigeria. Eugene then took Oha and Atilla to the Purcell Music School where they ran workshops for their students and for primary school children.

After returning to London from Mostar, I worked as a volunteer at the Spitz and helped Jane organise jazz evenings when she moved to Kings Place.

The Spitz was killed off by another betrayal. One of the most remarkable live-music venues in London replaced by yet another expensive restaurant to fill the bellies of those ever-hungry City bankers.

An early supporter of War Child and its work was the Japanese musician and entrepreneur Hiroshi Kato. When I first met him, Hiroshi was running the European office of the audio speaker company Fujitsu Ten. He had been living in London for over 30 years. He said that he'd arrived in the UK as a Japanese hippy, taking the trail from east to west and that he'd passed western hippies in Afghanistan as they went the other way.

After I'd been sacked from War Child, Hiroshi offered me a job with Fujitsu Ten. While I was working for him, we set up a new charity, Future Trust, to try and continue the work I'd been doing at War Child and at the PMC.

Hiroshi managed to get Japanese funding for 'In Site', a concert we organised at the Centre in October 2000. Performers included Brian Eno, Horace Andy of Massive Attack, Nigel Clarke from Dodgy and artists from Japan, the USA, India and numerous performers from across ex-Yugoslavia.

Now a trustee of Future Trust, Jane was there to help, along with Hideto Watanabe from Hiroshi's London office and Johnny Carmichael who'd been helping run War Child in Italy. The gig was broadcast on Bosnian TV and webcast in Japan. Not only was this an extraordinary event, but it raised enough money to help re-equip the Centre's studio.

Brian Eno said of the concert:

'It worked seamlessly. It was really wonderful – everybody had a great time and it must be the beginning of a new era for the Centre … This is exactly the kind of thing the Centre was set up for – I felt that this was a new bridge built in Mostar, probably more important than any of the other bridges being made there.'

The following year, in August 2001, and now working with Matt Black of Coldcut, Hiroshi and I organised the 'CanDU PirateTV' tour with gigs in Slovenia, Croatia, Bosnia and Serbia. At its heart was an interactive, multimedia circus incorporating the audio and visual talents of Ninja Tune, the pioneers who created and influenced a new generation of DJs. They had developed one of the first programmes to allow the manipulation of visual images as if they were musical instruments.

Arriving in town a day or two before each public performance, the visitors worked with young people who were then invited to take part in the gigs. The workshops were filmed and appeared within hours on six stage screens and 'timed' to the music. Meanwhile, Coldcut's and Ninja Tune's 'Solid Steel' show was syndicated to radio stations en route.

Oha was recruited as the tour manager and dealt with the complex movement of over 20 musicians and crew members across much of the Balkans, working from one mobile phone.

The PMC never collapsed. It just took to the road for a while and, thanks to Oha and his team, today it has returned home.

Neighbours

I have chosen to go to places where my life has been threatened, from bars in Brazil to besieged Sarajevo. But the closest I came to dying was no choice of mine, but back at home in suburban north London.

In August 2014 the President of the Royal College of Psychiatrists, Sir Simon Wessely, told the *Guardian* that two-thirds of psychiatric patients don't endure poor treatment – they get no treatment at all. 'Imagine it was cancer,' he remarked, adding that mental health provision in the UK was 'dangerously close to collapse'.

Anne and I live on the top floor of an Edwardian house. Across the street is a flat occupied by a woman I will call 'Sam'. She is in her mid-forties and has a long history of mental illness. She seems to have been in and out of prison more than in and out of hospital. At least twice a month, there are two, sometimes three, police cars outside her home and usually an ambulance.

Twice, armed police from the Specialist Firearms Unit have turned up. On the first occasion, I was walking home from the shops and saw an officer hiding behind a bush near her flat. He put a finger to his mouth to warn me not to give away his presence. Did he want me to hide behind a bush too?

On the second occasion, I was watching armed cops from my window. Sam turned the corner and walked up to her front door. The police did nothing. After she'd entered the house and closed the door, they rushed it, screaming. She was manhandled into the street.

Sometimes she's taken away in an ambulance and

sometimes in a police car, but every time she's back home that night or the next day. Perhaps poor Sam is used for exercise. 'What have we got on tonight, lads?' Silence. 'Let's go to Sam's.'

Madness, yes. But whose?

Living on the ground floor of our building was an ex-teacher, Roger Sutherland. He was a member of the Scratch Orchestra and a co-founder of Morphogenesis[1]. He also wrote the book *New Perspectives in Music*. He was an eccentric avant-garde composer, but we got on well enough – most of the time. He lived a quiet life and insisted that everyone else did too. He'd complain about the slightest noise, even going so far as to telephone the next-door neighbour when she put her pots and pans away.

The strangest example of his insistence on quiet was on December 31st, 1999. Just before midnight, Anne started to beat her Native American drum to welcome in the Millennium. Almost immediately the phone rang.

'Stop that noise,' Roger shouted. 'I'm trying to sleep!'

I told him my mother had died that day, that it was minutes from New Year and that he should get a life. I then turned the receiver toward the window as the whole of London exploded with fireworks.

Fast forward to four years later. February 5th, 2004, the night of a full moon, the time of month when police, midwives and hospitals acknowledge to be their busiest. I had gone to bed and Anne stayed up to watch *Six Feet Under*.[2] At midnight, she called up the stairs. 'David, I can smell gas.' She was right.

We called the emergency services and then Roger to warn him. Shocked and dazed, we stood at the top of the stairs, watching as firemen entered the building and police questioned him in the corridor below. We were astonished to hear that, after trying to take his own life and endangering ours, he was offered a choice as to what he wanted: the police cells or the Whittington Hospital. Not surprisingly, he chose the hospital.

As the officers escorted him out, he reached to turn on the hall light. A fireman shouted, 'Don't touch that switch. The place will blow!'

I woke up in the early hours to hear the front door opening, but went back to sleep.

Just after 6am, Anne woke me shouting, 'Smoke!'

Coughing, we ran downstairs where the smoke was so thick we couldn't see the bright blue numbers on the oven's digital clock. Anne rang 999 for the second time in six hours as I staggered through the blackness to the street.

Two firemen carried Roger out, naked and smoke blackened. Later we discovered that he had set fire to his foam rubber mattress which gave off cyanide fumes as it burned. For half an hour, I watched as they tried to revive him.

In hospital, he was put on life support. His daughter was told he was brain-dead and made the difficult decision to turn off the machines.

His estranged wife told us later that, in the previous month, she'd made over 50 calls to Roger's GP, desperately trying to get help for him. That the day before his death, he had turned on all the gas rings, trying to kill himself. Something she'd neglected to tell us at the time.

As compassionate as we felt toward Roger and his mental health problems, the reality was that, within the space of six hours, he twice came close to killing us. Our 'pots and pans' neighbours told us that the fire chief told them that the level of gas had been so high that, with one spark, not only our house would have blown up, but also the houses on either side.

Channel 4 TV came to interview us and our MP, Jeremy Corbyn, instigated an investigation as to why Roger had been allowed home in the middle of the night. At the Coroner's hearing, the hospital apologised that they didn't have sufficient resources to section him that night. The police claimed to have come round to us soon after Roger had escaped from A&E to warn us that he was back in the building. They testified that we hadn't answered the doorbell. The police had our telephone number, but their communication's systems didn't seem to have advanced much beyond the days of *Dixon of Dock Green*.

The Coroner ruled that Roger's death was due to 'unknown causes'. It couldn't be ruled as a suicide as Roger's finger marks were found on the wall beside his front door.

I came closer to death in my own home than I did in Sarajevo when I had to run across Sniper's Alley. The moral of this story? Your life can be threatened by wars abroad and by health and welfare cuts at home.

A Place to Go When You Sleep

'There is no longer any life pulsing under his
skin; it has been forced out already to the very
edges of his body, and death is working its way
through him, moving outwards from the centre.
It is already in his eyes … it's still him, but it isn't
really him anymore; his image has faded, become
blurred, like a photographic plate that has had too
many copies made from it. Even his voice sounds
like ashes.'
Erich Maria Remarque, *All Quiet on the
Western Front*

My father doesn't recognise me when I visit. Sometimes he
stares at me, trying to work out who I am and what is going on.
A week before his 101st birthday I arrive and he looks at me,
his face a question mark.

I bend over to kiss his head and ask, 'How are you?'

'Maturing nicely,' he says. 'Your artefact can go on the front
door. When will it be finished?'

'What artefact?'

'I need you to deal with the third man and the others.' He
looks at me. 'I don't know what I'm talking about, nor do you.
We've encouraged toe rags to conceal things. They are people
of doom, but the good will make more effort.'

He skewers me with an intense stare. 'What is it that holds
society together? This hub of ours is not a congealed mass. It's

a pact which we may not like and may want to change. But it is what it is. I'd like you to get all this into a hundred pages. You will do it well. I'll give you every encouragement.' He pulls the sheet higher and frowns. 'You'll need a good director. He or she will emerge. So far you've said sensible things. We don't need prototypes.'

He is quiet for a long time. 'I'm boring you. I needn't mention any names. You know them. They don't need a title.'

A nurse puts her head around the door and asks cheerfully, 'How are you, Ian?'

His hearing and eyesight is poor. He strains to see who she is.

She disappears and another nurse enters with a mug. 'Hello, Dr Ian. A cup of tea?'

Puzzled, he shakes his head in my direction as she puts it on his tray. She leaves the room and he says, 'Now you see them, now you don't. I'm glad I'm at the arse end of life. My family have had enough of me and so have I.' I bend over to kiss him goodbye. 'What day is it?'

'Sunday.'

'Good, one more out of the way. The Good Lord is waiting for them. But they don't know if he's there, or if he's where he's supposed to be.'

My visits to my father remind me that my early years have impressed themselves onto my life. Those Belsen photos in my father's desk are still there. They might have been thrown away, but they are there in my mind. Even the childhood house in Bromley which has long since been torn down.

I have a recurring dream which has repeated itself for decades. They all take place in that house on Westmoreland Road. The people and events are from the present or not so distant past. I may dream about Anne, about Ben and Jonny, Renata's parents, the house on Krk, about Mostar and Sarajevo, but it is all taking place in, or around, that house. Stranger still, whatever the subject of the dream, my parents are always there.

I have no idea what Freud would have made of this, but it reminds me of those cartoon films where a small house sits alone on top of a small planet. The planet is the house and the house is the planet.

I think the house is my filing system, the place which no longer exists, but where I go to try to make sense of my life. Where I try and make sense of everything. Where I pick up the pieces and reassemble them, give them new meaning, or fail to give them meaning at all.

My father can no longer make sense of his life, although I cannot be sure of that because he may still have a place to go to when he sleeps. But he is no longer in control of his life. I sit beside him and wonder if I am, or ever was, in control of mine.

Watching him at the end of his life has made me want to make sense of my own before I, too, become a prisoner of old age. There are so many things I want to ask my father, but there will be no further questions for him; he is already leaving us.

I arrive to see him staring at the window. 'Let go aft,' he says.

I haven't heard that nautical order from him since we sailed together in his dinghy.

'Who are you talking to, Dad?'

Without looking away from the window he answers, 'Paul and Nancy. You know them.'

I don't.

'Listen, you two. I'm not always wise, but on this occasion I am. Let's get going.' He turns his head towards me. 'I am very fond of them, but they are obstinate.'

'Where are you?' I ask.

'At sea and we must keep moving. If we don't, we'll be becalmed.' He raises his voice. 'You two would do well to listen to me. If you don't, I'll leave you here and sail on my own.'

Then he laughs, as though sharing a joke with his shipmates. He turns back to me. 'Thanks for coming, but next time bring soap, rough towels, fresh water and lots of food.'

'Why?'

'Don't ask silly questions. I'm in the Atlantic.' He pauses. 'No, maybe it's the North Sea, but I need supplies.'

I bend down to kiss his head. He smiles and shrugs his skeletal shoulders. I think he knows which sea he is crossing.

My father died on October 15th, 2013, aged 101 and 5 months.[1] One month later, my sisters and I scattered his ashes with those of my mother. Not on the Gower, but at the mill on the river Stour at Sturminster Newton, near Shaftesbury.

Greengrocer,
Vet and Judge

A year later, I had my own dangerous sea to cross. A few days before the end of November 2014, I started behaving strangely. I took a bath and when I'd finished, I annoyed myself by dropping the towel into the tub instead of onto the floor. Later, I pissed on the closed toilet seat. I went to the shops, came home with nothing and couldn't open the front door. I was using the wrong key. I stared at my computer. I had forgotten how to type.

On Sunday, November 30th, Anne and I went to the Victoria and Albert Museum with our friend Sebastian Balfour to see 'Disobedient Objects'. This was an exhibition of radical items from street demonstrations across the world. Hanging from the ceiling was a battered pan lid that had helped bring down the Argentine government in noisy rough-musik demonstrations. There was a slingshot made from the tongue of a shoe that a Palestinian had used against Israeli tanks and homemade shields made to look like book covers that had been carried by protesters in Rome. Students campaigning against austerity cuts in education had confronted the riot squad with Boccaccio's *The Decameron*, Dante's the *Divine Comedy* and George Orwell's *Homage to Catalonia*. The police would be seen to be attacking literature.

It was surreal and my already-muddled head started to spin. I couldn't read the text that accompanied the photos and displayed objects. With a splitting headache, I had to sit down. Was I finally being driven mad by radical politics?

We went to the café and Sebastian bought us tea. After eating the scones, I shocked the two of them by pouring my tea, not into my cup, but into the tiny strawberry jam jar. While we were there, Sebastian's wife, Gráinne, rang him, and when he told her how I was behaving, she insisted I go to A&E immediately.

On my way to the Whittington Hospital in north London, I tried to exit the Underground using my mobile phone instead of swiping my travel card. Even I realised something was seriously wrong.

In triage they were sufficiently alarmed to give me a CT scan. It wasn't political subversion that was scrambling my brain; it was a subdural haematoma, a slow veinous bleed in the head. There are two types, acute and chronic. The most serious is caused by trauma when an accident causes rapid bleeding to fill the area between the outer layer of the brain – the meninges – and the brain itself. This happened to Michael Schumacher and Natasha Richardson. Mine was the less serious chronic subdural haematoma.

You don't have to be a racing driver, skier or cyclist to get subdural haematomas. They can occur after a minor head injury, especially among the elderly, when small veins between the surface of the brain and its outer covering stretch and tear. Blood then collects below the dura, a tough tissue that encloses the brain. This creates a competition between blood and brain and when blood wins, the brain is moved off-centre. In severe cases, the lower part of the brain can become affected which is a dangerous situation because the brain stem is where respiration is controlled.

If an operation is required for either type of haematoma, blood has to be drained to alleviate pressure on the brain. Douglas Katz, Assistant Professor of Neurology at Boston School of Medicine, has said '[a] person may appear fine initially because the mass of blood in the head is expanding and there isn't too much pressure on the brain yet.' He refers to this as 'Talk and Die' syndrome. Others call it 'Walk and Die'. I was doing both at the time I was advised to get to A&E.

I was told that when a bed became available, I would be moved to one of two specialist hospitals for neurosurgery: Royal London or National Hospital for Neurology, Queen Square.

Over the next three days I became even more confused. Alarmed at my deterioration, Anne kept asking the Whittington when I was to be transferred, but Gráinne managed to discover the names and numbers of the bed managers at both hospitals and pestered them to take me as soon as possible. I later found out that Dorothy Byrne too had been actively pressing my case.

On December 3rd I was admitted to Queen Square and told I would be having an operation the next morning to drain two massive blood lakes on the left side of my brain. This was cancelled four times because of emergency cases. Anne refused to leave my bedside, afraid that if she did, I would be taken to theatre and she wouldn't be able to accompany me. Afraid that it might be the last time she saw me, she spent the whole day slumped over my bed rail.

I was operated on late that evening. When I woke up in the ward, I was speaking and functioning normally, but with the additional fashion accessory of a square, flat plastic bag. It was attached by tubing to one of the holes drilled into my head to drain post-op saline solution and any remaining blood.

But recovery, like life, is not always straightforward. Twenty-four hours after the operation, I had an unexpected relapse. I was unable to remember my name or date of birth. I dreaded the nurses who came constantly to take my blood pressure. Their first question was always, 'Where are you?' I would try and work out my answer as I saw them approaching.

I couldn't sleep and lay awake trying to work out what was going on. A cup of tea would be nice, except achieving it was difficult. I would walk towards the night desk, practising the words I needed. 'Please, can I have a cup of tea?' By the time

I reached the nurses' station, I couldn't get the words out, but they got used to me. As I stood there in silence, the duty nurse would smile, 'Go back to bed and I'll bring you some.'

I was now so confused I had no idea how to clean my teeth or use my mobile. When I went to the toilet, I couldn't remember if it was wipe, shit, stand or sit, wipe, shit. It was all very scary.

I could only say 'Yes' or 'No' to questions. Words on a page no longer made sense. I had lost the ability to speak in sentences or to read. A speech therapist came to my bedside with word exercises. At first, I was unable to read single-syllable words like 'book' and 'cold'. 'Peanut butter' was an impossibility.

I was given a sheet with pictures and the words underneath so patients who couldn't speak could point at an image to indicate what they needed to communicate. On the first row in the first box was a figure holding his head. The text underneath said, 'I'm in pain.' I struggled to decipher 'pain'. Stumbling over the tangle of letters, I finally managed to pronounce 'pain' phonetically. When the therapist asked me to read the next box with four figures holding hands that said 'I want my family', I repeated, 'Pain'.

My Brazilian guitar teacher, Deicola Neves, brought his guitar and played *bossa nova* to the ward. He left the instrument with me but, when I tried to play, I couldn't remember a single chord.

Anne knew more about my condition than I did. When she signed the consent form, just before my operation, they told her the procedure carried risks – seizures, infection, the possibility that I would not improve. Being left in a vegetative state, even death. Later she told me that, while I was in the operating theatre, she went to the hospital chapel and lit four candles for me: one from her and three on behalf of my sons and grandson. She then returned to the ward, staring at the empty space where my bed had been. She says she hoped for the best, but was preparing herself for the worst.

I don't recall being frightened from the moment I arrived at the Whittington to the moment I left Queen Square three weeks later. I wasn't even fearful when they took me to the operating theatre. I remember thinking, They're just taking me for a check-up downstairs. Anne has a different opinion and tells me that, as they wheeled me away, I had the eyes of a frantic bronco.

At time of death it is said that the body releases chemicals that ease the mind from feelings of panic and fear. Perhaps this also happens when your skull is about to be opened. My consultant told me that patients facing brain surgery somehow manage to hold themselves together to be able to get through it. She added that patients who worry the least take longer to recover because the mind which fights off fear at the most critical of moments only delays the trauma, but cannot avoid it altogether.

Four days after the operation and with no improvement, my consultant stood at the foot of my bed. She was unhappy with my progress because my ability to speak and read had deteriorated so rapidly. I was told I might have to have a second, more invasive operation, and that this would involve substantial risk. Anne asked what was involved. She explained that a window of bone would have to be cut out of my skull so the brain could be scraped. This procedure would remove the old, dried blood from previous bleeds in the hope that my ability to read and speak would be restored. There was, she said, no guarantee of success. Anne asked for the time frame before a decision was made.

The consultant answered, 'Two days'.

As soon as she left my bedside, I indicated to Anne to hand me the sheet the speech therapist had given me that morning. I had been able to read one word, pain. Miraculously, I slowly read out to Anne all the captions under all the pictures.

I have no explanation for this, except that a possible, more dangerous operation unlocked something in my mind. Without any other intervention, I began to speak and read. Within two hours, I was talking reasonably, and four days later I was home.

In my ward of six patients there was a greengrocer, a judge, a follower of Hari Krishna, a white Zimbabwean and an employee of Coca-Cola. I became friends with all of them, except the judge. The greengrocer lived by the principle of the Sufi, Abu Sa'id, who said, 'Whatever you have in your hand – give it. Whatever is to be your fate – face it.' He had faced two operations to remove a tumour on his pituitary gland. Four days after his discharge, he came to visit the ward and to give each of us a sack of tangerines.

The Hari Krishna kept offering me his vegan food. We agreed that, in the New Year, all things being well, we would walk together on Hampstead Heath.

Only the white African was a puzzle. In his 70s, he had served in the Rhodesian army and had then been a welder and businessman. He was nostalgic for lost 'Empire'. But he spoke a number of African languages, was adored by the nurses – many of them African – and was always sympathetically curious about their lives. He shared with me my dislike of the judge.

The Coca-Cola man was the only one in the ward with no bandages. When Anne worked up the courage to ask him why, he said he'd had a tumour behind his eye successfully removed through his nose. He told her this when he brought her a Costa coffee after seeing her looking distressed before my operation. He'd noticed that she hadn't left my bedside once. I warmed to him when he told me that he travelled the world for the company, but always refused to go to Israel. Then added that, although he drank 'American champagne', he knew it was a poison.

The judge treated the nurses as if they were on trial. Each day we were given a long menu (the food was excellent) and asked to choose our lunch and dinner. Once, when they brought the judge pasta, he complained he'd asked for spaghetti. They brought him the menu to show him that spaghetti was not on offer. 'Well, I ordered it,' he said. I wanted to tell him a neurological hospital is not the Ritz.

His wife rang one day and a nurse relayed the message to tell the judge she'd called. The nurse then asked him to tell his wife not to be so miserable because 'Life is short'.

In a neighbouring ward there was Bill, an old soldier, officer class, who kept trying to escape. He would shuffle into our ward and be obnoxious to the nurses who had to follow him around to prevent him from falling or straying too far. He would physically and verbally abuse them, not caring that he was often taking several of them away from their duties.

Just after my op, when I was able to speak, he passed my bed with three black nurses and muttered that he was about to be cannibalised. I got out of bed, prepared to hit him. One of the nurses warned me off and said they weren't allowed to touch him so I told him, 'Get the fuck out of here and stop insulting the staff.'

The greengrocer told me that Bill was suffering after his operation. Maybe, but he had clearly been an unpleasant man pre-op. Scarce NHS resources were being used to guard him.

The nurses and cleaners came from Zimbabwe, Nigeria, Uganda, India, the Philippines, Poland, Lithuania, Northern Ireland, England, Columbia, Spain, Portugal. The surgeons were from Italy, China, Ireland, the Philippines and north London. The surgeon who saved my life was from Nigeria. All of them were incredibly skilled, friendly and supportive.

Friends sent me flowers, fruit and cards and I received daily phone calls from my son in Barcelona. Lapsed Catholics lit candles, an Iraqi atheist friend who was in Tunisia made a Friday visit to the mosque to pray for me. Anne's sister-in-law in New Mexico invited 400 US Reiki practitioners to send me, a complete stranger, distant healing.

When I was well enough to leave the ward, Anne took me to the chapel where she'd spent an hour each day between the morning and afternoon visiting hours. On entering I saw a notice saying that 'This chapel is for all faiths'. It should be changed to '... all faiths and none'.

On a table near a bank of candles, there is a visitors' book.

In that book of hope and despair one inscription read 'Thanks to all gods and goddesses and the NHS.' Another was, 'Mum was always heading for heaven. But please, God, not yet'.

I wrote my own message. In place of the gratitudes to God, Jesus and Allah, mine said 'Let us thank the NHS'. I have no idea where I am heading but, wherever it is, my departure has been delayed. I am not lost at sea yet.

No Wrecks and
Nobody Drowned

La Torre de Dalt is a large *mas* (a Catalan traditional farmhouse) in the hills above Girona. It's the place where, for the last six years, Anne has run her annual writing retreats. When her course ended in June 2015, I hired it for a second week and invited friends and relatives to join me. I told them this was a celebration for my 70th year, but it also marked the completion of *Left Field* – bringing together some of those who have played their part in my life and without whom I would have had no memoir. One or two played their part in keeping me alive to be there at all.

Among the guests were Norman Boyer (Canford and Argentina), Eileen Davis, (Essex University), Sue Smith (college teaching friend), Anthea Norman-Taylor, Jane Glitre and Dorothy Byrne (War Child years), Liz and Peter Huhne (family), Alice Kilroy (Roger Sutherland's former wife), John Trent and Eva Zimmermann (neighbours from Muswell Hill and whose two daughters grew up with my two sons), Manuela Beste (early reader of a *Left Field* draft), Lee Pennington (La Torre chef and Mancunian wit) and Debbie Reid (sous-chef). Oha Maslo and Teo Krilic (my two Mostar sons) drove through the night from Bosnia with two small children to join us.

I had worried how these people from my past and present would mix: a political banner maker, a businessman, a bereavement counsellor, musicians, writers and journalists. I need not have. Widely and in some cases, wildly, disparate people spent the week talking, eating, drinking, walking and partying together. No one there will forget how we all fell in love with Alice as she encouraged us all, willingly or not, towards the Revolution.

We had *tai chi* classes, table tennis championships, swimming and, with a few writers there from the week before, writing workshops. I was told later that the *tai chi* with added yoga had been organised to help 'ground' me.

The writers soon became known as the 'murmuration of writers' as they met in corners of the building to create new work or read excerpts from their novels and poems. They seemed to swoop through the building like birds. In the evenings, during their 'open mic' nights, they read their work and invited the rest of us to join them.

Oha apologised for turning down their invitation to hear them: 'As soon as I see the first comma,' he told me, 'I go into a coma.' If I'd told him that one person was writing a novel about an unsuccessful whorehouse closing down, he might have forgotten his problems with punctuation marks.

In any case, his apology was adopted by Julian Herbert, one of the poets there, as the opening phrase for his paean to the week:

Comma coma?
Trace back through castles,
Until, until they're in the sky,
And we hold hands together,
While we fly.

We had musical nights and talent nights. Teo played guitar while Oha joined him on the cajón drum. He sang 'Na Klepeći Nanulama'.

Peter recited Marriott Edgar's 'The Lion and Albert' – made famous by Stanley Holloway and set in Blackpool where 'there was no wrecks and nobody drownded'.

La Torre looks across at the Cap de Creus above Cadaqués

where Dali had his summer home. Some guests visited his museum in Figueres, but they didn't need to go there to experience the surreal.

The week took on a weirdly wonderful quality when Oha told me that the nine-man Balkan rock group Dubioza Kolektiv were coming by. They had been gigging in Spain and were en route from Barcelona to France, on a tour which was to end at the Glastonbury Festival. When someone asked them where they were from, they answered – from practically every country of ex-Yugoslavia. 'What was that war all about?' said Mario. 'Here we are all together again.' With funky haircuts and dressed in black, they didn't touch the bottle of whisky they had brought for me, but drank tea and coffee and ate dainty biscuits.

The whisky was emptied that evening, but with no help from me. I am no longer allowed to drink much alcohol. This was a great surprise to earlier drinking partners, Oha and Teo in particular. They shook their heads in bafflement each time I turned down an offer of another beer or glass of wine.

The only advantage of not joining in, apart from staying alive, was that I was able to talk a bit more sense and on Lee Pennington's night off, manage to barbeque for 35 people without burning anything.

One of the things about getting old is that you sleep less. Perhaps nature is compensating you for diminishing your time left on the planet. 'Hey. Wake up. Make the most of what you have left.'

I woke up each morning in time to see the sun rise.

On the last morning I found Jane up as well. She told me that I said, 'There is always a sense of bereavement at the end of a holiday, but I have been feeling this every day.'

The death of my father, my illness and brief touch with death and now an upsetting family misunderstanding.

On the final night, Sue gave me a notebook with her drawings of La Torre, Manuela read her 'Thanks for the Memory' adapted from Leo Robin's and Ralph Rainger's poem and set to the music of Bob Hope's theme tune. 'Thanks for the memories, Of lunch from twelve to four and oh, so so much more, The dishes piled sky high, no matter how we try. By the way, what happened to that last huge dirty pot?'

Maureen Larkin composed a 'haiku' for me, which pretty well sums up my life:

70 miles speeding,
The cops have not caught me yet,
No point braking now.

HOOPTEDOODLES

Our lives are only chronological in that we think time is ordered into past, present and future and that events fit neatly into that timescale. *Left Field* has moved along that continuum until now. What follows are the parts of my life that can't easily be slotted into date order.

My wife, Anne, suggested that I call them 'Hooptedoodles'. Hooptedoodle is a term first used by John Steinbeck in his novel *Sweet Thursday*, when he wanted to include stories which didn't neatly fit into the logic of the rest of the book.

'Sometimes,' Steinbeck said, 'I want a book to break loose with a bunch of hooptedoodle – spin up some pretty words maybe or sing a little song with language.' But he goes on to say that the reader doesn't have to read them: 'I don't want hooptedoodle to get mixed up with the story.'

So you don't have to read my hooptedoodles either, but here they are and one of them isn't even mine. Linda McCartney asked to read Anne's 'Behind God's Back'. I'll never know for sure, but I think it was the reason why she donated 22 tonnes of veggie burgers to War Child.

Ships at Sea

One cold November Saturday morning in 1960 I was standing outside Bromley Library, the CND symbol proudly self-sewn on the back of my donkey-jacket. I was with a friend selling *Peace News*. Two men ran across the street shouting 'Bloody yids' and beat us up. They were from the British Movement, forerunners of the British National Party. They were probably at the library to return *Mein Kampf*.

With a black eye, a swollen knee and 'Bloody yids' ringing in my ears, I tracked down the Zionist Federation and bought a dozen yellow Star of David badges. The following Saturday my friend and I wore them and gave one away with each of the five copies of *Peace News* we sold that day. One of the fascists came back to harass us, but this time he just shouted obscenities. He wasn't brave enough to attack two pacifists on his own.

After being beaten up, my father supported me in my efforts to help change the world, but advised me never to be alone on the streets. My mother shook her head each time she saw me put on my jacket to head out to the High Street. 'What if my friends see you?'

'I'll try and sell them *Peace News*.'

'Why are you such a rebel? You're another Uncle Bill.'

Uncle Bill was my grandfather Rees's brother. He never had any money and used to tramp around south Wales. When he was desperate, he'd telephone Rees and demand £50. A huge sum in those days. If Rees refused, Uncle Bill would threaten to stand outside Briton Ferry steelworks selling matches, a sign around his neck, *I AM THE GENERAL MANAGER'S BROTHER*.

'Did he get the £50?' I asked.

My mother laughed. 'Of course he did. Every time.'

'Did you like Uncle Bill?'

She smiled. 'I adored him.'

At the height of the Cold War, nuclear weapons were to be deployed at five bases in Britain. In 1961, CND organised a weekend of protests at all five. I told my mother I was going to the West End to see *The Guns of Navarone*, but headed to the demonstration at RAF Ruislip in north-west London. I arrived to see thousands of people with placards and even ladders to scale the perimeter fence. Though I had no ladder, I was held in a police van for four hours.

This was my first arrest. Aged 16. My incarceration lasted a lot longer than *Navarone* so I rang from Ruislip station to tell my parents not to worry. My mother answered and I heard her shouting at my father, 'Ian, I blame you for this.'

Soon after Ruislip, a police inspector turned up at our house. He wanted to question me about a march I was helping to co-ordinate as secretary of South London Youth CND. 'Are you the organiser?' he asked.

'I'm one of them.'

'What is your role?'

I was being introduced to page one of the police training manual: locate the leader.

I said nothing, but my mother tapped him on the arm. 'He'll get over this,' she said. 'He's still growing up.'

As the front door closed, she pleaded with me. 'David, darling. Why can't you be normal?'

'What is normal, Mum?'

'Why don't you go into politics?'

'I am into politics.'

'Banning the bomb isn't politics. Why don't you join a party? You could end up in Parliament.'

Ambrose Bierce, the American wit, said that politics is 'a strife of interests masquerading as a contest of principles. The conduct of public affairs for private advantage.' Politics that you 'go into', takes place in a box with shared rules of engagement. If, like me, you believe there is nothing 'shared' about our world, the only place for politics is on the streets, not in a debating chamber full of Right Honourables who barrack and ridicule each other, then go off to have cosy lunches together.

For my mother, my extra-parliamentary activities made me an extremist. But it's like ships at sea. If a fleet of them are sailing together, a lone ship on the horizon is viewed as one which occupies an extreme position. However, from the point of view of the lone ship, you have to be a damn good sailor.

The next year ships were to play an important part in everyone's lives. With the 1962 Cuban Missile Crisis, nuclear war seemed imminent. If the missile-carrying Soviet vessels didn't turn back from Cuba, there would be war. Jackie Kennedy recalled that she insisted on sleeping with her husband – not something she often did. She didn't want to die alone. If she was scared, the rest of us had every right to be.[1]

As a result of the Cuban crisis, the anti-nuclear movement remained the focus of my politics. I read Robert Jungk's *Brighter Than a Thousand Suns*, the horrific telling of the bombing of Hiroshima and Nagasaki, with its account of the shadows of the dead imprinted on the earth. It left me in shock. The book's title is taken from Robert Oppenheimer's words when witnessing the first atomic bomb explosion in July 1945. He quoted the *Bhagavad Gita*, 'Now I am become Death, the destroyer of worlds.'

I started to self-educate myself with all that was not taught at Canford, following Bertrand Russell's axiom that 'Men are born ignorant not stupid. They are made stupid by education.' I read everything: from Marx to Dostoyevsky, from Bertrand Russell's *A History of Western Philosophy* to John Steinbeck's *The Grapes of Wrath*.

In 1966 I moved to Oxford and worked at Oxfam. I decided I wanted to go to university, but didn't have A levels. I took a correspondence course.

Two years later, I was at Essex University studying sociology. On the edge of Colchester, above the muddy River Colne, the half-built campus already seemed half-forgotten. We would change that. May came early for us. On March 17th, 1968, 40,000 people marched to the US embassy in Grosvenor Square to protest the Vietnam war. I helped a friend from the chemistry department make paint bombs, sealed inside plastic milk containers.

My most vivid memory is of linking arms behind a Vietnam Solidarity banner and running to the chorus of 'Ho, Ho, Ho Chi Minh, the NLF is going to win'. There was an attempt by anarchists to substitute this with, 'Hot chocolate, drinking chocolate.'

Few of our paint bombs made it onto the embassy walls and I watched as demonstrators rolled marbles under the horses' hoofs. Some of them were brought down, the horseshoes kicking sparks on the tarmac.

Two months later, the Sorbonne was occupied, French students were marching on the Renault factory at Billancourt and we were not going to let Colchester be left behind.

It only needed a spark to set the university alight and it came, appropriately, from the Chemistry Society. In May, scientists from the biological war research facility at Porton Down were invited to address chemistry students at Essex.

Led by David Triesman, 30 of us occupied the lecture hall. The police were called. Triesman was suspended and a General Assembly was organised with a motion to declare ourselves a Free University. Not expecting to win the vote, some of us left the meeting to blockade the Vice Chancellor's office. We used desks, chairs and filing cabinets. These had to be quickly removed when we 'vanguardists' were told that the university had voted in favour of the motion. No need to barricade liberated territory, comrades.

Students and staff met to change syllabuses and, in the Sociology Department, Emile Durkheim's *Division of Labour in Society* was replaced with Karl Marx's *Das Capital*. The head of the Department, Professor Peter Townsend, invited us to critique our lecturers. I argued that was going too far with Maoist self-criticism and that we would let him know if we weren't happy. He looked relieved when the meeting supported me.

I joined a delegation to inform other universities about a demonstration we planned in London against chemical and biological war research. I also had the task of alerting the media. The press considered Essex a flashpoint and asked me how many thousands of students would take to the streets. I stumbled a reply as I wasn't confident that we were going to get the numbers out.

On Sunday, May 26th, the day of the demonstration, it was pouring with rain. The paint from our posters, hastily made in Lincoln's Inn Fields the night before, dripped onto our feet. We were left to shout our slogans to an almost empty Oxford Street.

In some confusion, and in small numbers, we arrived in Whitehall. We banged on the huge front door of the Ministry of Defence. A side door opened and a janitor poked his head out. We handed him our petitions and he said he would pass them on to the 'relevant authority'. There was a brief sit-down in the street and the two mounted Household Cavalrymen at Horse Guards were, we later learned, persuaded by the *Sun*'s photographer to dismount and draw their cuirasses. In the absence of a student riot in the centre of London, the *Sun* had its picture. More *Monty Python* than *Battleship Potemkin*.

A year later the *Sun* got another photo. At the June 1970 General Election, I went to Colchester Town Hall to heckle the deputy leader of the Labour Party, George Brown, about Vietnam. I was sitting in the front row and shouting at him. He climbed off the platform and punched me in the face. The next day George's punch was on the front page of the *Sun* above a headline, 'Up and at 'em, George'.

This time my mother was unconcerned. 'My friends don't read the *Sun*.'

The miners went on strike in 1974. They won a 35 per cent pay increase after successfully closing down the massive coal stockpile at Orgreave in South Yorkshire. But things were going to change for the worse. It started with the defeat of a strike at Grunwicks, a photo-developing works in Willesden, north-west London. In August 1976 its workforce, mostly Asian women, dubbed by the media as 'strikers in saris', walked out over poor conditions and wages.

The dispute lasted two years. The total of over 500 arrests made during the strike was the highest figure in any industrial dispute since the 1926 General Strike.

One Monday morning I was standing on the pavement outside Grunwicks, holding a placard that said *ENOUGH IS ENOUGH*. Suddenly, Special Patrol Group officers attacked us. I was dragged across the street by my hair, bundled into a van, taken to Wembley police station and charged with assaulting a police officer.

A month later, at Willesden Magistrates' Court, the arresting officer read from his notebook, 'the defendant ran into the street and attacked me with his fists. I restrained him with difficulty.'

My solicitor passed a photo to the magistrate: me being dragged across the road. He looked at it and murmured, 'Case dismissed.' It seems perjury is never a crime when committed by a police officer.

A week later the Grunwick Strike Committee called for support from the miners. Just before scab buses were due to be driven through the picket line, several thousand Welsh and Yorkshire miners arrived. To roars from the crowd, they sealed the factory. The Welsh lifted some of the women on their shoulders and sang 'The Red Flag'.[2]

With little support from the TUC and none at all from the Labour Party, the strike was defeated.

Towards the end of the dispute, I remember a speaker calling for a march on Parliament. This was booed and someone shouted out, 'Don't disturb the dead.' I was not alone in my scorn for the 'parliamentary road'.

The next time I witnessed the solidarity seen at Grunwicks was during the 1984 miners' strike. I was teaching at Kilburn Polytechnic and my union branch set up a food support group for the Blaenant miners in the Neath Valley, south Wales. Their families had no money and the men had set up shooting parties to kill rabbits in the hills above their homes. Some local farmers supported the miners and supplied them with milk, eggs and, occasionally, fresh meat. I was one of those who drove groceries down to their families: tinned and fresh fruit and vegetables, cartons of long-life milk, pasta, cheese, biscuits, soft drinks and toiletries.

Our supplies were dropped off at the miners' social centres and distributed by the miners' wives support group who had precise information on every family's needs. Proof that a co-operative society can develop under the most extreme conditions.

I stayed with Pat and Selwyn Davies in Pen-y-Cae and, over the weeks and months of the strike, we became friends.

One weekend I travelled there with the North London Gay Liberation Front. They staged a benefit for the strikers and their families in the miners' club at the Onllwyn Miners' Welfare Hall in the Dulais Valley. It ended with a mass hug-in: miners and their wives and children embracing their visitors. That evening has been accurately represented in the 2014 film *Pride*.

Onllwyn is ten miles north-east of Pontardawe where my mother had lived. My grandfather would have been shocked by the GLF and even more so by his grandson's support for the miners. When I told my mother what I was doing, she answered in her confusion, 'You're helping the miners. Good. Do you sing with them?'

'Sing?'

'Yes,' she said. 'They sing such lovely songs. I hope you sing with them. They are very happy,' she said.

'Who?'

'The miners. The miners are happy. That's why they sing.'

The miners were defeated and their defeat marked the start of the neoliberal years of anti-union laws and privatisation. Margaret Thatcher had come to power in 1979 and her government's bludgeoning of the miners followed her Falklands War 'victory' two years earlier. Her obsessive attacks on society – 'And, you know, there is no such thing as society' – marked the end of the post-war consensus which had brought about the National Health Service and the welfare state. These years also marked my temporary withdrawal from political activity as I moved from teaching to the art world to film-making and then to aid work. It wasn't until the start of the second Iraq war in 2002 that I would return to activism.

When a military invasion of Iraq looked increasingly likely, Brian Eno agreed with me that we should do something to oppose impending war.

I had made contact with Noam Chomsky and he agreed to meet with Brian if we came to film in the US. We wanted him, and other interviewees, to appear in a documentary titled *Not in Our Name*. We had a meeting at Channel 4 TV to see if they would commission us to go to the USA and speak with opponents of an attack on Iraq. Nothing came of it and I apologised to Brian for wasting his time.

A few weeks later, I was contacted by ITN. Brian, they said, could meet up with Iraqis and design anti-war posters in his studio. A filmed collaboration with Chomsky in the US to poster-making in London didn't seem like a good idea to either of us. We declined the proposal, but nevertheless ITN went on to commission me to make a short film about how the Iraqi community in the UK felt about a possible military attack on their country.

With a £17,000 budget, I recruited the journalist Felicity Arbuthnot. She had researched for John Pilger's films and had worked with Dennis Halliday, former UN Assistant Secretary General in Iraq. I asked Edwin Maynard to be my cameraman. He'd worked with Brian and had come to Mostar on numerous occasions to film and photograph for War Child.

After a number of interviews, we quickly found that the Iraqi community in Britain were, not surprisingly, unexcited about an assault on their country, even those violently opposed to Saddam Hussein's dictatorship. The writer Haifa Zangana had been tortured and raped in Saddam's gaols, and academic Kamil Mahdi was a refugee from Iraq. Both were bitter opponents of the regime and were campaigning against the continuation of sanctions and in opposition to war.[3]

Haifa and Kamil spoke passionately to camera, and bravely. When we filmed at Haifa's house in north London, a black Mercedes was parked across the street. When I asked her whose car it was, she shrugged. 'They are Iraqi National Congress thugs.'

The INC were the CIA-backed politicians who were waiting to ride back into Baghdad on US tanks. A few days before our film, an ex-CIA operative commented on BBC Radio 5 that 'the INC are a greater threat to the world than Saddam Hussein'. Their leader in Germany had said that if democratic opponents of Saddam returned to Baghdad, they could expect to be hung from the lamp posts.

ITN were insistent that we include the Iraqi National Congress as a part of the Iraqi 'community' in the UK. Their Head of Press and Humanitarian Affairs in London was Ahmed Chalabi and we interviewed him at their office in Kensington. When we arrived, I noticed Chalabi's screen saver was a cruise missile with 'for Saddam' written on it.

Felicity got the interview off to a sparkling start. 'Mr Chalabi,' she said, 'why are Iraqis in this country as scared of you as they are of Saddam?'

Mr Chalabi shrugged and answered, 'Next question.'

The narrator for our film was Nadje Al-Ali, a young Iraqi academic. We included interviews with Dennis Halliday, ex-United Nations Humanitarian Coordinator in Iraq, and Ramsey Clark, former-US Attorney General. Brian Eno let us use the track, 'Regiment' from *My Life in the Bush of Ghosts*, the album he'd made with David Byrne.[4]

When we started to edit in Edwin's small studio in Belsize Park, we would get a daily visit from our ITN executive producer. Each day, she would take a tape of the current cut and return the following day with suggested changes. We were told it was to be edited to 12 minutes, then 10, until finally ITN asked for 8 minutes.

On the morning of transmission I delivered our film. We included contributions from all those we had recorded, including the INC. Nadje's narration carried the story and 'Regiment' was the backing track. I was told that it would be shown in its entirety.

At 7.30 that night they showed just four minutes and it bore no resemblance to the cut I'd delivered that morning. The narrator, music, statements and most of the interviews had been removed. There was no structure or logic to any of it. The film concluded with Mr Chalabi's interview and Nadje had been replaced by Simon Israel telling the viewers that he had been meeting with Iraqis in Britain.

The next morning, the executive producer rang me. She assumed I was unhappy.

'You're right,' I said. 'Simon Israel didn't meet any Iraqis.'

'Oh well. He met me.' She went on to add that her boss 'doesn't like to receive phone calls'.

I had cut short a holiday to make this film and felt that we had precisely kept to our brief. We had given voice to those Iraqis hoping that their country would not be attacked and destroyed. I shouldn't have been so naïve about the behaviour of the mainstream media. Others were going to learn this lesson once the war started.

As a sop to us, Brian Eno was invited to join a TV discussion on another night to debate the possibility of an impending attack on Iraq. He emailed me soon after.

'Dear David, I didn't feel I did that well, didn't land the killer blow. Shawcross is a sneering twat, a playground bully. Adelman is a classic cowboy zealot (I didn't mention it on air, but he was wearing cowboy boots). It was uncomfortable being stuck between them, but I was pleased that Adelman was goaded into an "America the Good" rap – because that was guaranteed to make the English public puke. After we'd finished, I asked the email girl what the drift of things had been. She told me that the emails had been increasingly in our favour as the evening progressed and that many of them had named Shawcross and Adelman as idiots (but she felt she couldn't say that on TV).[5] So I think we won by default if by no other means – by not appearing to be prats … I'm sorry they apparently chopped [your film] so mercilessly. At least you had them to blame – I could only put my half-hearted performance down to severe jet lag. Why is TV always always always always always always always always always always always so utterly fucking infuriating? Remember: regime change begins at home! Brian.'

At the time of the 2005 election, and three years after Iraq had been invaded, Brian told me he would put up money for an anti-war candidate to stand against Tony Blair in his Sedgefield constituency.

Reg Keys was the father of Lance Corporal Tom Keys, who'd been killed at Majar al-Kabir in Iraq. Tom and his fellow soldiers had been sent to a police station where they were ambushed. They had no radios and had been issued with limited ammunition. In Reg's words, 'They were let down in life by the men who sent them to their deaths and they have been let down in death by the people who continually deny responsibility.'

Reg was campaigning against the government and the Ministry of Defence and was planning to stand against the Foreign Secretary, Jack Straw, in Blackburn. Felicity Arbuthnot knew Reg and, through her, I made contact. He agreed to switch his candidacy to Sedgefield and I organised his first press conference at Brian's studio.

Chris Nineham and Andrew Burgin from the Stop the War Coalition were there and asked me if I'd help Andrew with press work. I accepted the offer and found myself dealing with media, writing articles and helping to manage the national office.[6]

Over the next few years and using the skills I had learned at War Child, I also organised fundraising music events. I produced a Tom Morello gig at the Scala in Kings Cross and in November 2005, working with Rikki Stein, the Rachid Taha Band performed with Brian Eno and Mick Jones at a gig at London's Astoria.[7] I also organised a number of fundraising evenings at St James's Church, Piccadilly.

Working with Anthea Eno and the publishers Verso, I helped put together two books for Stop the War: *Not One More Death* and *War With No End*. The first had contributions from Brian, Richard Dawkins, John le Carré, Michel Faber, Harold Pinter and Haifa Zangana. The second book followed a year later to mark the sixth anniversary of the US-led invasion of Afghanistan. We had contributions from Naomi Klein, Hanif Kureishi, John Berger and the cartoons of Joe Sacco.

My last fundraiser was a professional reading of *The Trainer*, a play I co-wrote with Anne, to raise money for the Stop the War Coalition and the Gaza Music School that had been destroyed by the Israeli attack on Gaza in December 2008. The Zionists who gave me the Star of David badges 40 years before would not have approved of this play, but they should take note of Primo Levi who said, 'Everybody has their Jews, and for the Israelis, it's the Palestinians.'

After leaving office as Prime Minister, Tony Blair gave a 'faith' lecture at Westminster Cathedral. I suggested we organise a 'rough musiking' for him, a popular form of protest in the Middle Ages when people played instruments, beat drums and made as much noise as possible to annoy and disturb the class enemy: the priest, the landlord, tithe and tax officials.

Two thousand protesters, with everything from drums to sound systems, marched around the building as Blair spoke. A journalist from the *Catholic Herald* had agreed to be my spy inside the cathedral and text me what was happening. She sent eight messages. They all arrived in my phone after midnight; they had been blocked. She'd been trying to tell me that Blair and his audience were well aware of the racket outside and that he looked unnerved.

Peter Mandelson made the mistake of leaving from the front entrance where most of the demonstrators were gathered. I followed him across Victoria Street, clanging a cowbell close to his ear, shouting over and over, 'Murderer, murderer, murderer.' He was furious and kept looking around at his two security men, as though expecting them to take action against me.

As we now know, thanks to Edward Snowden, the intelligence services are never far away. When I was involved with the Reg Keys campaign, Anne and I received anonymous phone calls every morning at exactly 3am. I decided to drop out when the campaign moved up to Sedgefield. The calls suddenly stopped.

When I mentioned this to Reg, he said that one day he was driving home to north Wales from London. He took a call on his mobile, asking him to come to a Birmingham radio station for an interview. Luckily for Reg, there was a traffic jam on the M6 and he was 90 minutes late. The 'radio station' was a trap. It was, in fact, a massage parlour. He said that he guessed that the 'interview' was a set-up and that there must have been a photographer waiting for him there who'd given up and gone home.

Tabs have been kept on me for half a century. One of my brothers-in-law was an officer in the Gurkha Rifles. In the 60s he was involved in one of the last gasps of Empire, fighting the anti-colonial insurgents in Borneo. When he was appointed Intelligence Officer in his regiment, MI6 asked him if he had any contact with me.[8] And those were the years before computers and the internet. It was staggering that they'd go to the trouble and the expense.

Those Bergen-Belsen photos were an early and striking lesson in the violence of fascism. I never asked my father why he showed them to me when I was so young. Was it out of rage and despair, or a call to action? Then the arrival of the Hungarian students who lived with us showed me that barbarism came in many forms. The family journey to the West Country in 1956, passing those tanks en route to Suez, was first-hand evidence that my own State had a tendency to exercise extreme violence.

For most of my life, I have been conscious of our common humanity: an injury to one is an injury to all. Sometimes those injuries have been personal. If my son Ben was, as I now suspect, a victim of the Glaxo Wellcome scandal, then the feelings of anger and bitterness don't get more political. With his struggles today to keep going in the face of the government's attacks on welfare benefits, my hatred of capitalism is, if anything, stronger than ever.

THOSE WHO MAKE REVOLUTIONS HALFWAY ONLY DIG THEIR OWN GRAVES. Forty-eight years later this Paris graffiti from '68 seems appropriate. The many graves I saw in the Balkans now stretch to Mesopotamia in the south and to the Hindu Kush, and beyond in the east. The dead in Africa from war, starvation and AIDS amounts to tens of millions. The years since 1968 have been ones of bloody imperialism. And yet, because of 1968, many of us who were politically active then, remain active today. We are, in Gramsci's words, 'pessimists because of intelligence, but optimists because of will'.

David Triesman was suspended from Essex in 1968 after leading us in the breaking up of that Porton Down meeting. Forty years later, and now Baron Triesman, he was a Minister at the Foreign and Commonwealth Office in Tony Blair's New Labour government.

In May 2007 he took part in a debate in the House of Lords and spoke in favour of this country's use of cluster bombs. 'The United Kingdom has concluded that these weapons have a real and significant military value when, and only when, they are used in compliance with both international humanitarian law and the United Kingdom's own rigorous targeting guidelines.'

I wrote to him asking whether he was the same David Triesman I had known all those years ago at Essex and, if so, what had happened to him.

I didn't receive a reply from his Lordship.

I'd rather be on my ship than his.

POSTCRIPT

October 2015: Despite my aversion to the 'parliamentary road' and not wishing to disturb the dead, I supported Jeremy Corbyn in the Labour Party leadership campaign. I helped work the phones and databased the media. I have now joined the Labour Party. Perhaps this is because Jeremy is one of the few MPs who is not dead. One of the few who offer an alternative to austerity and war, an alternative to the estate agents of New Labour. I have consistently voted for him as my constituency MP for these reasons and not because he belongs to the Labour Party. I write this on a Sunday afternoon in October after bumping into him on the street as he was cycling to visit his grandchild. He stopped to talk and asked me for permission to continue his journey! The next day he was addressing 7,000 people in Liverpool.

Simple Writings

One of my favourite films is Werner Herzog's *The Enigma of Kaspar Hauser*. Set in the 1820s, a young man is discovered at night in Nuremberg's town square, hardly able to stand. He is dumb and has been kept in a cellar, without human contact, since birth. Adopted by a local doctor, he learns to talk and proves to be wiser than those around him.

When I first saw the film, the friend I'd gone with told me the story reminded him of a character in a Hans Jakob Christoffel von Grimmelshausen novel. He said *Simplex Simplicissimus* was set in seventeenth century Germany at the time of the Thirty Years' War. If I wanted to borrow it, he had a copy.

I discovered that it had been translated into English in the 1930s. Even though the language was archaic, I loved Grimmelshausen's story of a peasant boy who'd been cruelly treated by his father and was hardly able to talk. As a mute, he was sent into the hills to watch over the family's flock of sheep.

When soldiers attack his family's farm, Simplex watches from the hillside as his parents are killed and his sister raped. He runs into the forest where he is befriended by a hermit who slowly and patiently educates him.

When the hermit dies, Simplex makes his way out of the forest and is found by marauding soldiers. Although he can discuss Plato's philosophy and Euclid's mathematics, he has no social skills. Thinking him a fool, Simplex is dressed as a goat and made a figure of fun. Since playing the idiot is infinitely better than killing, he willingly performs this role. He is eventually forced into one of the armies where he proves to be an invaluable military strategist.

I loved the book because its message was that humanity is basically good and is corrupted by social constructs and the institutions of power. What's more, the powerful are very often very stupid. I believed that *Simplex Simplicissimus* would make a great play. I jettisoned much of the original story, such as the absurd account of Simplex's return from Japan to Germany, but kept the essence of the narrative: a journey towards wisdom.

I felt Simplex had a resonance for my own time, an antidote to ten years of Margaret Thatcher. This is one of the first scenes I wrote:

SOLDIER   (*singing*) It's too long a war. It's too long a war.
A self-important MAJOR enters.

MAJOR   (*to SIMPLEX*) You're in the army now, laddie, although your beard needs to grow a little if you're to be a soldier.

SIMPLEX   I'm a match for any old man, Major. It's not the beard that marks the man, else billy goats would stand in high esteem.

MAJOR   If your courage is as forward as your tongue, perhaps you'll be useful. (*To SOLDIERS*) Now men, we're going to seek out our enemy in that village. (*He points*) They have to be disarmed as we have information they have a cache of weapons.

SIMPLEX   How do you know that, sir?

MAJOR   (*Laughing and winking at SOLDIERS*) Because we sold the blunderbusses to them, you fool.

SIMPLEX   This is a poor village, sir. We should travel further south. The peasants there are richer.

MAJOR   Who asked your advice?

SIMPLEX   If we raid this village, we will find little and there will be nothing left afterwards, then we will be forced south anyway. Travel to those villages now and there will still be something to return to. It's better than scraping at an empty barrel, even if that barrel is standing beside you.

SOLDIER   He talks sense.

MAJOR   Shut your mouth. Prepare to fire.

SIMPLEX   With respect, sir, wait—

MAJOR   Troop advance.

SIMPLEX   Sir, they know we are here. It would pay us to wait and watch where they hide their weapons, or whatever it is you are seeking. If we note their movements, it will save us time and blood. Here, sir. Take this pen and paper and please accept this as respectful advice.

MAJOR   (*Waves quill about, as he is illiterate*) You do it. I'm no clerk.

In 1986 I took the first draft of the play on holiday to Croatia. I would disappear from the family for hours to write under an olive tree in wild land above the sea.

Yugoslavia was beginning to fracture and the nationalism and aggression emerging from Milošević in Belgrade was finding its mirror image in Croatia, even among my wife's family of Partisans. My father-in-law would only smoke a brand of cigarettes called 'Croatia' and seemed to be breathing in the country's nationalism with the nicotine. The Simplex story took on added urgency.

Back in London, a friend suggested I contact Michael Walling, a young theatre director on the lookout for original plays. Mike was excited by it and agreed to direct. We staged it at the Duke of Cambridge Theatre in Kentish Town.

Michael adopted a Brechtian approach with minimalist set, songs to interrupt the action and the actors addressing the audience with Shakespearean asides.

Curiously, there had never been a dramatisation of this book in Germany, despite the fact that Brecht's *Mother*

Courage was adapted from another Grimmelshausen novel, *The Runagate Courage*. An opera, *Simplicius Simplicissimus*, had been composed by Karl Hartmann for chamber orchestra in the mid-Thirties. I'm sure that Hartmann must have toned down Simplex's radical message with the Nazis in power.

After a good review of my play in the *Financial Times*, ('witty, bawdy, and as profound as anyone cares to consider it'), German ZDF TV filmed a performance.[1] Excerpts were broadcast on their news channel, 'Here is a small pub in north London and an English writer has adapted our great classic for the stage.'

The three-week run was a sell-out.

At one of my afternoon visits to Gustav Delbanco, he told me a story about a Rembrandt that had made a journey from Amsterdam to the Soviet Pacific island of Sakhalin at the end of the Second World War. It had eventually fallen into the hands of the Japanese mafia, the Yakusa, and in the early 1950s turned up at a gallery in London.

With encouragement from Gustav, I used this story and my knowledge of the art world to write *The Old Master*. Set in a West End gallery and again with Michael Walling as director, rehearsed readings were given at the Old Red Lion in Islington and the Lyric Studio in Hammersmith.

My sister had met a TV producer from Los Angeles and told him about my play. He rang to ask if he could come to the Lyric reading. I was thrilled. Of course he could.

That was the last I heard of him until some years later. I was in New York on War Child business and told an American friend the plot. She said she recognised the story as one of a series on TV about art crimes. I asked her if she knew who the producer was. She didn't, but I did.

I have no copy of *The Old Master*. There was one in my house, as well as in a file on the Apple computer I left behind. Another victim of my divorce.

My next play had a connection with the art critic Mervyn Levy. After seeing *Simple Writings*, he wrote to me about a possible collaboration. He suggested that I might be interested in co-writing a play about Dylan Thomas. Mervyn had been to school with him and they'd shared a flat in Chelsea. In his letter to me Mervyn said, 'I can show you copies of the evidence concerning Dylan's stay in Macy's morgue, New York, and wonder whether something can be made of this fact. Dylan and I were totally obsessed with the Marx Brothers – we used to go to their films together and I would like to get them into the play. It would be good to work together on this venture since I think we cast a similar wry and humorous eye on the world … I can only hope that the idea appeals to you.'

Unfortunately, we didn't get much further with those discussions because the BBC *Arena* film and the War Child years got in the way. Mervyn died in April 1996 and it was only after I had returned from Bosnia in 2000 that I picked up his notes again. Among them was this account of his and Dylan's childhood years in Swansea. It had as its title 'A Temporary Measure, Swansea, 1925':

'Dylan was in the coal-house feeling May's tits. We had, as always, tossed a farthing for who went in first. Straggling home from the Grammar School, it was a game we often played about tea-time … May's breasts were as large as rugby balls, with rich brown aureoles and deep purple nipples that stood to attention as you felt and sucked … May sat on a pile of coal sacks to indulge our pleasures, our knees often grazed or bleeding.'

With these notes as inspiration I got going on the play.

DYLAN	Come and let me in and on. I'll kneel to you and latch upon those great balloons, my teatime marathon. Lovely, scrumptious, rumptious, tits like lemons.
WOMAN	No sultan could be better served.
DYLAN	Rugby balls, deep-purple nipples standing to attention.
WOMAN	Poke you in the eye though. Take care.

DYLAN	Salty-sweet, delicious on the tongue, crystallised fruits.
WOMAN	At Christmas.
DYLAN	Wet and warm.
WOMAN	Drive you mad.
DYLAN	Her eyes traps to ensnare my fluttering heart. Your breasts, twin sisters firmly grown. Two hills.
WOMAN	Oh no, oh no. (*DYLAN presses teats and they hoot*) Oh yes, yes.
DYLAN	How lovely youth is that flies us ever. Let him be glad who will be. There is no certainty in tomorrow.
WOMAN	Careful now. I'm not a cow. Oh, oh, give me cucumber and hooves.

Michael Walling suggested I set the play in Macy's morgue and that I include the Marx Brothers. Acting on his advice, *Spitting into the Sky* opens with Groucho and Chico talking about death. Harpo is running around the stage, opening caskets and introducing the audience to the characters in the play, stacked one above the other in mortuary drawers: Dylan, his childhood sweetheart, his parents, his wife and his lovers. The backdrop to all this is the New York skyline – a skyscraper graveyard.

As the play unfolds, Dylan's past emerges from the coffins, his childhood in Swansea, his time at the BBC in London and his visits to the USA. He delivers lectures and poems, falls in and out of love, argues with, and clings to, his wife, Caitlin, and wrestles with the two themes that obsessed him: sex and death. The boathouse in Laugharne is a place of peace and relative sanity in the chaos of his life. And it is all there, played out in Macy's morgue.

The first draft had too much poetry, and when Anne first read it, she reminded me that people went to the theatre to see drama, not hear long poems recited. There was also no second act and I didn't know how to expand it. She recommended

I read Caitlin's memoir, *Double Drink: My Life with Dylan Thomas*. In it, Caitlin tells how she arrived in New York as Dylan was dying and accompanied his body back to Wales. On the first night at sea, the captain put her below decks with her husband's corpse because she got so drunk she wrecked the bar.

Anne suggested that Act Two had to take place in the ship's hold. With a real sea captain in the play, there would be more than a nod towards Captain Cat and *Under Milk Wood*.

Ghosts are ever-present. Voices emerge from the gloom, reminding Dylan of a life he'd rather forget, but cannot escape, even in death. It becomes clear that, despite the alcohol and the women, he and Caitlin love each other. Towards the end, Groucho appears and he and Dylan discuss the hidden purpose of his humour and Dylan's poetry. Both, Groucho says, are avoidance techniques, a refusal to confront the reality of their lives.

After receiving praise from John Yorke, former controller of BBC Drama, and from playwright Terry Johnson, the play was given a rehearsed reading at the 2004 Dylan Thomas Festival at the Dylan Thomas Centre in Swansea.[2] The cast included Sion Probert, Stan Stennett and Liz Morgan.

In May 2009, Anne collaborated with me on *The Trainer*, the Gaza benefit play, which was performed as a professional reading at Oxford House in Bethnal Green and later at the Hackney Empire. The cast at both readings included Tim Pigott-Smith, Corin Redgrave and Roger Lloyd Pack. Sadly, it was one of Corin's last performances before his death in 2010.

The Trainer had its genesis in Keith Burstein's opera, *Manifest Destiny*. After the opera was performed at the 2005 Edinburgh Festival, the *Evening Standard* claimed that it glorified terrorism. The composer took the newspaper to court and, after losing in the Court of Appeal, he was ordered to pay the *Evening Standard*'s legal costs. Burstein was bankrupted by this decision and the Official Receiver seized possession of all his works, including *Manifest Destiny*.

The Trainer is a multimedia play set in a gym in the basement of a Mayfair gentlemen's club frequented by Court of Appeal judges. Their trainer is Leila, a young Palestinian who has a Jewish fiancé, Josh. Using video excerpts from the opera, news footage from Gaza and breakfast TV, the play deals with Burstein's bankruptcy, the love between Leila and Josh, and reveals the absurdities of UK terror laws. It delivers a darkly comic warning on the dangers of sleepwalking into a police state while, at the same time, highlighting the struggles taking place in Gaza.

As I write this, Gaza is once again under attack. Should Anne and I rework the play? It's too depressing to consider. Maybe my next play will be about mountain flowers.

Three Sisters

When my sisters and I were children, my mother's sister, Enid, spent most weekends with us in Bromley. Every Friday evening, she would walk up the hill from the station with her small black suitcase and large red handbag. She would extract from it Smarties for us children and a bottle of gin which she presented to my father as a gift for the weekend. He was a beer drinker and my mother had her sherry. Enid finished off the gin on the first evening.

For us children, there might be toothpaste, biros she'd found on the train, a comb she'd picked off the street. My mother would say, 'What are you thinking about, Enid? It's filthy. Throw it away.'

I'd watch my aunt's mouth turn into a hard line. 'Don't be silly, dear. Of course I'll wash it before David uses it.' Then turning to me, 'You like it, darling, don't you?' Putting me in the line of fire.

Enid was always heavily lipsticked and high-heeled, the higher the better. Her visits to the chiropodist were as regular as my mother's to the hairdresser. Although pretty, Enid never married. She worked as an assistant for a Harley Street dentist who was never without the latest model Italian convertible. Sometimes PK, as he was called, would drop her off at our house in Westmoreland Road. He was on his way home to West Malling to spend the weekend with his wife. Enid would throw her shoes onto the gravel driveway and, steadying her windswept hair, step out of his red Alfa Romeo Spider. My parents suspected that she and PK were lovers. I'll never know for sure but, when PK died, Enid developed alopecia and all her hair fell out.

My mother, not Enid, told me that the love of Enid's life had been an RAF Spitfire pilot killed in the Battle of Britain. His name was Peter and my mother used to tell me that Enid treated him badly. 'That poor boy was devoted to your aunt and she ... I can't tell you what she did to him.' And she didn't.

The two sisters had a love/hate relationship. My mother was jealous of Enid and her closeness to us children. 'It's all very well that sister of mine coming down here at the weekend and fawning over all of you. She doesn't have to get you up in the morning and put food in front of you.'

Without the responsibility of being the parent, Enid was generous with her time and her dotings. That dedication to us lasted all her life. When my sisters and I became parents, she was always a willing, and welcome, babysitter.

She spoke with a stronger Welsh accent than my mother, but declared herself to be a proud English woman. She had decidedly right-wing politics. 'The police are so marvellous.' 'I am so proud to be English.' And whenever politics entered a conversation, 'I've always voted Conservative, dear.' When I told her she spoke with a Welsh accent and was Welsh, it became even stronger as she raised her voice at me, 'Oh no, I'm not.'

She rented a room in a house in Allen Street in Kensington that was owned by a retired concert hall singer. Enid lived there for more than 30 years and when the singer died, she moved to Cricklewood and rented a dark, dank room in the house of an elderly Polish woman who shouted at my aunt every time she came home.

In neither place did Enid have her own kitchen. There was a small Belling cooker beside the bed and a handbasin in the corner of the room. When I was old enough to visit her, she would invite me round for dinner. It was always liver and bacon. 'Lovely to see you, darling. It's liver and bacon. I hope you don't mind.' I remember visiting her at the surgery in Harley Street and she would take me to the Prince Regent pub in Marylebone Road. 'Darling, the liver and bacon here is lovely.'

259

Not surprisingly, Enid didn't spend much time at home. In the evenings she sold programmes at the Royal Festival Hall. 'So wonderful there. Such gorgeous music.'

'What did you hear last night, Aunty?'

'I have no idea,' she would say in her Swansea lilt, 'but it was lovely.'

Enid was a wrestling fan and had a friend with whom she went to matches at Wembley Stadium. In Bromley, she'd sit watching it on ITV at 4pm every Saturday afternoon, along with 16 million others. Her favourite was Big Daddy.

I would annoy her with my commentary. 'Aunty, Big Daddy's real name is Shirley Crabtree. Shirley!'

'No man is called Shirley. Stop annoying me.'

'Wow, Giant Haystacks landed on Shirley and he didn't feel a thing. Aunt Enid, he's 48 stone! It's all a fix.'

'That's not the point. Now be quiet, dear, and let me enjoy this.'

She was always up and doing and that was her undoing because, when she reached her seventies, she would get lost travelling across London, putting us all to a lot of trouble.

Finally, she had to be put in a nursing home in Swiss Cottage. Like my mother later, she could not have survived out of care. She spent her days with other old people sitting in soiled plastic chairs, wearing clothes that were no longer hers and staring vacantly at the TV. She was treated kindly by the staff, but like a small child. 'Have you been a good girl and eaten your biscuit?'

After less than a year there, and short of breath, she was taken to the Royal Free Hospital. She was placed on a drip and it was left to my sisters and me to decide what should be done. Many times, she'd told us that she didn't want her life prolonged if she was incapable of living it fully. We asked the hospital to remove the drip. Within a few days, she died.

It was 1987, the year of the storms. She had loved walking in Kensington Gardens so my sisters and I placed her ashes there in a deep hole left by an uprooted oak tree.

I have a recurrent dream to add to the ones set in my childhood home. Enid is still alive and living in an old people's home. Nobody is visiting her and I am continually passing by, feeling guilty that I haven't dropped in to see her. I think she was very alone in life and my sisters and I were her only family. She was our second mother and it saddens me now to think that maybe we did not fully recognise the importance of that for her.

My two sisters turned out very differently to me. We were all sent to boarding school: I to Canford and they to St Margaret's in Hertfordshire. But there all similarities end. Though we are close in age, Elizabeth and Joanna were children of the Fifties and I was a child of the Sixties. For them, it was finishing school in Switzerland and secretarial college. While I walked round Bromley with a CND symbol on my donkey jacket, Liz and Joanna were playing tennis at Sundridge Park Lawn Tennis Club.

Liz married James Watt in 1962. Their first child, Joanna, was born three years later. I remember it was 1965 because I babysat my niece at their flat on Ham Common when she was a few months old. That morning I'd bought Bob Dylan's *Bringing It All Back*. The album had been released in the UK earlier that year. When I hear 'Mr Tambourine Man', I am back in that flat with that baby girl.

A year later my sister, Joanna, married a Sandhurst-trained army officer and went to live with him in Singapore.

It goes without saying that we have our political differences. As the black sheep in my family, I know that, for my sisters and their families, this has made me difficult to deal with. As the Uncle Bill of my times, I've not been the brother to invite round for a polite dinner party. From their point of view, I am that lone ship on the horizon, but I am proud to say that all my family were opposed to the Iraq war and, along with me, Liz took her opposition into the streets.

But it's not just political differences that separate us. Like many people from our background, we didn't share our formative years; we were sent away to school from a young age and that leaves its mark. 'If the Church of England is the Tory Party at prayer,' wrote John le Carré, 'the Public School system may be called the Tory Party in the nursery ... The British are known to be mad. But in the maiming of their privileged young, they are criminally insane.'

Today, both my sisters live more comfortably than Anne and I do in our one-bedroom flat. I don't say that out of envy. I wouldn't give up my life for theirs and, I'm sure, they think the same. We are just different. I am surprised that they have remained as friendly and generous to me as they have.

When I've been down and out – and that's been more than once in my life – both have come to my rescue. Mike and Joanna bought my Rabuzin silk-screen prints when I was struggling with the art world, helped host the artist's visit to the UK in 1989 and sold programmes for War Child at the Festival Hall.

When I was organising Coldcut's Balkan tour in 2001 with Hiroshi Kato, it was with sponsorship from Japan. Funding was suddenly removed and I found myself with 20 musicians in Dubrovnik who were unable to move, practically unable to eat. Joanna and Mike lent me the money so they could continue the tour.

Liz was a trustee of War Child; she went through a lot of anguish with the problems there and helped me in every way. She and her husband, Peter, came to Mostar three times to help out. The first time in December 1997, Peter persuaded the Hampshire police to loan them a Peugeot van which they loaded with donated shoes, clothes and candies. They then drove the 1,200 miles to Bosnia from London, crossing borders without any papers, arrived in Mostar and with hardly any rest, took part in the distribution of the aid directly to the families in most need. They then stayed on to help out at the opening of the Centre.

Not so long ago when, yet again, I was sinking under a mountain of debt, they gave me a loan which they insisted be written off.

As I get older, I have become increasingly aware of the importance of family. Maybe it is because of what Bertrand Russell called 'the terror of the cosmic loneliness'. In my own immediate, disunited family, I need to strengthen whatever remains that holds us together. My father's last years and my recent brain surgery have taught me that.

American Paint

America: drive-ins, pink Cadillacs the size of swimming pools, the Wobblies, Martin Luther King, Woody Guthrie, Joe Hill, Indians. Even as a boy, I always rooted for the Indians.

I fell in love with American literature when I was at Canford and asked the English master, Andrew Davis, why we couldn't have something contemporary and relevant like James Baldwin's *Go Tell It On The Mountain* as a set book. Why, I asked, were they all British – *Lord of the Flies*, *A Tale of Two Cities*, *Macbeth*, of course. I remember hating Golding's novel with its emphasis on how we are all born evil. He laughed and said he hoped I would overcome my infantile literary tastes. This only encouraged my passion for a hidden America that was ignored at Canford and marginalised in the States.

In the 1920s and 30s, American black jazz singers, Josephine Baker and Alberta Hunter, found their stardom, not in New York or Chicago, but in Paris and London. 'The Negro artists,' said Hunter, 'went to Europe because we were recognised and given a chance. In Europe they had your name up in lights. People in the United States wouldn't give us that opportunity.'

In the 1950s and 60s this happened again with the great blues singers who played to packed houses at London's 100 Club and the Marquee. It was Europe and the UK, in particular, that gave them the recognition they deserved.

When these musicians arrived in London, their first booking was often at the Bromley Court Hotel, Catford, a short bus ride from my home. Blues greats like Muddy Waters, John Lee Hooker, Howlin' Wolf and Bo Diddley appeared there with British stars such as John Mayall, Alexis Korner and Spencer Davis.

With his pencil moustache, red Telecaster, sharp suits and from Rolling Fork, Mississippi – as far from Catford as you could get – Muddy Waters 'Got my Mojo Working'.

The Bromley branch of CND used to hold meetings at the Swan and Mitre in the High Street, and I was delighted that being part of Ban the Bomb in south London meant I was among other blues fans. I remember one evening we cut the meeting short and decamped to the Bromley Court to hear Sonny Boy Williamson. I went home that night and dreamed of the Tallahatchie Bridge.

One American's arrival in Europe in the 70s was not as a jazz or blues singer, but as a ballet dancer. Anne Aylor was escaping from a border town in New Mexico where there was little culture of any sort. Her Dixie-born mother thought that ballet 'was about as useful as a tit on a boar hog'.

After travelling in Europe, she ended up in London where she lived hand to mouth, working at a shop in Great Marlborough Street that sold brass and wind music of the seventeenth and eighteenth centuries. This poorly paid job was supplemented by even more poorly paid work as an usherette at the London Coliseum. But the 30-pence-an-hour evening job enabled her to see opera for the first time and, during the summer season, the great touring ballet companies of the world. During these years, she became a writer of short stories, novels and plays and then a teacher of creative writing.

In 1991, I was struggling to expand my ideas for Dylan Thomas into a full-length play. Michael Walling recommended that I attend a playwriting course run by Steve Gooch and Nick Darke in Cornwall. I booked.[1]

The week-long workshop was held at a beach house in Porthcothen. There were ten of us and one of them was Anne. She and I were always the first up. We exchanged life stories sitting at the kitchen table. I was fascinated to discover that she had Native American ancestry, describing herself as a 'homeopathic Indian'. I laughed when she turned sideways to reveal her Indian nose. She said her maternal great-grandmother had been a full-blooded Cherokee and, although she didn't know much about her father's ancestry, he was hairless and dark-eyed. Both her parents were from Tennessee – Cherokee territory. She said that many whites from the southern States have Indian blood, whether they acknowledged it or not. 'Take a look,' she said, 'at Elvis.'

Anne talked about her career as a writer and ballet dancer. How she had hated her life in New Mexico and had escaped to California where she danced with the Oakland Ballet, then to New York and finally to Europe and London where she had been living for 20 years.

One morning at breakfast she told me that her play, *Children of the Dust*, had recently won a playwriting prize which resulted in its being produced by the Soho Theatre and that she was in the process of writing about the Russian poet Marina Tsvetaeva. The title, she said, was *Happiness is North of Here*, a line from one of Tsvetaeva's poems. Anne said that she shared many of the poet's obsessions. She, like Tsvetaeva, always had to be in love, though not always with the same person. 'I was madly in love with someone when I started writing this play,' she said, 'but like Tsvetaeva, the object of my obsession didn't feel the same way.'

When she told me her hometown was where Billy the Kid had escaped from gaol, she was home and dry. The Balkans might have seemed exotic, but the technicolour deserts of the southwest US – that was exotic and here it was on the north Cornish coast. I fell in love with the look of her, just a little before I fell for all of her. Her mermaid hair reminded me of the pale, beautiful women in Gustav Klimt's paintings.

Three months after the course, I received a Christmas card from her with a Zuñi prayer inside. It said:

May you have a powerful heart,

Strong spirit;
May you grow old;
May your roads be fulfilled;
May you be blessed with life,
Where the life-giving road
Of your sun father comes out,
May your roads reach;
May your roads be fulfilled.

She'd sent the same New Year's wish to several other friends, but because she'd signed it 'Love', I read more into it than was meant. I was so thrilled I put it under the mattress on my side of the bed so I could dream of her while I slept.

Anne had founded a writers' group and, because she liked what she'd heard of my Dylan Thomas play, invited me to join. I went to several meetings before I had the courage to invite her out for a meal. I suggested we meet at Joe Allens, the show business restaurant in Covent Garden. After dinner and a bottle of wine, I told her that I fancied her like mad, that I had been attracted to her from the first time I saw her, that I had been faithful to my wife for all my marriage but, after witnessing the war in Croatia, I realised how short life was. I did not want to die with any regrets.

Anne was shocked at my proposal for a discreet affair, but her father, to whom she'd been very close, had died earlier that year from a long, wasting illness. After years of fear and grief, she wanted to live again.

A few days after the meal, I rang to see if she would meet for a drink close to the City Lit where we'd both taught. She nervously agreed.

When we met, she told me she had to go to John Lewis to buy a vegetable rack. I said I'd come with her, but why not first go to a hotel in Russell Square? I tapped my pocket. I had come prepared.

She was taken aback by my suggestion, but not to the extent that she refused.

The Hotel President shared an entrance with the Imperial

and I tried to look like a tourist when I asked for a room. I fumbled over our fake names as the girl at reception handed me a key to Room 303. Anne pointed to the bar. 'I never drink in the day, but now I need one.'

Three stiff gin and tonics later, we made our way upstairs. When I tried the key, the door wouldn't open. I called to a cleaning lady who was chatting to a colleague at the end of the long corridor. She opened the door with her master key. Inside the darkened room I could see clothes and shoes.

We stood there with no luggage and I said, 'Those are not my shoes.'

The cleaner asked to see our key. 'You're in the wrong hotel, sir. This key is for the Hotel President.'

As we waited for the lift, we heard them giggling and started laughing ourselves.

In the right room, and with the vegetable rack waiting to be collected, I kissed her, or tried to. 'I don't think I can remember how to do this,' I told her.

'Me too,' she said.

Anne sat on the bed, nervously facing the window. I wasted no time and started to undress. When she turned around, her eyes told me she was shocked to see my nakedness. Later, she told me she'd been hoping for a slow, romantic seduction, but since I had already disrobed, she had to undress herself.

The first time 'the earth didn't move', but I had finally realised how hollow my marriage was and she, too, was in a relationship which was lonely in all senses of the word. That afternoon was the start of a love that had been sadly missing from both our lives for years.

On our way to the vegetable rack, I turned to Anne. 'It's been a long time.'

'For you or me?' she asked.

It was the start of a relationship that was to see me through the trials of a bitter divorce and much more. She helped me in my struggles with War Child, years of drama and trauma, and became a supportive stepmother to my two sons.

When I was Director of the Pavarotti Centre, she spent eight months there as a practitioner of Chinese medicine, treating the war-wounded and those traumatised by war with acupuncture. She also taught ballet at the Centre and got her students in London to organise donations of ballet shoes and leotards. Her classes were over-subscribed with young girls desperate to take part. When she left, a farewell party for her was organised. There were a lot of tears.

It was not just humans that were sorry to see her go. Anne adopted a feral kitten she'd found sitting on the rim of a tyre to escape the boiling sun. She named her Juba and this animal had amazing intelligence. There were no pet shops and so no litter trays to be had in Mostar. Anne trained her to use the garden below our flat at the top of the PMC. Once she knew the drill, we'd let her out and Juba would go to the garden and run back when Anne jangled her keys over the third-floor balcony. When we weren't there to let her out, Juba taught herself to squat over the toilet pan.

When we left Mostar for a few days, the cat was always there when we returned. That is, until Anne left for good in September 1998. I took Anne to Dubrovnik Airport for her flight back to London and, when I got back to the Centre, Juba had disappeared and was never seen again.

Anne has a way with animals. When we were staying with friends in Limerick, there were three horses pastured in a field behind their house. I watched as they approached her and took it in turns to nuzzle against the side of her face and try to chew her hair. When we got back to London, our friends rang to say that the horses had been wild before we came and, when the farmer moved them to a new paddock, he couldn't believe they'd been tamed.

They say we all have an animal double. Anne's is the American Paint. Mares from this Western breed are fast-witted, intelligent and independently minded. When you see them in a corral, they usually stand apart from the others as if in contemplation. When they do approach other horses, they like to rub their heads against the flanks of their companions. They are silent.

I cannot end this chapter without a story about one of the few books Anne brought to Mostar for her stay. In her suitcase was Dostoevsky's *Crime and Punishment*. A lover of Tolstoy, Chekhov and Nabokov, Dostoevsky was a writer she'd never been able to read because she found his prose too careless, too charged with melodrama and unbelievable coincidences.

Before I left for Bosnia to take up my post as Director of the PMC, I'd told her that the book had completely changed the direction of my life. That it was after reading this novel that I quit my job as a lawyer's clerk and decided to do something more worthwhile with my life. That it was this book that was responsible for me deciding to try to make the world a better place. She was curious to find out why.

In Mostar she started and gave up, started and gave up. When she had exhausted all her other books in English, she was forced to try again. After struggling through the 600 pages she said, 'I've spent weeks and weeks reading a book I didn't enjoy and I am no closer to understanding why it affected you so much.'

'*Crime and Punishment*?' I said, pausing for a moment. 'Maybe it was *The Brothers Karamazov*.'

She threw the book at me.

Behind God's Back

Anne Aylor

This hooptedoodle is something Anne wrote on her first trip to Mostar. *The New Republic* was interested in 'Behind God's Back'[1]. The editor asked for a shorter piece that focused only on the bakery. Anne felt a truncated article about a heroic city that had been under siege for so long would be a sell-out to the people of Mostar. She chose for it to remain unpublished rather than shorten it. Which is why it deserves an audience now.

26th July, 1994. Midnight, Dover. I am on my way to East Mostar, invited by War Child to visit their operations in Bosnia. As we sit waiting for papers from customs, a lorry full of cattle can be heard lowing. The word is too gentle for the terrible sounds they are making above the rumbling engines of sixteen-wheelers driving onto the Calais ferry. It is the cows' last night on earth and they know it.

Outside Nuremburg, I first see the white trucks of the UN, a sign that we are approaching a war zone. A bronze Buddha, which I have taken with me as a talisman, slides back and forth along the dashboard in the lotus position.

We are delayed for an hour and a half at the Austrian border because we haven't been given the right customs' stamp in Dover. In addition to transporting bakery supplies, medicines and parcels to people in East Mostar, War Child is carrying three bags of human insulin. Life in a bottle. Packed in melting ice, it is warming in the blistering heat.

Driving through Slovenia, we pass fields of corn, sunflowers, hops. Names with unusual patterns of consonants and more Js than you would see in a dozen English dictionaries. We pass a road sign to Vrnijka. Almost rhymes with Guernica.

In Croatia, near Karlobag, the hills are bare and rocky. Centuries ago, the Venetians stripped them of trees to build their city and ships for their fleets, which is why we can find no shade during a three-hour traffic jam on the road towards Zadar. We hear rumours that the delay is because a helicopter has been shot down. A sun-shaded army officer paces back and forth, screaming and cursing in Croatian. Two lanes blocked with traffic: a fire engine behind us, a bus in front. Utter chaos with no one in control.

Two hours later, we are told to drive up a small slip road, but there is no room for our pick-up. We are the last vehicle blocking the traffic and our driver is understandably anxious. We are in hostile territory with boxes addressed to people with Muslim surnames, clearly visible in the bed of the truck.

When the road has been cleared and we are given permission to continue our journey, we see what has caused the delay: two overturned container lorries that had been full of pigs. The ones that are alive are being hosed down by soldiers. What is eerie is that the animals are completely silent. They are traumatised, dead or dying in the 40 degree C heat. I wonder if it is the first time in history that an army has been deployed to help animals on their way to slaughter.

We pass the toppled containers and see dozens of UN vehicles facing the other way. It has been seven hours since the accident and these drivers will be here for many more. Seeing our War Child sticker, one of them waves at me. I ask him if he speaks English so I can tell him what is causing the delay. He shakes his head, says that he is German. 'Schwein,' I say, one of the few words I can remember from my high-school German, and thumb in the direction at the overturned lorries.

At Maslenica we drive across a pontoon bridge because the steel bridge has been destroyed by the Serbs. Piled high on either side are hundreds of old tyres. As we roll noisily across the pontoon's metal plates, the clanking sounds like shell fire.

On the other side of the bridge is an area which has been ethnically cleansed. Croatian houses damaged by the Serbs, or vice versa, have gaping holes or are roofless. Those belonging to the minority ethnic group in the area, the Bosniaks, lay in concrete heaps, dynamite charges having been placed at the four corners so that they collapsed neatly, like a pack of cards.

We arrive at our *pansion* outside Split where the UNHCR and other aid agencies have their headquarters. The family who own the *pansion* have been kind to Jim Kennedy, War Child's Field Director, whenever he is in town: treating him like one of their own, feeding him and relaying messages from his London office. Since the mobile bakery operated by War Child moved from Međugorje, where it had fed Catholic Croatian refugees, and is now based in East Mostar feeding Muslims, their attitude has been decidedly chillier.

When we arrive, Jim is sitting at a table in the dark, smoking. We are a day late and he's been waiting for us. He tells us that there has been an attack on a UN convoy into Sarajevo; a British soldier has been killed. 'Don't look like you'll get into Sarajevo with the insulin,' he says. 'The Serbs have no qualms. If they'll fire at the UN, they'll fire at anyone.'

The *pansion* where we are staying tonight is on the Magistrala. On one side the beach, the boats, the towels reserving bathing positions, vine-covered terraces, baked and sunburnt bodies, children skipping stones. On the other side, the war and the rumble of white-painted convoys as they roll into central Bosnia to distribute food and medicine to the ethnically cleansed, the dispossessed, the sick, the hungry. The street itself is a metaphor: of the peace that is so close to war.

The Magistrala is where you find the aid agencies, large and small. For some, but not all, this has been a good war: a little work, a lot of R&R. Spanking new white Land Rovers are parked along the roadside which seem to have rarely travelled into the war zone.

After picking up our UN cards, we enter the 'Muslim' ghetto that is East Mostar. We go first to the War Child bakery which has been installed on the HEPOK industrial estate. Pallets are stacked high with tonnes of US flour donated by the UNHCR. Stamped on the bags, in blue capitals, *NOT TO BE SOLD OR EXCHANGED. USE NO HOOKS*. On other pallets, sacks of Danish salt.

Fourteen local workers and six War Child volunteers are covered in flour, their arms and legs magnolia white like the Wilis in *Giselle*. A gloved Bosnian is using a long pole to pull the hot baking tins out of the ovens. Another leans over for a woman to brush the flour dust from his hair.

There are five mobile ovens for baking bread, but only three are operational because War Child doesn't have the funding to buy diesel to run the generator to provide enough fuel for all of them.

It is three o'clock in the afternoon and, after working since 5am, the bakery staff are ready to go home. In addition to the UN Spanish Battalion which is based close to the compound, there are soldiers from the Bosnian Republican Army to protect the bakery. The week before, there had been an armed exchange between the HVO, the Croatian army operating in Bosnia-Herzegovina, and the bakery guards. The HVO had climbed into the compound early in the morning and there had been small arms fire. One of the volunteers said that the attack had been provoked by the thousands of gallons of wine and *rakija* which are stored on the estate, but I think it is because the bakery, first situated in Croatian-controlled Bosnia, has moved into a Muslim enclave. Before the bakery arrived in Mostar two months ago, there had been no regular supply of bread in this part of town for over a year.

Like all of East Mostar, life in HEPOK is primitive, basic, hard. No electricity, no fresh food, no running water. The only water available is from the bakery bowser. Washing is done in a bucket, or in the River Neretva in town. Serbs on the hills to the east, Croats to the west, SPANBAT at the entrance. Everyone wants the jewel that is Mostar. On a building adjacent to the bakery is written *OPREZ MINIRANO*. Beware of mines.

I take my first drive into the city. Everywhere you look are cut railway lines dangling in space, UNHCR plastic on all the windows, a wall with *STOP KILLING THE CHILDREN* daubed on it. On the street are rows and rows of metal lockers. A flimsy barricade against snipers, they look like dented upright coffins.

We drive through terrible devastation to reach the one pharmacy warehouse that distributes medicine to all of East Mostar. The insulin we deliver, which should be refrigerated, is put in boxes on the floor. Two fridges have been donated to the warehouse, but they are empty because there is no constant power supply. A boxed computer also sits unused because a surge protector is needed to stop current spikes. The pharmacy doesn't have a desk or enough chairs. Their ashtray is a Petri dish which is normally used for growing cultures.

Before the war, the building had housed a large organisation with 40 employees. After the school had been destroyed across the road, the pharmacy improvised one in their former office upstairs. We ask if there are plans to rebuild it. They smile and say, 'Only in a basement.'

The director of the pharmacy tells us, 'My father is Serb, my mother, Muslim. What am I? I am married to a Croat. What are my children? What are they supposed to call themselves now? On the other side of the city they have everything. We used to have everything. Now we have nothing. We have only our lives.'

He is a refugee in his own city. When the war started, he had to flee to the other side. He hasn't seen his wife and children for almost two years. He says the Croats have stolen his flat.

'They stole my family. They stole everything. If someone steals something from you and they say they did it because, to them, you are nothing but a dirty Muslim, then you shrug your shoulders and say, "Oh well, it's unfortunate that that is what I am." At least there is some reason for it. But when they steal from you and that reason is not real, and the reasons they give for it are phoney and illogical, then there is no way you can live with that because you can't say, "I'm a Muslim, bad luck on me." I'm not. That is the crime. We don't want to be Muslims. We are so mixed. They want us to be Muslims.'

He adds that 90 per cent of Mostar wanted to live together; they always had. 'It is the scum who started this war. The fascists are a minority. The majority of people go along with it because of fear, and a few courageous people resist it.'

As we leave, lying in a triangle of land outside their office is an architect's blueprint with the lettering *Nova Podruma*. I carry it to the car and ask the driver what it means. He says, 'New basement.'

We pass a graveyard on the way back to HEPOK. The word for it in Serbo-Croat is *groblje*, a word that sounds as if it were a JRR Tolkien invention. Amidst the ruins of the city, this old Muslim cemetery is miraculously untouched. I mention it to Jim and he says they wouldn't waste a mortar on a *groblje*. But graveyards, I say, are the past, as much as any building. Destroy the graveyards, I say, and you destroy the memories.

'Mortars,' he says, 'are designed to get people into the cemetery and once they have accomplished that, they've done their job.'

Despite the destruction, Mostar is coming back to life after two years of siege, first from the Serbs and then from their former allies, the Croats. Some shops and bars are open. There is even an improvised outdoor cinema screen in the middle of town that a city official walked to Sarajevo for and carried back by hand.

That night we sit outside the bakery to have our only meal of the day. To the east, the Serbs, and to the west, the Croats. There are candles on the table and the sounds of a raucous wedding which echo across the valley.

We slap our arms and legs. The mosquitoes are out.

Jim says, 'They don't like the smell of yeast.' He brings a packet out of the bakery. I wet my finger and rub the dry yeast over my skin. The wedding grows louder: singing, clapping, shouting, laughter, then the sound of guns or firecrackers. War or celebration? It's impossible to tell.

At night, we sleep on the roof of the building next to the bakery. Improvised beds laid on flour pallets, positioned so that you will be in the shade when the sun comes up. But now it is night and the sky is clear and beautiful. Even without my contact lenses, I can see the Milky Way, a white river of stars. There is a breeze, the sound of cicadas. An owl hoots in the distance. I think to myself that we are light years away from Alpha Centauri, the nearest star. We are looking at history, at stars that might not even exist any more because they exploded aeons ago, their light still racing towards us. It is peaceful and still and, for a few hours, the war seems distant.

In the morning, I see an ashtray at the bakery, improvised from the end of a loaf of bread. A hole has been hollowed out of the centre and four grooves cut to rest cigarettes on. I think about a gypsy woman I had seen once in London with her young daughter. The child wanted a roll that her mother had in her purse, but it was too dry and hard to eat. The gypsy explained this to her little girl, then kissed the bread before she threw it away. This precious bread that people had been starving for only a few months ago.

Paddy, a black-and-yellow tom, is the bakery cat. Paddy belonged to an American aid worker who was living in Mostar at the height of the fighting. One day a friend came to visit and took a flash photograph of the ruins outside the aid worker's flat. Seeing the flash of light, an artillery gunner fired a shell through her window. She was cooking dinner at the stove when her body was torn in half. The photographer was unhurt. Paddy came to live at the bakery. In Bosnia, even animals have their stories.

Despite all this, what strikes me in this place is the struggle for normality in spite of everything. Another thing that strikes me is the number of toothless men. That is until I find out from Ahmet, one of the bakery workers, that his teeth had been knocked out by the HVO. He shows me his arms that are scarred where the Croatian soldiers had slashed him when they came to his house to take him away. Ahmet lied about his age, said he was 65, and was left behind with the women and children.

He limps a little when he walks because the canvas shoes he is wearing are too small. They belonged to his son and, along with a vest and the shorts he is wearing, are the only possessions he owns. His son, now safe in America, was taken to a concentration camp during the war. 'My son has been lucky,' Ahmet says, 'because the HVO would take 60 people and lock them in a garage until they died like pigs.'

Ahmet says that he went out at night to find berries for his granddaughter because there was nothing for her to eat. His life had been in danger because of the snipers on the hillside. He says they killed everyone, even the women who went out at night to wash clothes in the river.

I ask him what was the worst thing during the height of the fighting.

'Fear. You didn't mind being hungry as long as you were free. But fear, that was much worse than hunger. People were so frightened they would take four times the recommended dose of aspirin because it helped to prevent heart attacks.'

He shows me the hand-written ration card issued in his name by the Bosnian government, *OCTOBER* written at the top and the numbers from 1 to 31 ruled out by hand. A cross over a number indicated the days he was able to get food, a small bag of rice or beans. I count the Xs, twelve days in every month. A 14-day stretch with no food at all. He carries the ration card in his wallet. 'This,' he says, holding the limp piece of paper, 'shows what I have been through.'

Despite all he has witnessed and suffered, Ahmet is not bitter. He looks forward to the time when he can see his Serbian and Croatian friends again. He distinguishes between those who committed the cruelty and murder, and those who happened to share the same religion. I was reminded of something Martha Gellhorn wrote during the Spanish Civil

278

War: 'You have seen no panic, no hysteria, you have heard no hate talk. You know they have the kind of faith which makes courage and a fine future. You have no right to be disturbed.'

I ask Ahmet when he thinks life will be normal again. He shrugs, talking more with his shoulders than his tongue. Holding up both hands he says, '*Deset godina.*' Ten years.

On Sunday they have the jump into the River Neretva. It is an annual event in Mostar, but they haven't had one in the past two years because of the war. Competitors stand on the rickety suspension bridge that hangs where their beloved bridge once stood and jump, or dive, 24 metres into the ice-cold water. Most are Bosnians, but Matt, an Australian volunteer at the bakery, is participating as an act of solidarity with the local people.

After the competition, hundreds of men and women sit in the square at tables or on the marble steps. There is nothing to eat, but you can buy beer or juice if you are lucky enough to be an aid worker; no one else has any money. Disco music blares in the background.

At first it feels like a fiesta: women in their best dresses, waiters running up and down the steps with trays of drinks. It seems as if things are back to normal until you look more closely. At the tables people are talking, but there is no laughter. No one is smiling. All the children are quiet and, if you study the faces of the young men, they have the hard, dead eyes of soldiers. They are not looking at the pretty girls, but staring blankly into space. We are the only ones who look relaxed. After two years of living in cellars, they have put on a show for themselves. East Mostar is traumatised. This is an attempt at celebration.

On Tuesday we are invited to dinner by the foreman at the bakery. By three, the bake of 4,000 loaves is done and there is the possibility of a swim in the Neretva. We follow him through the narrow streets to his home. He pushes a bicycle ('my car,' he jokingly calls it), two half-kilos of bread under his arm.

His house is not his house at all. The flat he had had in Mostar has been destroyed, and the house he built in the nearby village of Blagaj was finished five days before the war started. His house was on the front line; he hasn't seen it for two years and doesn't know if it's still standing.

The flat he is living in now belongs to a Serbian-Croatian family who fled the Muslim side of the city when the war began. This, too, is on what had been the front line. Three houses at the end of his street are in ruins. He says the people in them were killed when the HVO rolled tractor tyres filled with explosives down the hillside.

His flat is cool and tidy. As in all Muslim homes, we leave our shoes in the hall. There is the Koran on the sideboard and a copper plate on the wall of an Arab leading a camel.

His wife talks about the day their flat had been bombed. Her husband was in the toilet when three mortars landed. She says they sat in the ruins laughing because they were grateful to be alive. 'You can cry,' she says, 'or you can laugh. Laughing is better.'

She has prepared a wonderful meal: *čevapčiči*, cheese and meat pies, barbequed chicken, a salad made from cabbage, tomatoes, onions and chickpeas. We are lucky to eat so well because in Mostar there is little food. Jim bought all the ingredients the day before from a Croat shop outside the city. It's the first fresh food all of us have had in days, not tinned beef or soup or pasta.

Before the meal, I was shown every photograph the family possessed: from the parents' childhood pictures to those of their son's. I was taken through one family's journey of 30 years. I was shown photographs of people who were no more, of a country that was no more. The old people had not died a natural death; they had died violently from sniper fire and mortar attack. Many of the young men smiling from the pages of her album – cousins, friends, a brother – had died at the front.

Proudly, the wife brought out a baby book that she'd made

for her son. She had neatly written his family tree, his first visitors at the hospital, his first words. '*Tata*,' she said a little wistfully, 'not *Mama*.' She turned page after page, carefully translating the captions she'd written. She brought out a lock of baby hair and the black stump of her son's umbilical cord which she'd kept for good luck.

By the time we'd reached his fourth birthday, there were only a few lines: 'We are refugees and things are very hard.' No picture, only some words. 'There was no photograph that year because we had no money for film.'

On her son's fifth birthday, the pages were completely blank. She said, 'Maybe I should try to write something.' She slowly shakes her head. 'No, maybe it is better that nothing is there.'

Now I understand why his father had said what he did when I first met his son. I asked how old he was and he said, 'My son is six years old, but he has had only four years of life.'

The following day we visit Azra Ratkusic's family in the middle of town. They are refugees from Stolac. Azra is a diabetic and has to inject herself twice a day. Her brother, Kamel, speaks English he taught himself from a book and Spanish which he learned from the SPANBAT soldiers based in Mostar since the beginning of the war.

We ask Kamel what it had been like for his sister during the fighting. He says that Azra had almost died twice after being in a diabetic coma because she couldn't get insulin and didn't have proper food to eat. We ask to see her insulin supply. The bottles she has been given by another charity are a year out of date.

Azra's grandmother appears at the door in her slip and offers to make us coffee. She is an old lady, but still has a glint in her eye. She giggles about the slip, then tells us she was driven out of her home by the Croats wearing what she has on.

The family had been well off before the war. They had had cars, videos, a summer home, vacations abroad. Sophisticated, cultured people, the old woman's children were doctors and lawyers. The ones that survived live in abject poverty, their homes and possessions stripped from them for no other reason than the fact they have a Muslim name.

That day the old woman's son swam across the Neretva. For two years he'd been living on the Catholic side of the city in fear of his life. 'He isn't here,' she says, crying. 'He is walking up and down the streets. He can't believe he's free.'

Azra's aunt comes in from work at the tobacco factory. Before the war, Zilla had been an economist. Now she does menial work to provide for her children. Like so many women here, she is a widow. She tells us that she watched as her husband was shot in front of her eyes. It is difficult not to cry with her. I do, hiding behind my dark glasses. 'How can you go on?' I finally ask.

She smiles sadly. *'Moramo biti herojia.'* We must be heroic.

The next day, a BBC reporter, who came to film War Child's activities in the city, goes with me to meet Hamid Custovic, the official responsible for food distribution in the city. Over whiskey, Hamid explains his view of the war. 'Before the war, the mosques were empty. Even now, after all this talk of us "Muslims", there are still only a few old women there at prayer time. The bridge was our life and they took that from us. They took what was most important. This war has nothing to do with religion. When you hear the muezzin call, you can tell the time of day.'

He adds, 'I used to live in West Mostar, close to the cathedral. I loved that cathedral and I loved its clock. I used to look out at it from my flat. When the clock stopped because some idiot damaged the building, I was very sad because I couldn't tell the time any more. Something important had been removed from my life. You know,' he said, 'that clock on the cathedral and the call to prayer from the mosque are one and the same.'

The reporter asks Hamid what the plans were for rebuilding the city. He smiles sadly, 'The people here don't feel they have a future. The fighting isn't over. They would like to think that it is, but they know it is not. That is the real sadness of this place. The West did nothing to stop this war, and they will let it happen again.'

It is our last day in Mostar. Earlier this morning, the UNHCR informed us that the town is on orange alert and that all aid agencies should leave the city centre and return to their bases. Sitting under the guns of both the Serbs and Croats, War Child is one of the few agencies that live and work on the east side of the river. It was advice that could only be ignored.

We sit with two bakery workers in the one black-market restaurant on this side of the city: fresh meat and salad in a town without fresh meat and salad at a cost that only foreigners can afford. None of us have eaten for two days and we are looking forward to the grilled trout, beer and vegetables.

We have just been served when the shelling starts, a loud explosion perhaps a street away. At first I'm not too frightened because one of the Bosnians explains that it's a *pat*. A word that sounds innocuous enough until he says that it's an air explosion that rains down shrapnel. 'Probably a Serb gunner who's had his first *slivovitz* of the evening,' he says. 'Nothing to worry about.'

Eleven violent explosions follow, one after another, causing masonry to fall into the street from a nearby building. My ears hurt; my stomach goes into spasm. Even though everyone has not eaten for days, the food on the table remains untouched. Conversation continues, everyone pretending to be unconcerned, but the much looked forward to meal remains unfinished.

'Are you scared?' one of our guests asks.

I am afraid I'll be killed, but I look across the courtyard at a baby crying, then at the men and women still walking past, unconcerned, in the street. To the people of East Mostar, this is nothing unusual. I reply with the only words possible. 'I have no right to be.'

There is a saying in the former Yugoslavia, that to be in

a terrible place is to find yourself behind God's back. East Mostar is behind God's back.

Acknowledgements

We enter life alone and – if we are lucky – are rarely alone again on our journey until we die. You will have been introduced to some of my fellow travellers in this book, but this is the opportunity I have to say something more about them. All of them have read it, commented, criticised and suggested and I thank them, but in no particular order.

Jane Glitre who's helped and befriended me over the years. I worked for her when she ran the Spitz music venue and later when she was organising jazz gigs at Kings Place. She read the script, more than once, and only had to say 'this isn't you, David' for me to get busy with my red pen. Hiroshi Kato who gave me a job after the War Child debacle. Sebastian Balfour and his wife, Gráinne, who are as close as friends can get without actually moving in together. I have known Seb since Essex University when he took the pseudonym of Mike Balfour. How can you agitate in a factory with a name like Sebastian? Gráinne may have saved my life when I developed the haematoma.

Eileen Davies whom I have known for 45 years and who is my third sister. She is one of the very few people I can share my intimate worries with and hope to come away feeling better.

Beverlie Manson who gave me a home after I walked out of my home. Some work too. She is an illustrator, famous for her fairies, and I helped out with one of her projects and invented its title, 'Long Ago But Not Forgotten'. She has always been there for me, allowing me use of her flat in Old Street for play readings and even a family wedding reception.

Her ex-husband, Roger Taylor, who gave me a job at Bleep,

his retail software company, in the interregnum between my work as an art agent and making the BBC film in the Croatian war.

Johnny Carmichael supported me in the long struggle with War Child and helped me more than he cares to admit.

Dorothy Byrne who recruited C4 and the *Guardian* to expose the misdoings at War Child. She also gave Anne and me a home when we re-decorated our flat. She, too, played a major part in keeping me alive when I was ill.

As a result of this book, I have re-established a connection with Roger Lavers and Norman Boyer and I owe them both a big thanks. Their memories of events and people at Canford and in Argentina are better than mine.

The same can be said of both my sisters. Liz and Joanna have corrected me when I have been wrong and reminded me when I have forgotten.

Berry Ritchie kindly read the chapters on War Child. He asked me what the book says about me and I was stumped for an answer. I set out to write a book about the events in my life. It's not a book about me, or is it?

A big thanks to David Sprecher. His delay in booking that Spanish holiday makes him responsible for much that has happened to me. No David S, no book.

I don't need to say much about Eugene Skeef. The reader will have realised his importance to me and to the young people of Bosnia-Herzegovina. I will just add that his talents, personality and good humour kept me – and many others – going.

Maja Drnda and Christian Martí, my two Barcelona friends, have supported me through thick and thin. I have been able to escape to their home and write in the centre of that city of homages. I pay homage to them here.

Deicola Neves of Camden Guitars not only taught me how to play the guitar, but his shop has been a musical sanctuary for me. Between the notes, he has listened to my problems as well as my chords.

ACKNOWLEDGEMENTS

Thom Hoffman took amazing photos of War Child and Mostar. I tracked him down in Amsterdam and he has kindly given me access to his work, which you can now see in this book.

Brian Eno has been a major part of my life in the last 20 years. First of all, his backing for War Child in its early days. His support for the Pavarotti Music Centre which was hands-on with his visits to Mostar. In this century, his work for the anti-war movement. He is one of very few well-known musicians who has taken a principled stand against Empire. He has performed, attended pickets and rallies, written and appeared on TV.

Everyone knows about Brian, and rightly so, but few know about the influence of Anthea Norman-Taylor, his former wife, who has had an effect on many of the events surrounding me in the last two decades. I owe my sanity to two women, my wife, Anne, and Anthea. Alongside my biological and Mostar 'sons', Oha and Teo, she is among the few to have travelled with me on the hard road I have taken. She has stuck with me when the asphalt gave out.

When mentioning the Enos, I can't leave out Lin Barkass, their PA, who was central to the organisation of the War Child fundraisers. I have been entirely dependent on her for the memories of these events. Also Opal's Jane Geerts, without whom neither Brian nor his office could function.

Both my sons have offered me their memories, sometimes painful ones, for all three of us. Ben and Jonny have been keen supporters of this book. When its working title was *Writing for the Attic*, it was with them in mind. If they are my only readers, then I have done well.

Manuela Beste also read the manuscript and bolstered my ego and determination to have it published. Robin Beste has been a regular and indispensable political 'adviser' and, thanks to him, I have been introduced to a myriad of informative weblogs.

My nephew, Peter Harrison, has kindly read it through in

his role as a lawyer. If I stay out of the courts, I have him to thank.

Thanks to Mathew Clayton at Unbound who showed enthusiasm for this memoir from the moment he read an early draft and gave me the title. Thanks also to Isobel Frankish, Unbound's editor-in-chief, Amy Winchester, Caitlin Harvey, Georgia Odd, DeAndra Lupu, Emily Shipp and Phil Connor. All of them amazing people and some with amazing names.

Canford School, which I hated so much, were the first to offer me the chance to give a talk about the book. Thanks and times have changed!

Without the supporters listed at the end of this book, *Left Field* would have remained 'writing for the attic'.

War Child today is under new management and the distant past is just that – distant. They continue to do great work with the children of war.

It's a cliché to say that writing is a lonely occupation, but it is. My writing group, The Group, has been invaluable in giving me an audience. I have learned much from them. Not only when they comment about my work, but from their own writing. Cecily Bomberg, Candyce Lange, Hekate Papadaki, Becca Bland, Tawnee Hill and, of course, Anne Aylor. Their criticisms and suggestions I ignore at my peril.

So finally Anne. She urged me to start writing this book ten years ago. Many times I have despaired at finishing it. She has always been there to call me back, lift my spirits and get me going again. She is my muse, my amanuensis and editor-in-chief. My Gordon Lish. Without her I might not be alive, and if alive, I would be dead.

Notes

The Gondola

[1] In *The Belsen Trial* by Raymond Phillips, 1949, Brigadier Glyn-Hughes describes the scene that the British found at Bergen-Belsen: 'The conditions in the camp were really indescribable; no description nor photograph could really bring home the horrors that were there outside the huts, and the frightful scenes inside were much worse. There were various sizes of piles of corpses lying all over the camp, some in between the huts. The compounds themselves had bodies lying about in them. The gutters were full and within the huts there were uncountable numbers of bodies, some even in the same bunks as the living. Near the crematorium were signs of filled-in mass graves, and outside to the left of the bottom compound was an open pit half-full of corpses. It had just begun to be filled. Some of the huts had bunks, but not many, and they were filled absolutely to overflowing with prisoners in every state of emaciation and disease. There was not room for them to lie down at full length in each hut. In the most crowded there were anything from 600 to 1,000 people in accommodation which should only have taken 100.'

Gaucho and Sailor

[1] The *Normandie, Queen Mary, Lusitania, Titanic*, and for me, *Arlanza*. The mystique that surrounds these ships hides a reality; they can be uncomfortable; they can make you seasick and they can sink. Designed to look like expensive hotels to encourage rich passengers aboard, the crews weren't fooled any more than the steerage passengers. A ship is a microcosm of society. The old liners represented Empire and class in a confined space and all the hypocrisy that goes with it. Behind the veneer of a white ship is the

hideousness of empire and the intention to destroy and subvert. Beneath the sipping gin and tonics, the holds stacked with crates of bibles and guns.

[2] These docks closed in 1980, and today the length of the George V Dock has been transformed into the single runway of City Airport.

[3] 'Argentina: The Country that Monsanto Poisoned'. *http://overgrowthesystem.com/argentina-the-country-that-monsanto-poisoned-photo-essay/* American biotechnology has turned Argentina into the world's third-largest soya bean producer, but the chemicals powering the boom aren't confined to soya and cotton and corn fields. They routinely contaminate homes and classrooms and drinking water. A growing chorus of doctors and scientists is warning that their uncontrolled use could be responsible for the increasing number of health problems turning up in hospitals across the South American nation. In the heart of Argentina's soya bean business, house-to-house surveys of 65,000 people in farming communities found cancer rates two to four times higher than the national average, as well as higher rates of hypothyroidism and chronic respiratory illnesses. Associated Press photographer Natacha Pisarenko spent months documenting the issue in farming communities across Argentina. Most provinces in Argentina forbid spraying pesticides and other agrochemicals next to homes and schools, with bans ranging in distance from 50 metres to as much as several kilometres from populated areas. The Associated Press found many cases of soya beans planted only a few feet from homes and schools, and of chemicals mixed and loaded onto tractors inside residential neighbourhoods. Yet Argentina doesn't apply national standards for farm chemicals, leaving rule-making to the provinces and enforcement to the municipalities. The result is a hodgepodge of widely ignored regulations that leave people dangerously exposed.

Salaam

[1] 'UK babies given toxic vaccines, admits Glaxo', Anthony Barnett and Tracy McVeigh, the *Observer*, June 30th, 2002: 'British drug giant GlaxoSmithKline has finally admitted that thousands of babies in this country were inoculated with a batch of toxic whooping

cough vaccines in the 1970s. Some experts believe that these Trivax vaccines – which had not passed critical company safety tests – may have caused permanent brain damage and even fatalities in young children. In 1992, the family of an Irish boy, Kenneth Best, who suffered brain damage from one of these toxic vaccines, was awarded £2.7 million in compensation by the Irish Supreme Court. Despite a long and fierce battle with the drug giant, the boy's family finally won this historic case after his mother Margaret made a startling find when sifting through tens of thousands of company documents. She discovered that the Trivax vaccine used on her son, from a batch numbered 3741, had been released by the company despite it having failed to pass a critical safety test. Documents revealed that the 60,000 individual doses within this batch were known to be 14 times more potent than normal. At the time the Irish judge accused GlaxoSmithKline – then known as Glaxo Wellcome – of negligence and attacked the company's poor quality control at its Kent laboratory. Immunology experts condemned Glaxo in court for what one US scientist described as an "extraordinary event". Last year an investigation by the *Observer* found evidence to suggest that vaccines from this faulty batch, which may have wrecked Kenneth Best's life, had also been used in Britain. Liberal Democrat MP Norman Baker raised questions in the House of Commons, asking whether vaccines from this batch had been given to British babies. Then Health Minister Yvette Cooper wrote to the company asking for information. Now, almost a year later, GlaxoSmithKline has replied that it is "highly probable" the toxic batches had been used in Britain. The Department of Health is under pressure to make efforts to trace the children who received the suspect vaccines. Last week in the House of Commons, Health Minister Hazel Blears said: "Unfortunately they no longer have details of the quantities of vaccine or the places where the vaccine was supplied. Since vaccines were not centrally purchased and distributed at that time there are no central records either. Information on individuals who received these vaccines will only exist if the general practitioner at the time of the immunisation recorded the batch number and the patient's notes are still available." Baker will now write to the Minister to demand that she asks health authorities to check the records to find out who received the vaccine. It is believed that at least one boy from Wales died after receiving a jab from toxic batch 3741, although the parents have never been informed. A spokesman for GlaxoSmithKline told the *Observer*: "We do not accept that these batches were harmful."'

Naïve
[1] *Rabuzin*, Mervyn Levy, Imprimis, 1990

The Artists' War
[1] 'Life is a Cabaret, Old Chum', Giles Smith, the *Independent*, March 7th, 1992: 'Imagine the scene; you're in the Croatian army, stationed on the front line, exhausted from skirmishing with the Serbs but enjoying, as best you can in the circumstances, a brief lull in the fighting. Suddenly a truck pulls into the camp and a small group descends, looking suspiciously like actors. They're actors, and within seconds, they've converted the back of the lorry into a makeshift stage-set with a sign in coloured lights above it, reading "Ad hoc Cabaret". It may have been one of the only consolations to you, as a soldier, that though the war zone was clearly hell, at least it minimised your chances of encountering a street theatre group; now you don't even have that anymore. Perhaps the only reasonable option is to lay down your arms, put your hands on your head, and set off on the slow trudge to enemy lines. Actually the particular troop of Croatian soldiers shown on *Arena* responded to the particular troupe of Croatian performers with laughter, applause and much waving of peace signs. They enjoyed the satirical songs (which the programme didn't bother to translate for non-Slav viewers); they looked appreciatively at the panels on the truck, which were flipped from behind to expose various challengingly abstract pieces of painting; they didn't even balk at the taped music, in which someone could be heard earnestly playing a home organ and a toy trumpet – or perhaps playing a home organ with a toy trumpet. When Croatia went to war, the artists decided to get involved – some to fight, the rest to do the cabaret, although those doing the cabaret didn't seem to recognise the distinction. One of

the members of the mobile theatre unit spoke of "fighting with our ammunition, which is art". You could test your feeling about the wisdom of this by asking yourself the following question: if civil war ever broke out here, would you rather have on your side a) the massed ranks of the Royal Tank Regiment or b) Simon Callow? As *Arena* got into its stride, you feared a programme burdened with difficult claims about art's ability to save us from ourselves; or, worse, one which attempted to convince you that a thoughtful piece of mime on the dynamics of violence was a capable match for an airborne assault. To which one possible response would be, if war is futile, what does that make street theatre? Here, though, the best part of the actors and artists and sculptors and the one jazz singer who addressed the camera, pointed out straight away how winning wars wasn't essentially part of their job description. Weighing the claims of the pen against the sword, many of them had opted for the sword, realising that if they didn't, someone was going to come in and steal all the pens. "Wearing this uniform," said a uniformed actor, "standing on the front line, is the only way I can be sure of my future." The programme doubled as an interview with the painter Ivan Rabuzin, now aged 70, so in no position to join up at the front, but able instead to offer a few sage notions on the impact of unrest on the artist's vision. Strangely, in a programme so questioning about art and its roles, there was little inquiry into the merits of Rabuzin's actual work – mostly pictures of skies filled with fluffy clouds and landscapes done up as puffballs. Rabuzin, it was said, "regards himself as a God in the sky of his paintings" . Even so, most of then looked like the kind of get-well card you might buy for someone you didn't know that closely. For once, it was better to hear from the artist than to look at his art. On the intrusion of war into his daily life, Rabuzin didn't seem to be making anything grander than an assessment of a personal dilemma when he wondered "Do I now paint a black flower instead of a church?" This was always going to be hard work in a film which included clips of people bombed to death and their families mourning them, for whom the matter of what Rabuzin did or didn't paint could not, right then, have carried much weight.'

Charity Virgins

[1] Letter in the *Guardian*, November 12th, 1992. 'Amidst discussions and votes on European integration, the European state of Bosnia disintegrates before our eyes. A day's drive from Maastricht will take you to a land of forced population movements, massacres, concentration camps, hunger and desperation. The latest estimates from UNICEF warn that, in addition to those already killed, maimed and made homeless in Bosnia, over one million children now face death from cold and hunger. All those appalled by Ed Vulliamy's article (47,000 flee down Vietnam road, *Guardian*, 2nd November, 1992) might be interested to hear about the War Child project, a three-day arts benefit which will take place in London in the new year. Its aim is to focus public attention on the plight of the children of war, and money raised from the event will provide direct aid for these innocent victims.'

[2] Andy Bearpark, Director General of the British Association of Private Security Companies (BAPSC), an independent trade association representing the leading UK companies in the specialist private security and risk management sector. Previously Mr Bearpark served as Director of Operations and Infrastructure for the Coalition Provisional Authority (CPA) in Iraq.

Ned of the Hill

[1] *Zlata's Diary – A Child's Life in Sarajevo*, Zlata Filipović, Penguin
[2] *Sarajevo Under Siege: Anthropology in Wartime*, Ivana Maček, University of Pennsylvania Press 2009

Del Boy

[1] Some years later, when I was at the Pavarotti Music Centre, I bumped into Pockets on the street. 'What are you doing here?' I asked. He tapped the side of his nose. 'That's for me to know and for you to find out.' That made me think back to Čapljina. Why had he wanted to go there and not return immediately to Split? What was he doing now in Mostar?

[2] In 1996 Jim was awarded an MBE. He rang me from Mostar after he had received the news. 'Is it any use, Dave?' he asked. 'It

will get you to the front of the queue in the betting shop,' I said. 'Mumsie must have had a hand in this,' he replied. I have no idea what happened to Jim. He is lost to me. There are no Google entries for him and he isn't the sort of person to be found on Facebook or Friends Reunited.

Little Pieces and Big Stars

[1] Brian Eno: 'My acquaintance with War Child began with Anthea, who'd been to a meeting and was quite fired up about it. She'd earlier been involved with the Nordoff Robbins Music Therapy charity, and seen how much money was flowing from the music business into that: her plan was to reroute some of that money towards War Child. She volunteered my engagement early on, before I really had a clear picture of what was going on in Bosnia. I'm sure you'll recall how confusing things were in those early days – it wasn't clear who was doing what. Anthea remembers that my initial inclination was somewhat towards the Serbs, though I have to say, I don't actually remember very clearly what I was thinking then. I do remember that Anthea was never in any doubt where her sympathies resided – with the Bosnians. I also remember that a very close friend of mine was a Serb supporter and this may have influenced my position. Anyway, what I realised quite early on was that it didn't really matter that much who was "right" and who was "wrong": the fact was that we had a major conflict in the middle of Europe – the first since 1945 – and not much was being done about it. There didn't need to be any politics involved. War Child was trying to help the child victims of the conflict and that seemed pretty uncontroversial. In time, of course, my sympathies went very strongly towards the Bosnians, not least because of the complete imbalance of power. In time I began to realise that it was the Bosnians who were the pluralists and hence the hope for a fairly shared future. Subsequently we all met up – you, Bill, Anthea, myself, and I think we both liked you and the way you were doing things. It had a "seat of the pants" feel which inspired my confidence.'

[2] Other contributors included: Anton Corbijn, four photographs; Vic Reeves, a drawing of 'Elvis and Frank on Their Way to the

Shops'; George Michael, his original drawings for the *Faith* album; The Edge, a Polaroid 'Self-Landscape'; Iggy Pop, 16 black-and-white self-portrait photos set one above the other like mug shots for 16 passports; Steve Reich, the first page of his 'Variations for Winds, String and Keyboards', three Davidoff cigars, two 18-carat nipple rings, a Ronson cigarette lighter and a Gold American Express card in a distressed resin cast; Joan Armatrading, an ink drawing; Michael Nyman, 36 Sony video prints from an original video of Ayers Rock (he actually sent a VHS of his holiday at Ayers Rock from which were produced the 36 prints). Contributions also came from Boy George, Kate Bush, Nick Rhodes of Duran Duran, Bob Geldof, Shane MacGowan, Adam Ant, Massive Attack and Russell Mills.

[3] *A Year With Swollen Appendages*, Brian Eno, Faber 1996: '"Pagan Fun Wear" went brilliantly – just the right balance between gorgeously stylish and improbably improvised. Lots of people came and they all seemed to have had a really good time. Anthea and I worked for two days and nights almost continuously without sleep in the run-up to this – so much to do and so many people to organise. Lynn Franks said this was "the most stylish charity event I have ever been to – and I've been to a few." So it was a tremendous relief at the end of the evening, at 12.30, when it was all successfully over and time to go home. I took one last walk round the various huge rooms of the pristine Saatchi Gallery to make sure no one had left anything behind. I was feeling fine. I'd especially pleaded with the staff at the Saatchi Gallery to use a room they don't normally let out – a particularly beautiful space. I'd promised them faithfully that there'd be no damage and they shouldn't worry and my word was my bond etc. "There won't be any mess at all, I promise you that." The walls and floor of the room had been squirted with huge jets of black, red, green and yellow paint. It turned out that some of the youngsters who worked for one of the record companies had got drunk and run amok. My heart dropped a thousand miles – and I set about scraping the whole mess off the walls. (It was poster paint, so it couldn't just be painted over – it would have mixed with the white paint.)'

[4] Lou Reed exhibited a small bottle of perfume labelled '*ODE* for

Ornette Coleman', blended by himself with the bottle's graphics designed by Laurie Andersen. Dave Stewart's homage was to Bob Dylan. Bryan Ferry's – Charlie Parker; The Pet Shop Boys' – *Saturday Night Fever*; Holly Johnson of Frankie Goes to Hollywood – the Beatles; Karl Hyde of Underworld – Captain Beefheart. John Squire – The Beach Boys. Tim Booth's homage was to Patti Smith's *Horses*.

[5] As well as these three major fundraising events, Anthea and her team also organised a set of Christmas cards in 1995 with contributions from Brian, Bowie, Kate Bush, Peter Gabriel, Oasis, Pulp, Iggy Pop, Radiohead's Thom York, The Blow Monkeys and Dave Stewart.

Rainbows

[1] 'Former Liberian president Charles Taylor is alleged to have gifted the diamonds to Campbell, who says she passed them on to Ratcliffe.' David Smith, *Guardian*, August 5th, 2010. 'Supermodel says she gave stones to charity boss to "do something good", but Children's Fund says it never had them. The man Naomi Campbell says she gave the bag of diamonds to refused to confirm if he still had the stones in his possession today. The British supermodel testified that she passed the "dirty-looking pebbles" on to Jeremy Ratcliffe, then chief executive of the Nelson Mandela Children's Fund, intending he use them for charity. She said she called Ratcliffe a year ago to ask what he had done with the stones, and he told her he still had them. Contacted by phone today, Ratcliffe did not deny receiving the diamonds, but claimed that legal restrictions bound him to silence. "The matter is *sub judice* and I'm not prepared to comment," he said. The Children's Fund today categorically denied ever having diamonds in its possession. Ratcliffe added only, "The fund is correct." Now chairman of JET Education Services in South Africa, Ratcliffe declined to elaborate and his phone failed to respond for the rest of the day. Calls to his homes in Johannesburg and Plettenberg Bay also went unanswered. There was no sign of him at his luxury three-storey house in Atholl, an upmarket neighbourhood in Sandton, Johannesburg's wealthiest

suburb. Ratcliffe's daughter, Claudia, answered an intercom to say that he was out and she did not wish to comment. The three-storey house is on a street behind a big security gate where guard dogs bark at the sight of intruders. It has whitewashed brick walls, brown shutters and window frames, a giant tree and neat row of bushes in its bricked forecourt. A sign warns that would-be burglars will be met with an "armed response". In court today , Campbell stressed she did not know personally whether the stones in question came from Taylor, after a party hosted by Mandela in Cape Town in 1997. She said she handed them to Ratcliffe on boarding a luxury train the following day. Campbell told the court: "I gave the stones to Jeremy. Immediately, I got on the train I looked for him … I said take them, do something good with them, make the children better, I don't want to keep them. Once I gave them to Jeremy, they were out of my hands." Oupa Ngwenya, a spokesman for the Children's Fund, said it had been unable to locate Ratcliffe today, and he could not be reached by phone. Ngwenya confirmed that Ratcliffe is still a trustee of the charity. He added: "We have no record of diamonds being in our possession." In a letter presented in court by the defence, the Children's Fund said it had "never received a diamond or diamonds from Ms Campbell or from anyone else. It would have been improper and illegal to have done so.'"
[2] http://www.edmundmhlongo.info/

The Opening
[1] Article in *Oslobođenje*: 'I understand that there have been criticisms from some politicians concerning the Pavarotti Music Centre – that it is too full of "Muslims". Let us start with the use of the word "Muslim". I am a Celt of Scottish and Welsh ancestry, with an English cultural background. I have a Jewish first name and a Christian family name, but am neither Jewish nor Christian, nor even, strictly speaking, English. I am still amazed that, at the far end of the twentieth century, in Bosnia-Herzegovina, where all people seem to be very much alike and where many are of mixed parentage, two groups are defined in terms of nationality (Croats and Serbs) while a third group is defined in terms of religion. This leaves aside

the number of families of mixed parentage. It would be amusing, if not so tragic, that ethnic definitions are based on the father's name and not the mother's. Why is a person defined as Muslim, Croat or Serb based on the male lineage when the mother might well be from one or the other of the newly selected ethnic groups? There is a missing logic here. That missing logic continues with criticisms of this Centre which has been set up for everyone, regardless of cultural, ethnic or religious background. As Director, I wish to involve all children and young people in our work since my own family is partly Croatian and I have a long and strong connection with Croatia. It is, of course, true to say that there are a lot of people with Muslim names in the Centre; hardly surprising considering what has happened in Mostar. This criticism is like saying that the Warsaw Ghetto was full of Jews. Yes, it was, and why were they there? Despite the continuing and shameful existence of the Mostar Ghetto, we at the Pavarotti Music Centre are determined to open the doors of this place to everyone. Those who criticise us will be disappointed to hear that many Croatian young people come here every day. Two weeks ago, we organised a percussion and performance evening led by our Director of Music Development (Eugene Skeef – mixed Zulu/Xhosa). Over 200 people were present, one third of them from the west side of town. From the west, we also have groups who regularly attend our rock school and we have been actively recruiting young Croats to join our team of guardians who look after the building during the day. In addition, the Centre carries out a considerable amount of work on the west side, with percussion workshops in two youth centres and we act as a meeting place for youth organisations from across the city and from as far away as Čapljina and Grude. This is a role we have recently taken on from the OSCE. We would do more. We would like to extend our music school work into western Herzegovina, working alongside the music schools in the west. It is politicians who make this impossible at the moment. I would also remind the public that the PMC is a War Child initiative, that our very first programme was a mobile bakery which started its work feeding refugees in Međugorje. We have also been a major supplier of diabetic medicines in West Mostar and western Herzegovina. We have, in collaboration with the Croatian Government, recently constructed an extension to the kindergarten in Pakrac (Croatia). Has all this been forgotten? We work in other parts of Bosnia Herzegovina: in Sarajevo, Goražde, in hospitals in Fojnica and Pazarić where, happily, we do not have to watch our backs quite so much as here in Mostar with criticisms of those we are working with. We have recently started work with young people in Republika Srpska. We do all possible to encourage attendance from all sides at the Centre and offer transportation to those who feel uncertain about coming here. Their uncertainty has nothing to do with fear of this place, but has more to do with what might and, on occasions, has happened to them when they return home. I would suggest that those who care to criticise us, take a good look at their actions and the behaviour of those in responsible positions, the police force for example, before telling anyone that the Pavarotti Music Centre is full of "Muslims". Those politicians and others who claim to be so proud of their ethnicity have history against them. Take a good look around the world – that is if you are prepared to raise your eyes from the puddle of your and other people's tears – and you will see that the greatest cultures of the world, the greatest literature, the greatest philosophies, art and music have been the result of a meeting of times, places, minds and peoples. To our critics I say, come to the Pavarotti Music Centre and you will be welcome guests. To those already coming here, I say that you have no reason to stop coming and, to those who have not yet come to the Centre, you are missing something that has been absent in all your lives for far too long – music and joy.'

2 *de Volkskrant*, Pay-Uun Hiu, (December 1997): 'Music Centre? Yes, yes. Of course, the taxi driver knows where to find it. Everybody in East Mostar knows it. Pavarotti, says the taxi driver and laughs. He points out at the bombed-out buildings. Boom, boom, he says. While driving over the newly-erected bridge, his hands move in a big circle around the steering wheel and form a big V; he seems to want to explain how the bridge was destroyed. Boom, boom. Then he stops the car in front of a brand-new yellow facade with terracotta ornaments, an unlikely fairy tale palace amidst the ruins; the Muzički

Centar Pavarotti which came to life at the initiative of the international aid organisation, War Child. The funds for the building, seven million Deutschmarks, were mainly raised by Luciano Pavarotti. Together with Brian Eno, and U2's Bono, he organised big charity concerts. Their song "Miss Sarajevo" alone raised £300,000. Director David Wilson does not waste time on greetings and formal chit-chat. Six days before the official festive opening on December 21, which will include Pavarotti, many other famous musicians and three hundred children, time is running out. The building was designed by British architects and arose from the ruins of an old primary school. The interior decoration, however, is far from finished. "Just follow me," says Wilson, while running on the shiny tiled floor through the courtyard to one of the performing areas, "we're just unpacking a grand piano". At the same time he explains about the building: the central courtyard where a fountain still has to be placed, a section for music education, a special section for music therapy, rehearsal areas, concert areas and a professional recording studio in the basement. Finally, there are two apartments in the semi-circled towers on the top-floor. These are meant mainly for guests, but Wilson also wants to use one of them as a healing and meditation area. This is Oha, says Wilson. Oha, very tall, crew cut, nineteen-years-old. He has impressively big hands with the nails painfully bitten off. He is the best *djembe* player in the whole of Bosnia, says Wilson. But Oha has more to offer. When he was 14, he was one of the youngest soldiers in the Bosnian army yet now he is one of the local helpers at the Centre. Oha and a group of other teenagers formed a club during the war for cultural activities, called Apeiron (from Greek philosophy: the Unending). Oha and his friends are both target groups and future cornerstones of the Music Centre. Of course the PMC also works with much younger children, but youngsters like Oha cannot be missed as interpreters, future workshop leaders and with the fieldwork in schools in and around Mostar. For these youths, the workshops and their other work for the Centre are an escape from the depressing void the war has left. War Child's philosophy is to finance and run the centre for another two years, and at the same time educate enough local helpers to take over and continue the work afterwards. This Sunday, Oha is very stressed, notes Eugene Skeef during the drum workshop. Skeef, born in South Africa and former co-worker of Steve Biko in the seventies, is a phenomenal drummer and has an equally phenomenal gift for music communication. In the small room, with a view of the strip of land where an aromatic herb garden is planned to bloom, it is impossible not to hear the forceful call of Skeef's *djembe*. With Skeef there is no place for quasi-serious or quasi-creative playing. "Focus," he demands, while rolling his dreadlocks into a ponytail. "Do not play before I ask you to! Concentrate! Watch each other. We want to get into the spirit of the music." Gradually the workshop takes on the air of an almost magical ritual. Every single player gets into the rhythm of his own rhythmic pattern which corresponds with the rhythmical pattern of the *djembe* trio formed by Skeef, Oha and Peter Vilk, a young English drummer and music psychologist. Through repetition of the pattern not a single part of the body is left unaffected by the sound. The lower *djembe* tones go right through your diaphragm and with their long waves provide a feeling of stability and calmness. The higher tones in the faster patterns work directly on the muscles and absorb all the concentration until everybody's attention is solely focused on the music. When this level of concentration has been reached, Skeef increases the intensity and complexity. He not only increases the tempo, but also the difficult rhythmic combinations and the tempo in which the patterns change. With extreme precision he moves every participant just a tiny bit over their limits, while stimulating them with his *djembe*. His voice has become like a hurricane: power, power, man! Keep going! Keep watching! Hands no longer feel pain, legs and feet are moving by themselves. Then Skeef lets his drummers go. The rhythms slow down and the drummers become Bosnian kids again. "Relax, relax. That was real power energy, man," he says. Oha's day has been made. He feels great after the workshop. Although Skeef wasn't easy on him. "I know you're under great pressure," he had said, "and that everybody demands a great deal from you. Oha, please help us with the piano, Oha, could you take those things there and there. But you are a musician and we still have to practise a lot before the opening.

Practise, practise, practise," Skeef had stressed. "You know," Oha later tells us while sitting on the battered old couch in Wilson's house, "it is like there is more and more growing noise inside my head which can be exorcised by the drumming." Afterwards it is quiet again and he has a moment of peace. Meanwhile the small living room is getting crowded and becoming more like a youth hostel. Everybody helps themselves to beer, coffee and tea. "I more or less adopted them," Wilson acknowledges. It is a bit unpractical to keep up the beer stock all the time, but guys like Oha, Teo or Crnji just don't have any other place where they feel at home. Wilson sees himself a "teacher, failed entrepreneur, manager and incidental playwright". At the end of 1992 he and film-maker Bill Leeson went to Zagreb to make a film about the war in Croatia, where his wife was born. Back in London he and Leeson founded War Child, named after a play Wilson once wrote. They organised a three-day benefit festival at the Royal Festival Hall, with artists like Julian Lloyd Webber. Their ideas about giving aid shaped the War Child philosophy, which contrasts sharply with the old colonial "we-relief-workers-know-what-is-good-for-you" mentality. Wilson, "if you are serious about doing something, for starters you have to become part of the community and then really listen to what is being requested instead of telling them what they need." Already during the war a bakery was set up in Mostar providing 15,000 people a day with bread. An insulin transport was set up for diabetic children and what became evident with all the visits was the repeated demand for music. As soon as the electricity was working again after a failure, children would immediately turn on their radios and play their CDs. War Child always left with a huge list of requests and came back with dozens of CDs and cassettes for the local radio. "Music forms an essential part in giving aid," Wilson determined. "Of course you need food and medicine, but you have to strive and keep people 'human' in an inhumane situation." The idea to deal with this request for music more systematically and to use music as a "healing force" came after War Child met up with Nigel Osborne in Sarajevo in 1994. Nigel, as intimates know is "larger than life". It is true that the composer and professor in music science at the University of

Edinburgh and the University of Hanover is a very tall figure with glasses, a beard and an impressive amount of untameable hair in the nostrils. Yet his reputation is mostly derived from the music workshops he organised in the basements of Sarajevo during the war. With his backpack filled with maracas, triangles, woodblocks, *crotales* and other instruments, he "sneaked" his way through the only good route to the city under siege; across Mount Igman, slipping by the snipers in the dark, through the tunnel at the airport. In the city Osborne set up different instrument depots, like soldiers do for their weapons. Through the "bush-telegraph" the time and place where workshops were taught was announced. At the workshops, for instance, he used a poem by Goran Simić, with whom he made a rock-opera which premiered in Sarajevo in 1995. "The end of the war is half an hour too late," the children sang, after three hours of democratic composing and orchestrating, for a public of 40 or 50. At present, Osborne (Head of the Music Department) and Skeef (Head of Music Development) are mainly responsible for the artistic content of the Music Centre. Osborne provides the typical Western European, academic approach and he wants to set up a clinical music therapy department with the help of medical specialists, focusing mainly on the treatment of trauma. At this moment his postgraduate students are already working at schools in the Mostar region with a programme combining music education and healing, where Skeef's African background is indispensable. Tuesday morning, one day later than planned, the first class of school children arrives at the new building to practise for the grand opening. Oha is there. "You know," Oha had stated before, "I was an impossible child." His parents' marriage was not great and he had "fire in his body". The war seemed exciting. "You are only a child, what do you know about it." His father was forced to flee to Germany and Oha became a soldier and fought on the Mostar front line. "It's because of all the films on TV," he thinks, looking back. "There you have heroes like the Terminator and children want to be like their heroes." He says he was lucky. That doesn't apply to all his friends. Some of them are gone for good, others he lost sight of because they were Croat. Just recently he ran into an old friend at the west side of the city. They talked and laughed as they had done in the old days, but it was not the same any more. "Everything seems the same, but it is not the same. Everything has changed," he notices daily. But music also changed his life. Eugene Skeef changed his life. After the war Oha went to Italy with other members of Apeiron. He just observed, observed a lot. The sea, the forests, the land. Kilometres of wide, safe areas. It brought calmness and in this calmness he decided he wanted to be a musician and work with children. And that he wanted children of his own and a close family life. Yet mostly, he wanted to live. For the first time, children's voices are heard in the high, light atmosphere of the Centre. The cleaning crew, the carpenters, the bricklayers and staff of the music centre are standing around the balustrades and glass doors looking around and enjoying the site. The children sing and Crnji, with his long black hair and known for his silent cigarette smoking, depicts, while flapping his arms, a bird spreading his wings across the ocean. Teo, who was interrogated about the whereabouts of his father during a surprise attack, and who then witnessed his father's murder and now has a hard time falling asleep, plays the snare drum while Oha plays his *djembe*. Just for a while they are no longer tough guys. They are no longer soldiers. They are back in what is left of their childhood. "It sounds romantic," Wilson knows, "but Mostar lost its bridge and the Music Centre could well be a new bridge, figuratively speaking: a bridge to the future, a bridge between music cultures, a bridge to the peace.'"

[3] Tiffany Hughes, PMC music therapist: 'It was cold, wet and almost dark, but we had to bear it. Pavarotti and his entourage would stop here first to hear the children of the Special School. The children were excited, clutching the toys they had been given by the Maestro and Nicoletta Mantovani. We waited, receiving conflicting information about the time of arrival, not knowing whether to take the children up the road or keep them by the school. They were growing restless and the atmosphere lay at the fine line between elation and frustration. Adrenaline ran high, mine and theirs, for different reasons. Through the rain in the distance, with a powerful serenity, descended two helicopters. This was a sign for me of how

long we had to make our decision. None of the children noticed. By now they were singing their way through every song that we had ever taught them. The decision was made to take them to the road so that they would be nearer Pavarotti. We ran in the rain and discovered there was only a muddy strip of wasteland for us to occupy, but it was better than being fenced in. More waiting. I thought the moment would never come, but at long last a slow procession of vehicles approached us. The children sang for all they could, only until the cars stopped. A door opened and in the damp, cold night, a great beaming warmth drew in the children with his smile. The voices drifted off into an amazed gasp and shrieks of excitement. The song was lost, but it no longer seemed appropriate anyway. Whatever the Maestro actually felt at this point, all he showed these children was his heart. They hadn't noticed the helicopters, but no one could miss how the smile dispelled the cold and the waiting. Pavarotti had arrived in Mostar and these children, if any, deserved his attention first.'

[4] Letter from Tom Stoppard: 'The thing I will remember longest is the long straight road which was the walk from the Music Centre back to the hotel; walking the gauntlet between ruins shelled and shot to pieces, trying to imagine what it must have been like. Knowing it was impossible to imagine. Someone pointed out a place where a dance class continued to practise underground during the fighting. I didn't feel comfortable in Mostar: to have suffered nothing and to be made a fuss of by people who suffered much, and lost so much, and now had regained so much between the ruins, is not comfortable. I only felt normal with children too young to remember anything; and how young those had to be. But – somehow – the experience was uplifting too.'

Music and War

[1] Western orchestral music would not have been possible without Pythagoras' visit to a blacksmith. Hearing a hammer strike an anvil he asked if he could weigh the hammers. He found that one was two-thirds the size of the first. He showed that by continually dividing by two-thirds, an infinite spiral of notes emerges. He had hit upon

'natural harmonics'. He concluded that the cosmos was a harmonic ratio, that we lived in a musical universe and that music obeys the laws of physics.

[2] Look at the honeybee to see how this is true for beings other than mammals. In *Following The Bloom: Across America with the Migratory Bee Keepers,* Beacon Press, Boston 1991, Douglas Whynott says that bees produce 'sustained wing vibrations and measured sound pulses. Tempo corresponds to distance. [Bees] remain in the hive dancing through the day and into the night, altering the straight run to create a gravity symbol that refers to the sun's position on the other side of the earth – a position the bee has never seen.'

[3] *Book of Sound Therapy,* Olivea Dewhurst-Maddock, Fireside 1993.

[4] The International Helsinki Federation for Human Rights acknowledged in their 1993 report that 'what is taking place in Bosnia-Herzegovina is attempted genocide – the extermination of a people in whole or in part because of their race, religion or ethnicity', with the international community (the parties to the Geneva Convention and the United Nations) 'displaying nearly incomprehensible incapacity; having failed to put an end to a war between one of the best equipped armies in Europe and a civilian population, who were neither psychologically or physically and materially prepared for it.'

[5] My opening remarks made at the Anne Frank Exhibition, PMC, September 3rd, 1998: 'The PMC is honoured to host the opening of the exhibition. On a personal note and, as one born right at the end of the Second World War, my politics, in fact my presence here at the PMC, has been shaped by Anne Frank. My father was one of the first British doctors to enter Bergen-Belsen and I still have his photographs of the emaciated survivors imprinted on my brain. He told me that he had been ashamed at how many died after Liberation because British soldiers fed the people too much, too quickly. Anne Frank would recognise Bosnia and Herzegovina. We should not hide from the facts. Nothing was learnt from her experiences and we sit here today in the Mostar Ghetto, a place where thousands of Anne Franks ate grass soup for ten months at the worst time of the war. We also sit inside a European country where events took place

which were the equal of those that happened during the time of the last European Holocaust. It is to our shame that the same speeches were made, the same eyes were averted, Munich went transatlantic. And it goes on. The twentieth century has been the century of Anne Franks. From the Armenians at the beginning of the century on to the Nazi terror, the Stalin Gulags, Cambodia, Rwanda and onwards to Iraq. It has been estimated that in the last decade we have had millions of Anne Franks: two million children killed in wars, four million orphaned and some ten million psychologically traumatised. One survivor of Auschwitz, Bruno Bettelheim, said that there is no meaning at all to life but we must behave as though there is. Anne Frank lived that dictum almost to the end of her short life. If she was here now – perhaps she is here now in all of us present – she would understand and enjoy what we are doing here.'

6 'Music is the weapon' declared the Nigerian musician Fela Anikulapo Kuti (from the 1982 film about Kuti of the same name by S Tchal-Gadjieff and J-J Flori). Aware of that fact, politicians around the world use music and musicians to achieve their goals or try to control musicians who they perceive as a threat to their power; the treatment of Kuti, for example, in Nigeria or Victor Jara in Pinochet's Chile. Even instruments are sometimes seen as a threat and are banned.

7 'Your Child's Brain', *Newsweek,* February 19th, 1996, presented evidence for the brain's need for rhythm. The article described the stress produced when the brain is deprived of this basic need.

8 For those interested in the aid debate as applied to former Yugoslavia, I would recommend Barbara E. Harrell-Bond's 'Refugees and the Challenge of Reconstructing Communities Through Aid', in *War Exile, Everyday Life*, published by the Institute of Ethnology and Folklore Research, Zagreb. For an overall political perspective, see Noam Chomsky, *World Orders and other writings on Cold and post-Cold War International Politics.*

Missing Elton

[1] 'Further to our telephone conversation earlier this week, I confirm that Hydrogradnja would be pleased to accept the return of the 40,000 DEM gift provided to you, and we fully understand your reasons for not being able to accept this. Please arrange the transfer of funds back to our account in Sarajevo. We will forward confirmation that the funds have been received back into our account. Yours sincerely, Mehmed Drino, General Manager.'

[2] Excerpt from Minutes of the Trustee Meeting of February 5th, 1997: 'The Trustees decided that all monies should be returned as soon as possible to the contractor ... the Trustees expressed their unease with Mike Terry's role in this matter and questioned whether he could bring War Child into disrepute in future. The Trustees noted that he, as Project Director of the Music Centre, is vital to the successful completion of this major project. The decision of the Trustees was to keep MT in his position as Project Director of the Music Centre but to restrict his involvement in future projects.'

[3] Letter from Anthea Eno to the War Child Trustees, September 23rd, 1998: 'As a member of the Board of Governors of the PMC and as one of War Child's earliest supporters, I am writing to you and to the key personnel in War Child to express my total support for David Wilson and my absolute dismay at his being asked to resign. The recommendations made are mostly to do with improving efficiency. Other comments I recognised as very much David's ideas for making the place less 'designer-style' and more child-friendly. If a Director is asked to resign then surely there must be some very serious things that he has done wrong. No top-level executive can be asked to resign for such spurious reasons as 'being irrational and manipulative'. When that director is also a key person in the whole organisation and co-founder of it, then these reasons become even more outrageous. David's courage, and the creativity he has employed in dealing with a very difficult situation in Mostar, seem to have been totally ignored, let alone praised. I am more than happy to take this opportunity to do so. What on earth is going on here that I don't know about? I cannot understand what he is being accused of. To me, David is not ill and he has done and is doing a

fantastic job that no one has actually criticised. If there were reports of misappropriation of funds at the PMC or if David was just sitting around drawing a fat pay cheque while the building stood empty and neglected, then of course resignation would be in order. Whereas the only complaints I have heard are of a personal nature or concern his creative use of the space. This reflects pretty poorly on War Child, who I always supported because it did not make strict, clinical rules for a given situation, but seemed able to move and change with it. Anthea Eno.'

4 Bill named me 'Spreadsheet Man' because I was responsible for the charity's finances. Bill was also responsible for Anne's nickname. At the time she was studying to be an acupuncturist and was required by her college to turn in a minimum of 20 tongue diagrams each week. She was often in the War Child office taking pulses and notating tongues. Both can indicate disharmony, or disease, in specific parts of the body.

Whistleblower

1 Brian Eno's letter to the Trustees: 'Dear Mr Spencer, On Friday, 7 May 1999, the Patrons of War Child were informed of the resignation of nearly the entire Board of Trustees of War Child UK. At the Trustee meeting of 5 May, Trustee Ed Morris resigned, followed by Keith Turner. We understand that Andy MacDonald also wishes to resign, but is barred legally from doing so as no trustee board can exist with only one member. These resignations effectively leave War Child UK without a functioning Board of Trustees. We believe that this incredible and utterly avoidable calamity is the direct result of your failure, as Chairman of the Board of Trustees, to appreciate the severity of the current situation and to take the necessary actions agreed upon between the Board and the Patrons at our joint meeting of 9 April. You had been informed at some time before that meeting of Nicoletta Mantovani's letter of 7 March to Bill Leeson requesting an explanation of two extremely serious issues involving War Child UK's management: 1) Generally, the 1996 incident concerning the construction of the Pavarotti Music Centre, in which Bill Leeson and Mike Terry allegedly were involved in financial irregularities

with the Bosnian firm Hydrogradjna; and, specifically, 2) An accounting of the $500,000 disbursed to War Child UK for the Pavarotti & Friends Liberian Children's Village, construction of which has yet to begin. At the joint 9 April meeting the Trustees and Patrons present agreed on the following measures: the immediate dissolution of War Child UK's Management Committee; the retirement of Bill Leeson; the appointment of a new War Child UK Chief Executive; the immediate handover of the Pavarotti-funded projects to Nicoletta Mantovani, with administrative control thereof assigned to War Child Netherlands (the Pavarotti Music Centre); War Child Italy (the Pavarotti & Friends Liberian Children's Village); and War Child USA (the Pavarotti and Friends Guatemala project). Despite this joint agreement, the only change undertaken thus far is the unexplained firing of John Carmichael, who it was agreed at the 9 April meeting would assist War Child Italy in its implementation of the Liberia project. As far as we know, no other action has been taken. As a direct result of your inaction, War Child UK is left without a functioning Board of Trustees. The faith of the Patrons in War Child UK has been finally exhausted. Because we have always taken our positions as Patrons of War Child seriously, we feel now obliged to fulfil our responsibilities by ensuring the proper resolution of the present crisis. Due to your apparent lack of a similar sense of responsibility, coupled with the disintegration of the Trustee Board, we support the reporting of the situation as it now exists to the Charity Commission on Tuesday, 11 May. This will raise the question why you, as Chair, failed to resolve the situation, and the reason for the resignations of your fellow Trustees. We would like to be able to report to the Commission that some progress, however minor or belated, has been made toward remedying War Child UK's untenable position. While time is quite short, we recommend that the following actions be taken by the remaining Board of you and Andy MacDonald … so that they can be notified to the Commission at the meeting of 11 May: 1) The appointment of three neutral Trustees, recommended by the Patrons, with no affiliation whatsoever to the War Child UK Management Committee, so that their impartiality vis-à-vis the management of War Child UK is guaranteed; 2) Written confirmation that the course of action decided upon at the joint Patron/Trustee meeting of 9 April has been implemented, or, at the least, initiated; on completion of 1 and 2, the resignation of yourself as Chair and Trustee. We believe that the carrying out of the above would enable the Patrons to indicate to the Commission on Tuesday that some progress has been made toward resolving War Child UK's internal crisis, progress mitigating against the need for the Commission to intervene as it determines legally necessary. Nothing short of these three steps will begin to restore the faith of the Patrons in War Child UK, and prevent us from taking whatever steps are necessary to protect our good names. We anticipate your immediate response. Brian Eno on behalf of (most of) the Patrons.'

[2] Bill Leeson, quoted in *The Sunday Times,* December 10th, 2000: 'Bill Leeson, co-founder of the charity War Child which was set up in 1993 to help victims of the war in Bosnia, is trying to cut celebrities out of the loop. "I would like to phase celebrities out of War Child completely and let the work the charity does speak for itself," he says. Leeson, more than anyone, knows the benefits that celebrity endorsement can bring: when he first wanted to raise money, "the situation was an emergency and I used celebrities mercilessly". The result was a compilation CD, *Help*, which climbed high in the charts thanks to contributions from Blur, Oasis and the Manic Street Preachers. But then Leeson found the charity was becoming more famous for its celebrity endorsers than its work and he had to reassess things. "We suddenly became fashionable and all sorts of undesirables, more interested in promoting their flagging careers than doing anything worthwhile, tried and failed to jump on the bandwagon."'

[3] Letter from Amela Sarić, Director of the PMC to War Child Trustees, October 9th, 1999. 'I am writing to you for the first time as PMC Director, but I find it really necessary. Last few weeks I was in contact with David Wilson hoping that he will be one of the crucial internationals willing to help Pavarotti Centre in the future. But from that contact I realised that he is too depressed by problems with War Child and with the fact that he has to work from home and not to

be welcome in the organisation he founded. The fact that he may be made redundant would be wrong and disaster for the PMC. As you all know, he was the PMC Director for the first two years and most of the successes and good reputation of PMC we have to thank him for. He found enough strength and courage to stay with Bosnians, leave very quiet and secure position in War Child and fight for the Centre in the middle of a divided city. Pavarotti Centre became the oasis of peace, place for the children and young people of Bosnia mostly thanks to his vision and hard work. The only independent centre from all kinds of politic games. He was brave enough to fight against some local politicians who wanted to destroy us, to destroy the idea that the Centre is for all people in Bosnia without regard to their names, nationality or confession. He was brave enough to give a chance to young people to have a job, responsibility and hope to find a way to become normal human beings. And this is not just my or PMC staff opinion. He has respect of local people and politicians, important people in OHR, UN, OSCE, BiH politicians. His speeches are still remembered in Mostar and BiH and he was given a lot of media attention and strongly respected in my country. Even Croatian press was nice about him. Most of the international journalists that visited us in the last few weeks asked me what is happening with him, is he still in War Child, what is his future role? He is the best ambassador for us and without him the PMC future is in doubt and we will lose our best supporter and friend. And at the end he was the only member of War Child London who cared about this project. I still believe that through good and continued work of PMC as one of the biggest projects of War Child, War Child can benefit. We are the best example of War Child success for possible donors of future War Child projects. I write this letter as Director of PMC supported by people working here. We are very willing that one of us come to London and speaks with you directly if you find it necessary.'

[4] Letter to Raymond Chevalier, December 19th, 1999: 'I don't know how bad the financial side is at War Child, but I am pretty certain that they have been dipping into PMC monies (the underspend and the "Miss Sarajevo" income). The PMC will grind to a halt

in February without at least the underspend being sent down ... I realise how delicate the situation is for you, but the fact is that, as a founder of War Child, I am unable to work from the London office because of the susceptibilities of others who should be the ones in exile and not me. It is deeply frustrating and depressing and prevents me from getting on with my work. People are beginning to ask me why, when I am in London, I communicate all the time from a home address. I should be writing on War Child letterheads to MEPs and the Directorate General X at the EU to get monies to the PMC which are owed. I should be setting up meetings at DFID for future funding, reapplying to the UK Lottery and so on. I cannot do this and it is an absurd situation.'

[5] Brian Eno's draft letter, January 30th, 2000: 'Dear Trustees of War Child UK, As you know, for the past year we, as the patrons of War Child, have been waiting to hear that the troubles that blighted the charity were behind us. We made some suggestions concerning the London office and we were glad to hear that a new CEO had been found. We have now been informed that Raymond Chevalier, hired as Chief Executive by the Trustees in November to, we presume, implement reforms and seek answers, has suddenly resigned. We have now also heard that funding for the Pavarotti Music Centre in Mostar is uncertain, and that a crisis at the PMC looms. It appears that there is a resistance within War Child UK to support the Pavarotti projects and to produce answers to serious financial questions. As our professional reputations are linked to War Child, and because we still believe in the vision of War Child as it once was and can be again, we believe it imperative that the following be implemented immediately: We propose the immediate appointment of an interim Chief Executive Officer, to work with the remaining co-founder of War Child, David Wilson, toward the restructuring of War Child UK. Because the current state of crisis does not provide adequate time to go through the process of applications and headhunting, we propose the appointment of a previous candidate for the CEO position, as interim CEO. This appointment should be for six months, reviewable by the Trustees at the end of that period in consultation with the Patrons. During that

time, the Trustees may wish to conduct another application process, which may include consideration of the interim appointee. We urge that the Trustees provide the interim appointee with a narrow and focused remit: namely, to retain a completely independent professional auditor, whose role it will be (with facilitation from David Wilson) to examine every aspect of War Child UK's finances and make a complete report to the Trustees and Patrons as soon as possible. During this examination, we believe the interim appointee should carefully administer and control incoming and outgoing funds, with weekly reports to the Trustees on all financial and programme activities. All existing programmes and employees should be closely scrutinised for financial – and results – effectiveness, and no additional initiatives or appointments should be made during this interim period without the full agreement of the Trustees, in consultation with the Patrons. During this time, David Wilson should work with the interim appointee to resolve the funding and morale crisis at the PMC. This person should also work with the Patrons, Trustees, and other relevant War Child offices to ameliorate this crisis and work toward short- and long-term support for all of the Pavarotti projects. We, the undersigned patrons, wish to maintain our status as War Child patrons, but feel unable to do so unless the above urgent actions are taken … We await your earliest response.'

[6] Letter to War Child from James White, Finance Director, Universal Records, August 19th, 1999: 'I am pleased to be able to present War Child two cheques, the first for £133,259, representing the balance of monies due for worldwide royalties due on the "Miss Sarajevo" single and the same song on the *Passengers* album. The second for £7,961 (after deduction of Gift Aid) for the profits on the UK single release. This represents accounting up to 31/12/98. Future accounting will be dealt with directly by our royalties department; Andy Harwood is the contact. Recently I spoke with the representatives of the artists involved and was asked to convey their wish that these monies be passed directly to the Pavarotti Music Centre in Mostar. Please don't hesitate to call if you require further information.'

[7] Note on War Child Trustees: Twelve Trustees resigned as a direct result of the crisis in War Child: (as of Feb 2001) Sylvester McCoy (actor); Tim Spencer (lawyer) first resignation; Khawar Qureshi QC, Chair (barrister); Berry Ritchie (journalist); Liz Huhne (Justice of the Peace); Ed Morris (charity adviser); Keith Turner (accountant); Tim Spencer, Chair (lawyer) second resignation; Andy Macdonald (record producer); Anthea Norman-Taylor (music publisher); John Gaydon (music promoter); Kate Buckley (lawyer).

[8] Anthea Norman-Taylor's letter of resignation from Trustees, February 13th, 2000: 'Dear All, After our meeting on Thursday, Kate summarised the situation to me again by saying the choices are to either split it up or wind it up. I have thought long and hard about this as I am sure we all have. I would like to reiterate what I have been trying to say for a year, which is not either of the above options. The Patrons and the music business were attracted to War Child because of its aim to think long-term about children in war zones, not to just deliver aid, as so many charities do already. The concept of the Pavarotti Music Centre epitomised that aim ... to provide a 'safe haven' from ethnic conflicts through the medium of music making. An ancillary part of this is music therapy. Although it cost a lot to build and run, the building was actually given (not sold) by the city authorities because they were convinced this was a valuable addition to the town and might help it heal the divide. I know I need not say more about the Centre because I know you all support its existence. But Pavarotti, Nicoletta and the many people in the music business who helped this happen are now being told by War Child that that project was an aberration, that in fact all War Child wants to do is send money to existing 'in the field' NGOs to provide immediate aid with food, clothing, medicine etc. You must be able to understand that this is deeply upsetting to Pavarotti (and the other Patrons) when so much time and thought and money has gone into researching other long-term projects to help children of war zones in other parts of the world. And as you know, he was also justifiably very concerned about the lack of financial controls over his other projects when being handled by War Child London. It is clear that the London office was/is being run by a management

team who do not want to work with Pavarotti's projects. I am astounded that Kate listens to the London office's "expertise" on the subject, rather than the people who have actually been there and been involved (i.e. Nicoletta Mantovani, Johnny Carmichael, Tom Ehr and David Wilson). But that seems to be where we are. It is a difference of vision, I guess. The London office, with Kate's support, are saying they want to go their own way. They suggest Pavarotti and those who think differently to them split off, basically that there be a divorce. My preference would be not to split and not to fold, but to have all the offices working together. But this just cannot happen with people who are against the Pavarotti projects running the London office. Kate seems to believe that our priority is to make David Wilson redundant. That would certainly make the London office happy. But this would not help the situation in that the other offices (certainly Italy, USA and Canada) cannot work with the London office because it is staffed by people antagonistic to their aims. As you know, I was in favour of David going back into the London office, but not as CEO. I had imagined a situation where we could have a London office being run by a new CEO and David working for a new body, War Child International say, which took care of long-term projects involved in healing through cultural exchange etc., i.e. to co-ordinate with the Pavarotti projects and hopefully a whole lot of new ones. David has many ideas on this front; he is a creative and hard-working person. I had thought then maybe we should wind it up … that it was a total impasse. However, I know there are lots of ghastly implications and that lawyers and accountants would descend like vultures (sorry Kate), quite apart from the press. I cannot vote to wind it up, but neither can I vote to split it up. I cannot justify to myself or to the supporters I have brought in from the music business that War Child London would be a charity worth supporting. Their little projects from safe-play areas to diabetic medicine or food deliveries are being handled already by other charities. I would rather money went directly to GOAL, for example, to help the Sudanese situation. I cannot explain why the money has to first go to a London office where ridiculous overheads are maintained and deducted, then on to another charity.

I find it especially galling that the public are then misled by press stories implying War Child are directly involved in creative projects for children of war. Furthermore, I see the staff are saying they have not had their pay rises. I have no alternative but to tender my resignation herewith and to inform the Patrons that I am doing so, giving my reasons as above. In any event the Patrons who signed the letter to the Trustees of February 10 will step down as Patrons since their views have been ignored. No doubt the London office will be delighted by both these moves and no doubt Bill Leeson and Bob Close, who are in close contact with the London staff, will feel vindicated. This is what they wanted all along. I am sorry to leave you all with such a situation, but as you know, I have put a tremendous amount of time and energy into War Child. However, I can no longer justify that devotion. With best wishes, Anthea Norman-Taylor.'

[9] My redundancy letter, February 29th, 2000: 'Dear David, I am writing following recent discussions amongst the Trustees. The Trustees have considered your report of November 1999. We apologise that it has taken some time to respond to this. The Trustees wished to have the view of Raymond, as Chief Executive at the time, on this report. That is why you received no immediate response to it from the Trustees. Raymond reported at a meeting of the Trustees in January and said that he did not believe that the report identified any sustainable role for you and that the charity could not justify creating roles given its present financial condition. That view is shared by the current Trustees and, moreover since the date of your report, it seems that the Patrons will have a reduced role in the light of Anthea's resignation as Trustee, Brian's resignation as a Patron and Anthea's indication that many of the other Patrons will also resign. Moreover it is clear that relations between you and the staff in the office are strained. In the circumstances, and in the light of the present financial uncertainty of War Child, the Trustees have decided that they cannot identify any post to offer you at the present time and have accordingly concluded that it is not appropriate to continue to employ you. I am writing therefore to give you notice of termination of your employment by reason of redundancy. You are entitled to a week's notice for every year that you have worked. I

believe that you have worked seven full years and on that basis give you notice that your contract will end on 19 April, 2000. You are also entitled to a redundancy payment. This is calculated at £345 for each year of service. The Trustees do not require you to work during your notice period. Accordingly, I enclose a cheque for £5,470.42, being your pay during your notice period and your redundancy payment. There is an outstanding issue in relation to your claim to expenses. The Trustees have considered these and given the uncertainty of your position since September have exceptionally decided to pay the majority of these expenses even though many of them were unauthorised. The Trustees are not prepared to sanction the trip to the United States. Authority for expenditure of this size should have been sought before it was incurred. Accordingly I enclose a cheque for £621.73 in relation to these expenses. With regard to property and papers belonging to the charity we should be grateful if you could return these to the offices of War Child. If you have any information in relation to the Music Centre or otherwise that you believe should be known to the charity, please forward this to the office as well. Yours sincerely, Kate Buckley, Chair of Trustees.'

[10] I prepared a letter in reply to Kate which I never sent. In it, I wanted to ask why value was given to Raymond's opinion when he had been in post for such a short time and seemed to have fled to Thailand. I wanted to remind her that the Patrons and most of the Trustees had resigned in support of me and that the new Trustees had never met me. That it could not be the case that relationships between myself and the War Child office staff had been 'strained' since 1997 when I'd been in Mostar; most of them had never met me. That the argument that my trip to meet Pavarotti in New York should have been sanctioned was ridiculous. Was I supposed to have contacted Bill and asked for his permission to take a flight to report on his misdoings? I wrote a report to the Charity Commission, but they, and the War Child lawyers, refused to read it or see me. Their grounds were that they could only deal with the Trustees and that I was no longer employed by War Child and therefore had no official position. Catch 22.

[11] http://wikipedia.qwika.com/de2en/World_Award

[12] *Guardian* articles on War Child: 'Stars Quit Charity in Corruption Scandal', David Hencke, January 10th, 2010. 'It Seemed Close to Deceitful that Our Money Hadn't Gone Where It Ought to', Interview with Brian Eno, January 10th, 2010. 'Charity Returns £41,000', David Hencke, *Guardian*, January 17th, 2001.

[13] 'The Commission Has Been Too Slow to Act', *Guardian* editorial, January 10th, 2001. 'War Child UK, the charity set up to help victims of the Bosnian war, is in serious trouble. Luciano Pavarotti and five other celebrity patrons have walked out of the high-profile overseas aid charity. Eleven trustees have resigned. A joint investigation by the *Guardian* and Channel 4 News shows that Bill Leeson, one of its co-founders, and Mike Terry, a consultant, took a bribe from contractors building a Bosnian music therapy centre, named after the Italian tenor. Though it was later repaid by the charity, the two men are still involved with the charity. There is also grave concern about high administrative expenses, poor accounting, inadequate management structures. A spokesman for Mr Pavarotti said yesterday that he did not want to be associated with anything corrupt. He had asked about a Liberian children's project, but had had to wait for a year before he could get the accounts to discover that administration had absorbed much of the expenditure. As a result, he personally directed that all future money from him for former War Child UK projects in Yugoslavia, Liberia and Guatemala should be funded by different charities, following which, when the Kosovo crisis broke, a $1m donation was sent to the United Nations refugee agency. Nigel Osborne, professor of music at Edinburgh University and former Director of Music for the centre, described the bribe as "a catastrophic betrayal". It was the revelation of the bribe that prompted the patrons to act. They called for the retirement of Mr Leeson, the dissolution of the management committee, and the transfer of the Pavarotti project out of War Child UK's control. But nothing happened, leading to an exodus of patrons and trustees. It was a sad development in a charity that won the support of a new generation of pop stars. Many of the biggest names helped raise money for it in the mid 1990s. Other patrons included Sir Tom Stoppard, the playwright, and Juliet

Stevenson, the actor. What lessons can be learned? The Trustees clearly behaved responsibly. Thwarted by the charity's management, they wrote to the Charity Commissioners in June 1998 about the lack of reports to Trustees and the refusal to arrange suitable meetings. They also complained of the "financial impropriety". Two further letters were sent the same year complaining about the lack of financial information, the reluctance of Mr Leeson to cooperate, and the need for a full-time paid trustee to fill in the gaps in their knowledge and to examine whether Mr Leeson could be dismissed. The Chairman of the Trustees called in an independent auditor and independent solicitors. Yet they were still unable to budge the charity's management. Hence the decision of 11 Trustees to resign. The Charity Commission is conducting a financial audit but has moved much too slowly. It is 30 months since it was alerted to serious problems in the charity and yet it has still not produced a report or made public any recommendations. The Commission's procedures are notorious for being ponderous and antiquated. John Stoker, the Chief Charity Commissioner, is planning to upgrade its monitoring role, helped by a two-year 40% boost to its funding that begins in April 2002. But with a current £20m budget and a staff of 500, it should already be able to move more quickly to deal with a serious complaint. Quite separate from its regulatory role, the Commission needs to review the advice it gives trustees. War Child Trustees wanted to dismiss their unsatisfactory managers but failed. With better advice, they should have been able to get their way.'

[14] Bill Leeson: 'Do-Gooders Need Not Apply'. Cheryl Dahle, May 31st, 1999 and published in June 1999 issue of *Fast Company Magazine*. 'Bill Leeson, the outspoken co-founder of one of Great Britain's most high-profile charities, believes that you can do good works without being a do-gooder. "I am a deal maker. I make deals to get my story out." Bill Leeson doesn't have much patience for do-gooders. Ask him to talk about most nonprofits – outfits bound by tradition and filled with self-importance – and the hot-headed Brit finds it hard to contain himself. "I hate the idea of charities as holier-than-thou organizations that set themselves apart from the world, as if they are the chosen ones that will fix things," Leeson complains.

"We are the do-gooders that will sort out all of these problems. You just give us the money. That's a bloody crock." Think of War Child, the organization that Leeson co-founded six years ago to aid children in strife-torn regions, as the anti-charity charity. It has delivered nearly 8 million pounds ($13 million) worth of aid and services to young people in the former Yugoslavia and in Africa – but it has a staff of just 15, and it operates on a lean 4% overhead. Its more ambitious projects (a music-therapy center for children in Mostar, Bosnia, completed in 1997; a soon-to-be-completed children's-education center in Liberia) are decidedly unorthodox. And no matter how obscure the countries that it's working in may be, War Child maintains a glamorous image in its home country, where it hosts "eat-ins" at chic restaurants and puts on concerts featuring Luciano Pavarotti, U2, Spice Girls, and Oasis. In short, Leeson has created a new breed of nonprofit – one that combines sympathy with savvy, noble ideals with self-interest, and good works with smart business. Leeson, now 55, got his first close-up view of war in 1993, when he traveled to Croatia to film a documentary on artists. His experience there changed his life – not just because of the violence that he saw, but because of the effect that the violence had on young survivors. Walking through the streets of Zagreb, he saw children's drawings hanging in shop windows. "They were just what you'd expect of children's artwork – stick figures drawn with brightly coloured crayons," he says. "Except that they were pictures of guns and corpses. It was all stuff that these kids had seen with their own eyes. It was horrifying. I found it terribly difficult to go back to my normal job again." So he didn't. Soon after returning to London, Leeson organized a fund-raiser. Friends encouraged him to take personal control of how the money that he raised would be spent – instead of donating it to a charity whose overhead (according to War Child) would take as much as 12% off the top. Ten days later, War Child was born. From the start, Leeson recognized that his competition was not other charities – it was indifference and ignorance: "When people watch TV, they see a ten minute news program with half a dozen wars, each reduced to a 30-second sound bite. People get desensitised, and they flip the channel." One

322

of the organization's first efforts was to sponsor a mobile bakery in Mostar. Instead of delivering rations to thousands of people for just a day, War Child supplied fresh bread to one village for several months. Donors who suffered from compassion fatigue suddenly heard stories about their dollars buying warm bread for families. War Child has also helped reforge the link between rock music and good works – a relationship that had become decidedly unhip to teenagers, who saw earlier efforts (such as the *We Are the World: U.S.A. for Africa* recording) as cheesy. "We had a generation of young people in the UK who felt that charity had nothing to do with them," Leeson says. "We wanted to show them that charity could be cool." War Child was able to persuade some of the UK's hottest bands to write songs for an album. The CD, titled *Help* and produced by Brian Eno, raised £1.5 million ($2.4 million). Leeson also understands the power of the media. Starting with his first fundraiser, a concert in London's Royal Festival Hall, he has always drawn impressive coverage. Part of War Child's media success has been the result of connections: it helps to have friends who control the cameras. Plus, as the fighting in the Balkans has received more and more exposure, the plight of people in Bosnia and Croatia has gained in "popularity." But neither of those reasons explains how War Child has managed to get such sustained coverage while so many other non-profits toil in obscurity. Leeson explains it this way: "I am a deal maker. I make deals to get my story out." He's not talking about bribes; he's talking about working with the media to generate compelling footage and dramatic stories – a form of collaboration that is deemed taboo by many traditional charities. "The media world and the aid world have completely different agendas, but few nonprofits bother to try to understand what the media agenda is about." source: http://www.fastcompany.com/37241/do-gooders-need-not-apply
[15] Ed Vulliamy, 'War Child and The Bosnian War 15 Years On', *The Observer*, Sunday, July 4th, 2010

Tie a Knot
[1] Frederick Francj: 'After I saw a human in Hiroshima, burned into a concrete wall, a human shadow the moment the Bomb struck, I

was haunted by it. Returned home I took a steel plate, and with a blowtorch cut out the contour of this volatilised fellow human. When the outline was complete the human form dropped out, leaving a gaping hole surrounded by frames of steel. I placed both components so that, through the empty negative, the human image can be seen rising, like a phoenix from its ashes.' http://www.dayspringchurchmd.org/resources/43

Neighbours

[1] Morphogenesis was an experimental music group specialising in improvised music and unconventional instruments. Set up in 1985, Roger Sutherland was, with Mike Cosgrave, one of the founding members. Stewart Lee shared a flat with Mike and here is what he wrote about them. "Morphogenesis moved out of the gloom to take their places: a half a dozen or so shady individuals who looked like they should have been manning a Baader-Meinhof Group terrorist cell, or else researching the growth of unusual moulds in an underground room somewhere. What followed was not music or entertainment as I understood it, but an undulating, formless wash of drones, clicks and bubbles, that resisted all formal development and didn't even allow any room for a solo on those carefully arranged elastic bands. There sat Mike, a man who could pick up any tune instantly and play it back to you note perfect, reduced to dropping matches onto his frets in absurd concentration, while a man stood behind him making irritating squeaking noises by rubbing a partially deflated pink balloon And when the balloon promptly burst in his hands, he reacted only with a smug expression which suggested the object's implosion was not actually a mistake, but part of a far greater artistic whole which I would never be able to understand. After 45 minutes or so the sounds mercifully subsided, and I hurried downstairs to get a drink, barely able to suppress my laughter at the most pretentious and pointless display I had ever witnessed."

[2] Despite having gastric flu, Anne forced herself to stay up on the night of February 4th, 2004 because she couldn't bear to miss *Six Feet Under*. Had she not done so, she would not have smelled the gas. In the early morning she woke up uncharacteristically early because

of abdominal pain. It was only her stomach flu that prevented us being overcome by smoke and fumes.

A Place to Go When You Sleep

[1] *The Times*, October 24th, 2013: 'As editor of *The Lancet* from 1965 to 1976, Ian Douglas-Wilson joined a long series of radical editors which went all the way back to Thomas Wakley who worked with the social reformer William Cobbett in the 1820s. Douglas-Wilson's predecessor, Sir Theodore Fox, was a pacifist ambulance driver in the First World War, and *The Lancet's* current editor, Richard Horton, has not hesitated to speak out against government "reforms" to the NHS and the last government's war policies. After taking part in the D-Day landings, Douglas-Wilson found himself treating shell-shocked troops. He committed his experiences to paper, and his article on what was to become known as post-traumatic stress disorder was published in the *British Medical Journal*. He was one of the first Allied medics to enter Bergen-Belsen concentration camp. Later, he would tell his family that he felt guilty because the first British troops to arrive fed the famished prisoners high-calorie rations and many died because they were unused to food. He kept photos from Belsen in the bottom drawer of his desk. His study doubled as his children's nursery, and they used to open his desk and look in horror at the skeletal bodies of inmates. After the war he was interviewed for a job at the *BMJ*, but was advised by its then editor, Hugh Clegg (Nick Clegg's grandfather), that he was too radical for their publication and that he should apply for a job at *The Lancet*. He stayed there for 30 years, the last 11 as editor. Douglas-Wilson was a modest man. When interviewed on BBC, he would insist they didn't mention his name but refer to him as "*Lancet* editor". This modesty didn't restrict his outspokenness. When Lord Moran, president of the Royal College of Physicians and physician to Winston Churchill, published the former Prime Minister's personal health details, he felt the lash of Douglas-Wilson's tongue. He was a vociferous opponent of routine peer review, believing that it cowed original research. Under his editorship, potential contributors received a quick response which gave them time to search out alternative

publications if articles were refused. Douglas-Wilson was an early advocate of receiving osteopathy into the medical "family" and after his retirement was delighted when acupuncture was accepted into the NHS. In 1964 Douglas-Wilson travelled across Africa and came back to write *Health Prospects in Africa*. This was one of the first post-colonial observations into illness and healthcare provision on that continent. His radical approach to medical journalism was reflected in his personal life. Returning from Germany in 1945, he and his wife Betty invited German PoWs to spend Christmas with them and their children. The Douglas-Wilsons sent money to refugees and, in 1956, offered a home to two students who had fled from Budapest during the Hungarian Revolution. There were always interesting people visiting the Douglas-Wilson home in Bromley, Kent. His Danish friend, Karl Henrick Køster, arrived each Christmas, looking a bit like Santa with his two-metre frame and Viking beard. This was the man who had helped Jews escape to Sweden and who, after his death, was the subject of the Disney film *Miracle at Midnight*. Douglas-Wilson's closest friend was Thomas Dormandy, a chemical pathologist and leader writer for *The Lancet*. Dormandy covered a range of topics from medical ethics to Chekhov and the Royal Academy Summer Exhibition. Dormandy was himself a painter and author. Until his death, he would regularly turn up at Douglas-Wilson's care home to read him instalments of his latest book. Douglas-Wilson's wife Betty died on Millennium Eve, aged 91, and he spent the next 13 years on his own until he had to enter a care home. His sense of humour lasted to the end. In the final months of his life, he suffered from dementia and his son remembers a ramble on one visit which involved setting sail across the North Sea. Douglas-Wilson concluded with, "I don't know what I am talking about, nor do you." As an editor, he was a stickler for proper use of language. Here he followed George Orwell, all of whose works were on his bookshelf. "Good writing is like a window pane," wrote Orwell, and Douglas-Wilson followed his advice. He treasured examples of deficient punctuation, such as "Let's eat granny", or unintended ambiguity such as the *Daily Express* headline at the time of the El Alamein campaign in 1942:

"British Push Bottles Up Germans". Orwell wasn't on his shelves just for the clarity of his prose. Douglas-Wilson liked him for his no-nonsense honesty. "Do remember," wrote Orwell, "that dishonesty and cowardice always have to be paid for." Douglas-Wilson lived by these words, honest to his family and friends and never afraid to stand up for the sick, the displaced and difficult causes. He was an early supporter of CND and took his teenage son on one of the first Aldermaston marches. Unloved by a cold mother, Douglas-Wilson had difficulty releasing his emotions. At home, he spent all his time at his desk, poring over next week's editorial and covering the floor with rolls of copy text, children banished to their bedrooms or the garden. He retired early to nurse his sick wife and his capacity to love and be loved increased. With a growing family, he ended his long life giving and receiving empathy and compassion. When his son cleared his desk after his death, the Belsen photos were no longer there. Nor was the family tree that a cousin had meticulously prepared, suggesting that Douglas-Wilson wanted to walk through life unencumbered with his own history. He leaves two daughters and a son. (Dr Ian Douglas-Wilson, physician and editor of *The Lancet*, 1964–76, was born on May 12, 1912. He died on October 15, 2013, aged 101).'

HOOPTEDOODLES

Ships at Sea
[1] At the height of the Cuban Missile Crisis, President Kennedy telephoned Jacqueline, at their weekend house in Virginia. From his voice, she would say later, she could tell that something was wrong. 'Why don't you come back to Washington?' he asked, without explanation. 'From then on, it seemed there was no waking or sleeping,' Mrs Kennedy recalled. She begged her husband to remain with him. 'If anything happens, we're all going to stay right here with you,' she told him in October 1962. 'I just want to be with you, and I want to die with you, and the children do, too'. She told all this to Arthur M Schlesinger, the historian and Kennedy aide.
[2] The Labour Government commissioned an Inquiry which

recommended both union recognition and re-instatement of the workers, but the employer, backed by the right-wing National Association For Freedom and the Conservative Party, rejected the recommendations. The TUC subsequently withdrew their support and the workers' strike committee announced the end of the dispute in June 1978. The repercussions for British industrial relations were far-reaching, significantly weakening the British trades union movement. For the Conservative Party and the right-wing this was seen as a major political and ideological victory, preparing the ground for their success in the 1979 general election and their subsequent curbing of union power in the 1980s.

[3] Haifa Zangana and her husband have since become good friends of mine. She is a novelist, poet and polemicist and I recommend *City of Widows* and *Dreaming of Baghdad*.

[4] *My Life in the Bush of Ghosts*, Brian Eno/David Byrne, Sire Records, 1981.

[5] William Shawcross is Chairman of the Charity Commission of England and Wales and a right-wing commentator. He was a supporter of the war on Iraq. Kenneth Adelman is a long-time Washington insider closely aligned with neoconservatives. He was a member of the Defense Policy Board during the George W. Bush administration.

[6] 'There are Weapons of Mass Destruction in Iraq. They are ours', Futuretrust.org; 'The Gloucester Weapons Inspectors', Counterpunch.org, January 30th, 2003; 'Collapse of Iraq's Health Care Services', Counterpunch.org, October 14th, 2006; 'Bush in London', Counterpunch.org, June 18th, 2008; 'What a Strange Way to Protect Civilians, Depleted Uranium and Libya', AntiWar.com, April 16th, 2011; 'The Terror Weapons Israel is Using in its War against Gaza', Stopwar.org. July 23rd, 2014; 'Famous Jews Who have Opposed Israel', Stopwar.org, August 12th, 2014.

[7] 'Stop the War Benefit at the Astoria', DVD with Brian Eno, Rachid Taha Band, Mick Jones, Nitin Sawhney, Imogen Heap.

[8] When he told me this story, he added that he and my sister had been visited in Singapore by a young woman who I had dated for a month when I was sixteen. Her name was Jane Smith and she was in

Singapore en route to Australia. She told them she had applied for a job at the Foreign Office and had been asked if she had ever had a boyfriend who was in CND. She said 'No'. They accused her of lying and she didn't get the job.

Simple Writings
[1] *Simple Writings* reviews, the Duke of Cambridge, May 30th–June17th, 1989. Claire Armitstead, *Financial Times*, June 13th,1989 'David Wilson's dramatisation, originally made for television, comes to the stage with a cast of ten who give themselves ably and ebulliently to the task of peopling Grimmelshausen's world. A succession of scenes takes us from the orphaning of the child Simplex, through his conversion and education by an old hermit and his adventures as an innocent adrift in a bad world, to his final return to contemplative solitude. In the background and sometimes the foreground, rages the Thirty Years' War. The astonishing thing to emerge from this production is that the novel has not been dramatised before: it is witty, bawdy, and as profound as anyone cares to consider it.' Ann McFerran, *Time Out*, June 7th, 1989. 'Based on Grimmelshausen's *Simplicianic* Writings, writer David Wilson unfurls a sprawling, vibrant, bustling canvas of 17th-century German peasant life in the Thirty Years' War as he tells the story of a naïve boy, Simplicius, who, like the original author, was separated from his parents in adolescence. Since the action is continually counterpointed with the naïve wisdom of Simplicius' philosophy, the play at times works like a painting by Breughel, in its juxtaposition of the ingeniously fanciful and the gruesomely horrific.' *Ham & High,* June 10th, 1989. 'David Wilson's *Simple Writings* brings to often uproarious life a 17th-century German novel with overtones of Fielding and Rabelais, but with its own contemplative force besides.'
[2] John Yorke, former controller of BBC Drama: 'A powerful and beautifully written piece of theatre, and I have to say that your mastery of language isn't far off Thomas's himself. I thought you did an excellent job of interweaving between the man himself and the world of the plays and the poems, and adding the Marx Brothers

into the brew lent a wonderfully surreal tone. Much as I enjoyed the piece as theatre, I think that's exactly what it is, theatre ...'
Terry Johnson, Director, *One Flew Over The Cuckoo's Nest* (West End, 2004) and playwright (*Insignificance*; *Hysteria*; *Dead Funny*; *Hitchcock Blonde*; *Cleo, Camping, Emmanuelle and Dick*, etc.): 'I read *Spitting into the Sky* and I loved its imaginative spiralling. I loved the setting and the theatrical gifts it allows you to indulge. I love the idea of the Marx Brothers taking us through the play: I think the language is grand, and worthy of the man. I think it's very good.'

American Paint
¹ After recovering from a stroke in 2001, Nick was diagnosed with cancer and died, aged 56, in 2005. His wife, Jane, and son, Henry, continued his legacy in film. Written and directed by Jane, *The Art of Catching Lobsters* is a moving account of the grieving process and was premiered on BBC 4 in September 2007. Nick was a playwright, fisherman, environmentalist and beachcomber. A great workshop leader, he had written a play for the Royal Shakespeare Company, *The Dead Monkey,* a dark comedy featuring a childless couple, their monkey and a sexual liaison between the wife and the pet. A film producer saw the play in Washington DC and invited Nick to Los Angeles to write the film script, all expenses paid. He returned from the West Coast to his Cornish cottage and Cornish poverty and waited for the call which would change his life. Some months later, a fax arrived from the producer. 'Dear Nick,' it said, 'This is America. We can have a monkey. We can have a dead monkey, but we can't have a fucked dead monkey.' Nick was not one to compromise. It was the end of his Hollywood dreams. With Anne, a slightly different story. Her first novel, *No Angel Hotel,* was published in London by HarperCollins. When it appeared under the imprint of St Martin's Press in New York, the title had been changed to *Angel Hotel.* 'This is America,' she was told. 'A negative title won't sell.'

'Behind God's Back'
¹ Letter from *The New Republic*, September 19th, 1994: 'Dear Ms Aylor, Thank you for submitting "Behind God's Back" to us

for consideration. We enjoyed the piece, but in its current form, it is too long for publication. We might consider publishing a 1,500–2,000 word piece on the bakery, however, and we invite you to submit something of that length. Sincerely, David Greenberg, Managing Editor'.

SUPPORTERS

Unbound is a new kind of publishing house. Our books are funded directly by readers. This was a very popular idea during the late eighteenth and early nineteenth centuries. Now we have revived it for the internet age. It allows authors to write the books they really want to write and readers to support the writing they would most like to see published.

The names listed below are of readers who have pledged their support and made this book happen. If you'd like to join them, visit: www.unbound.co.uk.

Kareem Aboualfa
Alison Acton
Frank Ahern
Dragan Andjelic
Katrina Austin
James Aylett
Anne Aylor
Mary Alice Ross Aylor
Sebastian &
   Grainne Balfour
Jason Ballinger
Lin Barkass
Nick Barlay
Jenny Barraclough
Andrew Bax
Paul Belben
Carolyn Belson
Manuela Beste
Robin Beste
Becca Bland
Justin Bolognino
Cecily Bomberg
Martin Bowes
Fling Boyer
Norman & Fling Boyer
Jim Brann
Sue Brock
Chris & Nicola Brooker

Andrew Burgin &
   Kate Hudson
Noeleen Butler
Dorothy Byrne
John Byrom
Johnny & Niki Carmichael
Laureano Carrasco
Nigel Castle
Mary Chamberlain
Michael Clark
Wendy Clarke &
   Hume Cronyn
Nicholas Cohn
Jeremy Corbyn
Anna Cornelius
Jonathan Crook
William Cullen
Eileen Davies
David Dawson
Steve Day
Bill & Sandra Denne
Margaret Dewey
Kevin Donnellon
Gabriella Doran
Elizabeth Dormandy
Jonny &
   Maria Douglas-Wilson
Tiffany Drake

Maja Drnda &
   Christian Marti
Thomas Ehr
Carolyn & Ivan Ellison
Brian Eno
Darla Eno
Irial Eno
Vincent Espagne
Imogen Evans
Alaistair & Trish Fraser
Geoff Gamlen
Carole Garley
John Gaydon
Jane Geerts
Simon Glinn
Jane Glitre
Ben Griffin
Aimee Hansen
Brent Hansen
Nancy Hardy
Jason Hares
Osy Harris
Tanya Petra Harris
Joanna Harrison
Mark & Zoe Harrison
Michael Harrison
Peter Harrison
Alastair Hatchett

Julian Herbert
Peter Hickey
Tawnee Hill
Yannick Hill
Charmian Hislop
Virginia Hjelmaa
M A Hockey
Tansy Hoskins
Susie Howard
Gillian Howell
Chris Huhne
Liz & Peter Huhne
Mustafa Humo
D.H. Jayaraja
Malcolm Jones
Gerry & Helen Judah
Hiroshi Kato
Andrew Kelly
Sanford Kelson
Hilary Kemp
Clare Kenny
Peter Kerner
Dan Kieran
Alice Kilroy
Teo & Sanja Krilic
Andreas Kuhlen
Candyce Lange
Geraldine Lanser
Mary Larkin
Patricia Lawlor
Charles Leach
Kathryn Leander
Anna Leibowitz
Simon Leibowitz
Roger Levy
Kran Lin
Haakon Lovell
Chrystyna Lucyk-Berger
Shade Majekodunmi
Beverlie Manson
Miriam Margolyes
Gill Marshall-Andrews

Oha & Masa Maslo
Edwin Maynard
Gez McCoy
Paul McNaught
David Metz
Rosemary Mitchell
John Mitchinson
Gwendolyn Modder &
   Shane DeBeer
Ken & Jan Montague
Merilyn Moos
Carlo Navato
Annemarie Neary
Dawn Neely-Randall
Deicola Neves
Leora Neves
Julie Newman
Anthea Norman-Taylor
Jack O'Donnell
Anna-Maja Oléhn
Professor Nigel Osborne
Andreea Paciu
Grainne Palmer
Hekate Papadaki
Chantal Papini
Scott Parker
Hugo Pascal
Liz Peet
Lee Pennington
Wendy Perriam
Jennifer Pittam
Van Pittsenbargar
Philip Podmore
Justin Pollard
Jan Pooley
Raphael Prais
Jason R B
Gwynne Reddick
Debbi Reid
Berry & Carol Ritchie
Terri Robson
Sue Ruben

Richard Salmon
Dilshini Sandhu
Tom & Beryl Sandlund
Patricia Sharp
M Shire
Goran Simic
Richard Simmons
Eugene & Azra Skeef
Sue & Ali Smith
Jon Snow
David & Kay Sprecher
Tanya Squires
Rikki Stein
Tom Stoppard
Anna Sullivan
Stephanie Sutherland
Jeremy Swift
Roger Taylor
Gerald Tenenbaum
Bo Treadwell
Eva & John Trent
Tabitha Troughton
Elise Valmorbida
Peter Vilk
Fra von Massow
Michael & Nisha Walling
Anne Walsh
Alexander Watt
Joanna Watt
Nick & Rebecca Watt
Simon Willock
Ben Wilson
David Wilson
Peter & Suzanne Wilson
Jane Woolley
John Youle
Mary Zajicek
Haifa Zangana &
   Mundher Adhami
Eva Zimmerman